The Politics of Collective Violence

Are there any commonalities between such phenomena as soccer hooliganism, sabotage by peasants of landlords' property, incidents of road rage, and even the recent events of September 11? With striking historical scope and command of the literature of many disciplines, this book seeks the common cause of these events in collective violence. In collective violence, social interaction immediately inflicts physical damage, involves at least two perpetrators of damage, and results in part from coordination among the persons who perform the damaging acts. Professor Tilly argues that collective violence is complicated, changeable, and unpredictable in some regards – yet that it also results from similar causes variously combined in different times and places. Pinpointing the causes, combinations, and settings helps to explain collective violence and its variations and also helps to identify the best ways to mitigate violence and create democracies with a minimum of damage to persons and property.

Charles Tilly has published more than twenty scholarly books in addition to monographs and edited volumes on political processes, inequalities, and European history. Professor Tilly has held research and teaching positions at the University of Delaware, Harvard University, the University of Toronto, the University of Michigan, and New School University prior to his current position as the Joseph L. Buttenwieser Professor of Social Science at Columbia University.

Cambridge Studies in Contentious Politics

Editors

Doug McAdam   *Stanford University* and *Center for Advanced Study in the Behavioral Sciences*
Sidney Tarrow   *Cornell University*
Charles Tilly   *Columbia University*

Other Books in This Series

Ronald R. Aminzade et al., *Silence and Voice in the Study of Contentious Politics*
Jack A. Goldstone (Ed.), *States, Parties, and Social Movements*
Doug McAdam, Sidney Tarrow, and Charles Tilly, *Dynamics of Contention*

The Politics of Collective Violence

CHARLES TILLY

Columbia University

CAMBRIDGE
UNIVERSITY PRESS

CAMBRIDGE UNIVERSITY PRESS
Cambridge, New York, Melbourne, Madrid, Cape Town, Singapore,
São Paulo, Delhi, Dubai, Tokyo, Mexico City

Cambridge University Press
32 Avenue of the Americas, New York, NY 10013-2473, USA

www.cambridge.org
Information on this title: www.cambridge.org/9780521531450

First published 2003
Reprinted 2004, 2006

A catalogue record for this publication is available from the British Library

Library of Congress Cataloguing in Publication Data

Tilly, Charles.
The politics of collective violence / Charles Tilly.
   p. cm. - (Cambridge studies in contentious politics)
Includes bibliographical references and index.
ISBN 0-521-82428-1 - ISBN 0-521-53145-4 (pb.)
1. Violence. 2. Political violence. 3. Collective behavior. I. Title. II. Series.
HM886.T55 2003
303.6 - dc21   2002074067

ISBN 978-0-521-82428-6 Hardback
ISBN 978-0-521-53145-0 Paperback

To Doug McAdam and Sid Tarrow,
still friends despite years of collaboration.

Contents

Preface

Human life is one mistake after another. We make mistakes, detect them, repair them, then go on to make more mistakes. Errors and error correction fill our days. If we are lucky, smart, or surrounded by helpful critics, error correction outweighs error, so that competence and knowledge actually improve – at least for a while. Certainly my own experience as a student and teacher of political processes has told me so. Repeatedly I have thought I had identified an important principle, proved a crucial point, or found a superior way of communicating an argument only to discover that the principle suffered exceptions, the proof failed to convince, or the new rhetoric caused misunderstandings I had not anticipated.

My first book refuted my doctoral dissertation, a fact at least guaranteeing that the author under attack would not complain. This book's vision of violence corrects mistakes I made during the 1970s. At that time I denied that collective violence constituted a causally coherent domain, but argued that "most" collective violence occurred as a by-product of negotiations that were not in themselves intrinsically violent. Another thirty years of work on political conflict helped me see the error of my earlier ways.

Although I still deny the existence of general laws from which we can deduce all particular cases of collective violence, I now believe that a fairly small number of causal mechanisms and processes recur throughout the whole range of collective violence – with different initial conditions, combinations, and sequences producing systematic variation from time to time and setting to setting in the character, intensity, and incidence of violent encounters. I also see that my own research of the 1970s led me to exaggerate the prevalence of the forms of collective violence that this book calls scattered attacks and broken negotiations while neglecting brawls, opportunism, coordinated destruction, and violent rituals. Live and learn.

Brutal airborne attacks on New York's World Trade Center and Washington's Pentagon occurred when this book was well under way. They – and (even more so) the public discussion they initiated – caused this book to say more about terrorism than I had originally planned. I still think that terror is a recurrent political strategy adopted by a wide variety of actors rather than a creed, a separate variety of politics, or the work of a distinctive class of people. But public concern about terrorists has led me to deal more extensively with sudden or clandestine attacks on civilian targets than I had intended and to spell out relations between such actions and other forms of political conflict at greater than my planned length. I hope my analysis will help readers rethink both their own understandings of terror and public policies designed to combat it.

A number of discerning readers helped me live and learn. Heartfelt thanks for criticism, information, and advice go to Rod Aya, Thomas Bernstein, Christian Davenport, Carmenza Gallo, Herbert Gans, Michael Hanagan, Hanspeter Kriesi, Fernando López-Alves, David Stowell, Sidney Tarrow, Sudhir Venkatesh, Elisabeth Wood, Viviana Zelizer, and two anonymous readers for Cambridge University Press. Audiences at Yale and Columbia universities also subjected fragments of the book to salutary criticism.

I have adapted a few passages in the book from "State-Incited Violence, 1900–1999," *Political Power and Social Theory* 9 (1995): 161–79.

It is now your turn to find mistakes and perhaps to correct them as well.

1

Varieties of Violence

Three Violent Vignettes

1. Cowboys Shoot Cowboys   "Cowboys used their guns," reports David Courtwright of the American West,

> to act out any number of roles, the deadliest of which was _nemo me impugnit_, "no one
> impugns me." Harry French, a Kansas railroad brakeman, witnessed a fight between
> cowboys riding in the caboose of his cattle train. It began during a card game when one
> man remarked, "I don't like to play cards with a dirty deck." A cowboy from a rival out
> fit misunderstood him to say "dirty neck," and when the shooting was over one man lay
> dead and three were badly wounded. (Courtwright 1996: 92)

Whenever young, single men like the cowboys congregated for long periods
under other than stringent discipline, Courtwright argues, violence ensued.
Where the congregation had access to liquor, gambling, and guns, violence became more frequent and more lethal. American history featured an exceptional
number of such congregations. Most of them resulted from the rapid migration of young men to new opportunities such as frontier settlements, expanding
cattle ranges, railroad building, and gold mines. But their equivalent has arisen
recently in major cities, as drugs and unstable households have interacted to put
large numbers of young men on the street in each other's company. So, reasons
Courtwright, virulent violence in major cities stems from their resemblance to
frontier towns; both places harbor uncontrolled, armed concentrations of young,
single males.

2. Villagers Attack Combines and Landlords   Political ethnographer James Scott
has been following social life and social change in a Malaysian village since the
1970s. Early in his studies, he observed an episode of violence quite different
from the gunfights of America's Wild West:

When, in 1976, combine harvesters began to make serious inroads into the wages of poor villagers, the entire region experienced a rash of machine-breaking and sabotage reminiscent of the 1830s in England. The provincial authorities called it "vandalism" and "theft", but it was clear that there was a fairly generalised nocturnal campaign to prevent the use of combines. Batteries were removed from the machines and thrown into irrigation ditches; carburettors (*sic*) and other vital parts such as distributors were smashed; sand and mud were introduced into the gas tanks; various objects (stones, wire, nails) were used to jam the augers; coconut trees were felled across the combine's path; and at least two machines were destroyed by arson. Two aspects of this resistance deserve emphasis. First, it was clear that the goal of the saboteurs was never simple theft, for nothing was actually stolen. Second, all of the sabotage was carried out at night by individuals or small groups acting anonymously. They were, furthermore, shielded by their fellow villagers who, even if they knew who was involved, claimed total ignorance when the police came to investigate. (Scott 2000: 200)

Most of the time, Scott emphasizes, the same peasants maintained decorous, deferential public relations to the same landlords despite incessantly muttering among themselves, dragging their feet, stealing rice from the landlords' fields, and otherwise deploying what Scott calls "weapons of the weak." Although landlords would not have hesitated to prosecute a machine breaker or thief caught red-handed, landlords found themselves caught in a confining set of relations that would cost them standing, influence, and access to labor if they engaged in vindictive violence or generated open rebellion.

3. Rwandans Slaughter Each Other   Neither of these episodes matched Rwanda's bloodletting of 1994. In July 1973, Rwanda's senior military officer, General Juvénal Habyarimana, had seized power by means of a relatively bloodless coup. Soon he was establishing a one-party regime that lasted for two decades. A Hutu from the northwest, Habyarimana ruled with the help of his wife and her powerful family. But they faced opposition from Tutsi-based military forces in Uganda and along Rwanda's northern border as well as from Hutu political leaders based in the south. Since 1990, the primarily Tutsi Rwanda Patriotic Front (RPF) had been advancing from its base near the Ugandan border, Hutu peasants had been fleeing the Front's advance, and Hutu Power activists had been organizing local massacres of Tutsi in response to the threatened return of the previously dominant Tutsis to power.

On 6 April 1994, President Habyarimana's aircraft was approaching its landing at the Rwandan capital, Kigali, when someone using sophisticated missiles shot it down. In that crash, not only the president but also Rwanda's army chief-of-staff General Nsabimana, Burundian president Cyprien Ntaryamira, and several others died. Habyarimana and Ntaryamira were returning from a meeting of African heads of state in Dar es Salaam, Tanzania, where participants had discussed (and perhaps agreed upon) installation of a broad-based transitional Rwandan government. Both inside and outside Rwanda, a number of power holders had reasons to oppose such a settlement.

Whoever instigated Habyarimana's killing, within a day one of the twentieth century's greatest massacres had begun. From the start, military men and Hutu Power activists targeted not only members of the Tutsi minority but also prominent rivals among the Hutu. "At first," in the words of Alison Des Forges,

assailants generally operated in small bands and killed their victims where they found them, in their homes, on the streets, at the barriers. But, as early as the evening of April 7, larger groups seized the opportunity for more intensive slaughter as frightened Tutsi – and some Hutu – fled to churches, schools, hospitals, and government offices that had offered refuge in the past. In the northwestern prefecture of Gisenyi, militia killed some fifty people at the Nyundo seminary, forty-three at the church of Busogo, and some 150 at the parish of Bursasamana. A large crowd including Burundian students and wounded soldiers took on the task of massacring hundreds of people at the campus of the Seventh Day Adventist University at Mudende to the east of Gisenyi town.

In Kigali, soldiers and militia killed dozens at a church in Nyamirambo on April 8 and others at the mosque at Nyamirambo several days later. On the morning of April 9, some sixty Interahamwe [members of a Hutu militia originally formed by the political party of dead president Habyarimana] led by Jean Ntawutagiripfa, known as "Congolais," and accompanied by four National Policemen, forced their way into the church at Gikondo, an industrial section of Kigali. They killed more than a hundred people that day, mostly with machetes and clubs. (Des Forges et al. 1999: 209–10)

Eventually several hundred thousands of Rwandan civilians took part in massacres of Tutsi and of Hutu accused of siding with Tutsi. Between March and July of 1994, assailants slaughtered perhaps 800,000 Tutsi as well as 10,000–50,000 Hutu. But the bloody victory of Hutu supremacists did not last long. Genocide mutated into civil war in Rwanda that spring; after the massacre, the RPF drove Hutu leaders out of the country or into hiding, then took over the government. Tutsi Paul Mugabe became Rwanda's head of state.

American gunfights, Malaysian sabotage of combines, and Rwandan massacres do not greatly resemble each other, but they all involve *collective violence*. They have in common episodic social interaction that:

- immediately inflicts physical damage on persons and/or objects ("damage" includes forcible seizure of persons or objects over restraint or resistance);
- involves at least two perpetrators of damage; and
- results at least in part from coordination among persons who perform the damaging acts.

3

Collective violence, by such a definition, excludes purely individual action, nonmaterial damage, accidents, and long-term or indirect effects of such damaging processes as dumping of toxic waste. But it includes a vast range of social interactions.

Critics could plausibly raise any of three quite contradictory objections to using the same term for this range of phenomena. First, could such disparate events possibly have anything in common? Second, aren't all of them expressions of a general human propensity to inflict damage on others, and therefore indistinguishable in principle from individual violence? Third, why make such a big deal of direct physical seizure and damage? Shouldn't collective violence also include totalitarian regimentation, environmental degradation, exploitation, and injustice, whether or not anyone damages persons and objects in the short run?

Could such disparate events possibly have anything in common? Although no universal law governs all episodes of collective violence, similar causes in different combinations and settings operate throughout the whole range. Collective violence resembles weather: complicated, changing, and unpredictable in some regards, yet resulting from similar causes variously combined in different times and places. Getting the causes, combinations, and settings right helps explain collective violence and its many variations. More than anything else, this book organizes around an effort to identify relevant causes, combinations, and settings.

Don't all sorts of violence express general human propensities to inflict damage on others, propensities that simply activate more people simultaneously in collective violence? Although regularities that determine individual aggression against persons and objects surely apply within complex interactions as well, collective violence is not simply individual aggression writ large. Social ties, structures, and processes significantly affect its character. A rough distinction between individual and collective violence therefore focuses attention on how social ties, structures, and processes affect change and variation in violent incidents.

What about nonviolent violence? Questions of injustice, exploitation, and oppression unquestionably arise across a wide variety of collective violence. What is more, physical seizure or damage often occurs as a contingent outcome of conflicts that greatly resemble each other, many of which proceed without direct short-term damage. Nevertheless, to spread the term "violence" across all interpersonal relations and solitary actions of which we disapprove actually undermines the effort to explain violence (for a contrary view, see Weigert 1999). It blocks us from asking about effective causal relationships between exploitation or injustice, on one side, and physical damage, on the other. It also obscures the fact that specialists in inflicting physical damage (such as police, soldiers, guards, thugs, and gangs) play significant parts in collective violence. Their presence or absence often makes all the difference between violent and nonviolent outcomes.

Ideas, Behavior, and Social Interaction

These are, appropriately, contentious matters. Broadly speaking, observers of human violence divide into three camps: idea people, behavior people, and relation people. The three camps differ in their understanding of fundamental causes in human affairs.

Idea people stress consciousness as the basis of human action. They generally claim that humans acquire beliefs, concepts, rules, goals, and values from their environments, reshape their own (and each other's) impulses in conformity with such ideas, and act out their socially acquired ideas. Idea people divide over the significance of the distinction between individual and collective violence, with some arguing that individual and collective ideas inhabit partly separate domains, while others argue seamless continuity between individual and society. In either view, ideas concerning the worth of others and the desirability of aggressive actions significantly affect the propensity of a person or a people to join in collective violence. To stem violence, goes the reasoning, we must suppress or eliminate destructive ideas.

Behavior people stress the autonomy of motives, impulses, and opportunities. Many point to human evolution as the origin of aggressive action – individual or collective. They argue, for example, that among primates both natural and sexual selection gave advantages to individuals and populations employing aggressive means of acquiring mates, shelter, food, and protection against attack. Hence, runs the argument, propensities to adopt those aggressive means entered the human genetic heritage. Others avoid evolutionary explanations but still speak of extremely general needs and incentives for domination, exploitation, respect, deference, protection, or security that underlie collective violence. Still others adopt resolutely economistic stances, seeing violence as a means of acquiring goods and services.

Behavior people often take a reductionist position, saying that ultimately all collective phenomena sum up nothing but individual behaviors or even the impacts of particular genes. Because motives and impulses change at a glacial pace, runs this line of argument, violence rises or falls mainly in response to changes in two factors: socially imposed control over motives and socially created opportunities to express those motives.

Relation people make transactions among persons and groups far more central than do idea and behavior people. They argue that humans develop their personalities and practices through interchanges with other humans, and that the interchanges themselves always involve a degree of negotiation and creativity. Ideas thus become means, media, and products of social interchange, while motives, impulses, and opportunities operate only within continuously negotiated social interaction. For relation people, collective violence therefore amounts to a kind of conversation, however brutal or one-sided that conversation may be. Relation people often make concessions to the influence of individual propensities but generally insist that collective processes have irreducibly distinct properties. In this view, restraining violence depends less on destroying bad ideas, eliminating opportunities, or suppressing impulses than on transforming relations among persons and groups.

Each group of thinkers has a point. Ideas about proper and improper uses of violent means, about differences among social categories, and about justice or injustice undoubtedly shape people's participation or nonparticipation in collective violence. James Scott's villagers followed an elaborate code of civility as they attacked their landlords' harvesting combines. Deep behavioral regularities surely affect the readiness of different categories of people to inflict violence on each other. As David Courtwright's cowboys illustrate, segregated groups of young, single males figure disproportionately in collective violence over the world as a whole. Relations certainly matter as well; in Rwanda and elsewhere, previously existing organization and intergroup relations channel who visits violence on whom.

Recognizing that interplay, some analysts of violence offer combinations or compromises among ideas, behavior, and relations. Classic Marxists, for example, derived shared interests especially from relations of production but then saw interests as determining both prevailing ideas and interest-oriented behavior. Violence, in that view, generally resulted from and also promoted class interests. For Marxists, relations had priority, but relations, ideas, and behaviors interacted. Classic liberals replied that properly instilled ideas (sometimes, to be sure, reducing to simple person-by-person calculations of gain and loss) generated appropriate behaviors and social relations. They thus combined ideal and behavioral explanations while relegating relations to secondary importance.

In a less abstract way, David Courtwright himself combines ideal and behavioral explanations.

The geographically and ethnically uneven distribution of American violence and disorder to the end of the nineteenth century can be explained by three sets of factors, one cultural, one racial, and one demographic. Cultural beliefs and habits, like southern sensibilities about guns and honor or the Irish penchant for aggressive drinking, help explain why some regions or groups consistently had higher rates of murder and mayhem. Racism was important both because it encouraged and exacerbated conflict with minorities, such as the Indians, and because it contributed to the economic marginalization of black men and restrictions on Chinese immigration. Then there were local and regional variations in population structure, notably the age and gender imbalances on the nonagricultural frontier. Through a combination of pooled biological tendencies, widespread bachelorhood, and male group dynamics, these produced more drinking, gambling, prostitution, quarreling, carrying of weapons, and other traits associated with bad ends. (Courtwright 1996: 170)

Thus Courtwright treats behavioral causes as fundamental, sees ideal causes as modifying their effects, and makes a gesture or two toward relational processes. Despite many such attempts to combine perspectives, however, analyses of collective violence have divided sharply over the relative priorities and connections among ideas, behavior, and social relations. Strongly competing explanations for collective violence have therefore emerged (Aya 1990).

This book proceeds mainly along relational lines. While calling attention to influential ideas and behavioral regularities where necessary, it concentrates on ways that variable patterns of social interaction constitute and cause different varieties of collective violence. At the same time, it shows how similar causal mechanisms appear in disparate modes of violence, producing parallel short-term effects but yielding distinct overall outcomes as a function of their settings, sequences, and combinations. It stresses relational mechanisms – those that operate within interpersonal transactions – but sees them as producing their effects in conjunction with environmental and cognitive mechanisms.

A relational emphasis has its limits. For example, this book does not definitively obliterate the possibility that, deep down, the extent of collective violence depends heavily on how many genetically predisposed young people gather in the same place without firm discipline imposed upon them. Indirectly, this book raises doubts about the adequacy of simple behavioral accounts; it does so by identifying historical changes and variations in collective violence that surely result from variable social processes rather than from alterations of impulses, inhibitions, and population distributions. But in fact its conclusions leave open a great many questions concerning individual propensities to engage in violence.

Nor does the book provide a full account of the anger, fear, lust, gratification, and empathy that, variously combined, often dominate feelings of participants in collective violence. It does show that, for all their grounding in individual predispositions, such strong emotions arise from social interaction and respond to changes in social settings. But it does not trace out moment-by-moment connections between physiological changes and fluctuations in collective violence. Steadfast behaviorists may therefore leave the book still insisting that inhibitions and opportunities for expression of strong emotions ultimately determine how much violence occurs, on what scale, by whom, and to whom.

The book's challenge to idea-based explanations of collective violence does not extend far beyond insisting on the importance of social interaction in the generation, diffusion, and implementation of violence-promoting ideas. It leaves open the possibility that my great teacher Barrington Moore rightly sees monotheistic religions as fostering gross intolerance, hence readiness to kill outsiders, because of their sharply drawn distinctions between the worthy and the unworthy, the pure and the impure (Moore 2000).

Even if Moore is right, however, the relational analyses to follow clarify what social processes intervene between acquisition of a violence-promoting idea and direct participation in mayhem. After all, most holders of views that justify violence against one sort of human or another never actually abduct, maim, or murder anyone. That such ideologues should enlist others (who are often not especially ideological) to abduct, maim, or kill on their behalf raises precisely the kinds of questions about social processes that we are pursuing here.

A relational approach maintains a dual orientation to conventional writing on violence. On one side, analysts of violence commonly reconstruct the motives, interests, circumstances, or beliefs of one actor at a time, then divide between condemning or defending the actor. After the major police–civilian battles, property destruction, and looting in predominantly black sections of large American cities during the 1960s, commentators divided sharply between (a) interpreting the events as an understandable response to deprivation and (b) justifying repression of disorderly youths who were merely seeking short-term gratification (for the two views see e.g. Feagin & Hahn 1975; Banfield 1970, esp. chap. 9). By locating causality in negotiated interactions, a relational approach makes individual assignment of praise, defense, or blame more difficult.

The same writing on violence, however, also commonly offers judgments on what would reduce violence – how to prevent genocide, deter terrorism, open up nonviolent paths to justice, mitigate the damage from brawls, and so on. All such judgments rest, implicitly or explicitly, on causal arguments concerning what produces the violence that occurs and what would produce alternative outcomes. For example, a blue-ribbon panel on violence convened by the National Research Council characteristically recommended new research and reporting, but its action program emphasized these measures to reduce violence:

- intervening in the biological and psychosocial development of individuals' potentials for violent behavior;
- modifying places, routine activities, and situations that promote violence;

- maximizing the violence-reduction effects of police interventions in illegal markets;
- modifying the roles of commodities – including firearms, alcohol, and other psychoactive drugs – in inhibiting or promoting violent events or their consequences;
- intervening to reduce the potentials for violence in bias crimes, gang activities, and community transitions; and
- implementing a comprehensive initiative to reduce partner assault (Reiss & Roth 1993: 22).

Such recommendations rest primarily on the assumption that violence results from a balance between individual impulses and inhibitions on those impulses. Although it leaves some room for ideas, the implicit argument centers on behavioral causes. It assigns almost no weight whatsoever to effects of social relations except as they work through impulses and inhibitions.

If this book does its job well, it will make superior causal arguments to those now available in behavioral and ideal accounts of violence. It will thus clarify which proposals to reduce violence would, if implemented, produce what effects. If its arguments are correct then – for a given amount of effort – attempts to modify individual behavior, place greater restraints on impulses, or banish bad ideas will have significantly less effect on prevailing levels of violence than will intervention in relations among contenders.

Let us not assume automatically that any social policy reducing violence is a good thing in itself. Whatever else readers learn from this book, they will find that political regimes differ in the levels and kinds of violence they generate; in choosing political regimes, to some extent we also choose among varieties of violence. Personally, if forced to choose between a nonviolent tyranny based on stark inequality and a rough-and-tumble democracy, I would choose the democracy. I hope the book will help readers see how to create democracies with a minimum – but not a total absence – of damage to persons and property.

In stressing relational mechanisms rather than ideas or individually motivated behavior, this book extends recent analyses of contentious politics (McAdam, Tarrow, & Tilly 2001; Tilly 2001a). Contentious politics consists of discontinuous, public, collective claim making in which one of the parties is a government. A government is a substantial, durable, bounded organization that exercises control over the major concentrated means of coercion within some territory. Collective violence does sometimes occur quite outside the range of governments; however, above a very small scale, collective violence almost always involves governments as monitors, claimants, objects of claims, or third parties to claims.

When governments are involved, collective violence becomes a special case of contentious politics. That insight will serve us well when it comes to explaining variation in the character and intensity of large-scale violence. It will help us to see the influence of political regimes on the sorts of violence that occur within their territories.

The book also draws on recent work concerning social inequality (for critiques and syntheses, see Tilly 1998b, 2001b,c). In that line of analysis, two fundamental relational mechanisms generate and sustain a wide range of inequalities between categories of humans. *Exploitation* comes into play when powerful, connected people command resources from which they draw significantly increased returns by coordinating the efforts of outsiders whom they exclude from the full value added by that effort. *Opportunity hoarding* operates when members of a categorically bounded network acquire access to a resource that is valuable, renewable, subject to monopoly, supportive of network activities, and enhanced by the network's modus operandi. Once exploitation and opportunity hoarding are at work, inequality also depends on adaptation (creation of practices that articulate people's lives with unequal arrangements) and emulation (transfers of relevant practices, beliefs, and relations from site to site). For present purposes, however, exploitation and opportunity hoarding do the critical explanatory work.

Both exploitation and opportunity hoarding gain in effectiveness when the categorical boundary in play corresponds precisely to a boundary that operates widely elsewhere in social life and thus brings with it a set of supporting beliefs, practices, and social relations. Boundaries of ethnicity, race, religion, gender, or nationality reinforce exploitation and opportunity hoarding. In their turn, exploitation and opportunity hoarding lock such differences in place by delivering greater rewards to occupants of the ostensibly superior category.

Governments always do a certain amount of exploitation and opportunity hoarding, with government officials and ruling classes being the typical beneficiaries of the two mechanisms. They commonly incorporate categorical boundaries that already operate elsewhere, for example by excluding women or followers of heterodox religions from full citizenship. How much and exactly how governments exploit and hoard opportunities varies tremendously; much of political theory concerns just that variation. Inequality based on control of governments figures significantly in collective violence – both because it makes control of governments worth fighting for or defending and because it almost always includes differences in access to violent means.

Nongovernmental inequality also affects collective violence deeply. Governments usually side with beneficiaries of existing inequalities, for three reasons:

first because rulers and ruling classes figure among those beneficiaries, second because beneficiaries have superior means of organizing and influencing government, and third because governmental resources (such as tax revenues, soldiers, weapons, ships, food, and information) flow to the government from systems of inequality whose challenge would threaten those crucial flows. Only in times of conquest or revolution do we regularly see governments intervening to replace existing systems of exploitation and opportunity hoarding. Although collective violence certainly occurs in conquest and revolution, it more frequently results from governmental use of violent means to defend beneficiaries of inequality from challenges by victims of inequality.

Beneficiaries and victims of nongovernmental exploitation and opportunity hoarding (e.g., mine owners and mine workers) often engage in their own struggles over the proceeds of their joint effort, sometimes use violent means in the course of their struggles, and occasionally attract intervention in the form of attacks by the government's armed forces against one or both sides, especially the challengers. Parties to relations of exploitation or opportunity hoarding regularly seek governmental support either to maintain or to overthrow existing advantages, which in turn generates new collective violence.

Political action, finally, is a way of creating, defending, or challenging nongovernmental systems of exploitation and opportunity hoarding, for example property rights to minerals, exclusive control over sacred sites, and customs that require workers (but not their employers) to keep their contracts. The extent to which governmental categorical distinctions (e.g., citizen vs. noncitizen or legislator vs. constituent) coincide with nongovernmental categorical distinctions such as gender, race, religion, and ethnicity affects the form and stakes of political struggle, hence the character of collective violence. As Hutu–Tutsi struggles show, under some circumstances lying on one side of a categorical boundary or the other becomes a matter of life and death. These insights will help us understand the surprising prominence of "us–them" categorical distinctions in all varieties of collective violence.

Collective violence presents a series of puzzles for which no one has yet arrived at satisfactory solutions.

1. Why does collective violence (unlike suicides and individual homicides) concentrate in large waves – often with one violent encounter appearing to trigger the next – then subside to low levels for substantial periods of time?
2. How and why do people who interact without doing outright damage to each other shift rapidly into collective violence and then (sometimes just as rapidly) shift back into relatively peaceful relations?

3. In particular, how and why do people who have lived with their categorical differences (often cooperating and intermarrying) for years begin devastating attacks on each other's persons and property?
4. Why do different kinds of political regimes (e.g., democratic and authoritarian regimes) host such different levels and forms of collective violence?
5. How and why do peacekeeping specialists such as police and soldiers so regularly and quickly switch between violent and nonviolent action?

So far, neither ideal, behavioral, nor relational analysts have provided credible explanations of collective violence that address more than one of these questions at a time. Nor has anyone assembled reliable evidence for proposed answers to any one of them taken singly. We face the challenge of using relational insights to construct superior and mutually consistent answers to these questions.

Types of Interpersonal Violence

What must we explain? The great majority of interpersonal transactions proceed without violence – without immediate short-term physical damage or seizure of at least one party or that party's possessions by another. Even in zones of civil war and widespread brawling, most people most of the time are interacting in nonviolent ways. Yet nonviolent interactions do turn violent, people who have coexisted peaceably start killing each other, cowboys shoot, villagers sabotage, and Rwandan Hutus slaughter their designated enemies – sometimes. When, how, and why do shifts between nonviolent and violent interaction occur? In particular: when, how, and why do people get involved *collectively* in inflicting damage on other people? Collective violence takes many different forms, so what determines its social organization and character?

In order to arrive at satisfactory answers to such difficult questions, we must pick our way carefully through four distinguishable problems. First, what causes people to make collective claims – violent or nonviolent – on each other? This book draws heavily on previous analyses of collective claim making. Except for applying those analyses explicitly to violence, however, it does not add much to existing ideas on the subject.

Second, what causes people sometimes to damage other people and objects in the course of collective claim making, but other times to employ nonviolent means? The book says much more about this issue, but it does not arrive at grand general statements on the sheer presence or absence of violence. We will, in fact, discover some gray areas where no more than minor contingencies make the difference between otherwise similar political processes in which violence does and does not occur.

Third, when people do employ violent means of claim making, what determines the extent of damage? Later chapters give the extent and intensity of violence considerable attention, examining both what sorts of social circumstances produce high levels of violence and by what kinds of social processes violent claim making reaches a large or small scale.

Fourth, what causes collective violence to take so many different forms, from cowboy brawls to peasant machine breaking to genocide? The problem of explaining variation in the character and social organization of violence takes up much more of the book's energy than do the first three problems. This book stands or falls on the extent to which it clarifies what causes collective violence, when it occurs, (a) to vary so greatly in form and (b) to make significant shifts, sometimes quite rapid, from one form to another.

In order to discipline our inquiry into the fourth problem, we must specify the sort of variation we are trying to explain. Let us construct a two-dimensional map of interpersonal violence, including individual attacks of one person on another or on that person's property. Call the first dimension *salience of short-run damage*. We look at interactions among the parties, asking to what extent infliction and reception of damage dominate those interactions. At the low extreme, damage occurs only intermittently or secondarily in the course of transactions that remain predominantly nonviolent. At the high extreme, almost every transaction inflicts damage, as the infliction and reception of damage dominate the interaction. Routine bureaucratic encounters that occasionally lead to fisticuffs stand toward the low end of the range, lynching parties toward the high end.

The second dimension represents *extent of coordination among violent actors*. The definition of collective violence offered earlier incorporated a minimum position on this dimension: it insisted on at least two perpetrators of damage and some coordination among perpetrators. Below that threshold, we call violence individual. Nevertheless, collective coordination can run from no more than improvised signaling and/or common culture (low) to involvement of centralized organizations whose leaders follow shared scripts as they deliberately guide followers into violence-generating interactions with others (high). At the low end we find such events as scuffles between drunken sailors and military police; at the high end, pitched battles between opposing armies.

This way of setting up analyses of collective violence emphasizes its connections with nonviolent political processes. Obviously we could conjure up other interesting dimensions of collective violence, such as scale, duration, destructiveness, asymmetry, and proximity to established governmental institutions. In fixing on salience and coordination I follow my hunches that: (a) they identify significant, coherent variations in relevant combinations of outcomes and causal mechanisms; (b) they locate clusters of collective violence within which similar causes operate; and (c) for those reasons they help explain variation with respect to scale, duration, destructiveness, asymmetry, and proximity to governmental institutions (for some confirmation, see Bonneuil & Auriat 2000).

How much coordination occurs among violent actors and how salient damage is to their interactions with others, for example, help pinpoint and explain the degree of destruction resulting from those interactions. Broadly speaking, destructiveness rises with both salience and coordination. Where salience and coordination both reach high levels, widespread destruction occurs. Of our three opening vignettes, Rwandan genocide best illustrates combined high levels of salience and coordination.

Figure 1.1 presents a preliminary typology of interpersonal violence that follows from such a two-dimensional classification. For the moment the diagram includes individual aggression in order to specify its relation to other larger-scale forms of violence. Later I will give reasons for separating the analyses of collective and individual violence. Here is how the classification works: First, we locate a clump of violent episodes in the salience–coordination space, for example in the upper left-hand corner, where high coordination among violent actors and relatively low salience of damage in all interactions among the parties coincide. Then, we name the location for the most common kind of episode in that location. The upper left-hand corner gets the name "broken negotiations" because of the frequency with which longer-term nonviolent bargaining processes that go awry result in low-salience, high-coordination collective violence. Proceeding in approximately clockwise order from the upper right-hand corner, the types include

- *Violent rituals:* at least one relatively well-defined and coordinated group follows a known interaction script entailing the infliction of damage on itself or others as it competes for priority within a recognized arena; examples include shaming ceremonies, lynchings, public executions, gang rivalries, contact sports, some election battles, and some struggles among supporters of sporting teams or entertainment stars.
- *Coordinated destruction:* persons or organizations that specialize in the deployment of coercive means undertake a program of damage to persons and/or objects; examples include war, collective self-immolation, some kinds of terrorism, genocide, and politicide – the programmed annihilation of a political category's members.
- *Opportunism:* as a consequence of shielding from routine surveillance and repression, individuals or clusters of individuals use immediately damaging

Varieties of Violence

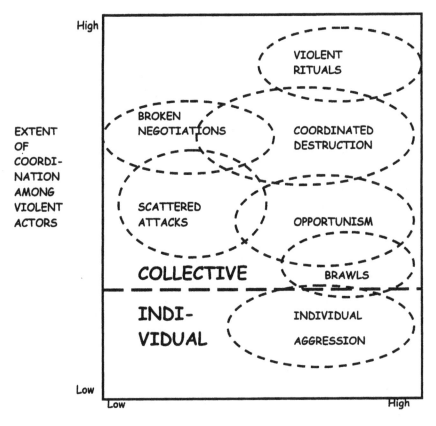

Figure 1.1 A Typology of Interpersonal Violence.

means to pursue generally forbidden ends; examples include looting, gang rape, piracy, revenge killing, and some sorts of military pillage.

- *Brawls:* within a previously nonviolent gathering, two or more persons begin attacking each other or each other's property; examples include barroom free-for-alls, small-scale battles at sporting events, and many street fights.
- *Individual aggression:* a single actor (or several unconnected actors) engage(s) in immediately and predominantly destructive interaction with another actor; examples include single-perpetrator rapes, assaults, robberies, and vandalism.
- *Scattered attacks:* in the course of widespread small-scale and generally nonviolent interaction, a number of participants respond to obstacles, challenges, or restraints by means of damaging acts; examples include sabotage, clandestine attacks on symbolic objects or places, assaults of governmental agents, and arson.

15

- *Broken negotiations:* various forms of collective action generate resistance or rivalry to which one or more parties respond by actions that damage persons and/or objects; examples include demonstrations, protection rackets, governmental repression, and military coups – all of which frequently occur with no more than threats of violence yet sometimes produce physical damage.

Figure 1.1 shows these types as overlapping ovals to emphasize that the concrete episodes involved necessarily have imprecise boundaries. Violent rituals such as sporting events, for example, sometimes convert into broken negotiations (ushers' attempts to expel rowdy spectators produce attacks on ushers and the stadium) or opportunism (spectators or players take private revenge on their enemies). But an even larger share of violent ritual overlaps with coordinated destruction – feuds, gang fights, and similar contests that look much like war except for their smaller scale and greater containment.

The typology names each segment of the coordination–salience space for the most common process that produces its particular combination of coordination and salience. Most often, for example, extremely high levels of coordination and salience result from activation of a familiar script by parties already specializing in doing damage with monitors who contain their interaction; the term *violent ritual* describes that sort of process. Now and then, however, two armies at war – and therefore engaged mainly in coordinated destruction – move into the zone of extremely high coordination and salience, stylizing and containing their interaction. I name the low-coordination but relatively high-salience territory near the individual–collective boundary *brawl* not because every interaction in the territory actually begins with a nonviolent gathering within which pairs of people begin to fight, but rather because such a sequence does regularly result in low-coordination, high-salience violence. The typology provides a handy reminder of on-the-average differences in dominant social processes occurring at different locations within the coordination–salience space.

Variation in participants' motives neither defines nor explains differences among the types of collective violence. No doubt participants in opportunistic violence feel greed and lust more often than participants in broken negotiations, while anger and fear frequently well up in broken negotiations. But (as later chapters will abundantly show) many a participant in opportunism acts with righteous indignation or fear, and greed recurs throughout the full range of violent interactions. The classification locates types of collective violence in terms of the social processes that generate them, not in terms of the motives and emotions carried by damage-doing people.

Later chapters will spend little effort locating the exact boundaries of these types or deciding which incident belongs to which type. On the contrary, they will repeatedly trace processes by which events start out at one location in the coordination–salience space and end up in another – how scattered attack, for example, moves step by step toward coordinated destruction, or vice versa. Later sections of the book will show the large parts played by brokerage and activation of us–them boundaries in the more highly coordinated forms of collective violence: violent rituals, coordinated destruction, and broken negotiations. Where brokerage and boundary activation loom large, the evidence will show, they commonly override previously existing social relations among participants – so much so that people who live peaceably together one day begin slaughtering each other the next.

Conversely, previously existing social relations among participants (including previously hostile relations) exert greater influence in the zones of lesser coordination: opportunism, brawls, and scattered attack. We will likewise discover systematic relations of salience to social contexts, notably how accessibility of violent means and/or specialists in violence such as thugs and troops promotes high-salience collective violence.

In these terms, we can place the three episodes described by David Courtwright, James Scott, and Alison Des Forges in different parts of the coordination–salience space. Cowboy gunfights usually conformed to the model of brawls, although they occasionally mutated into opportunism, violent ritual, and even coordinated destruction as a consequence of shifts in the salience of short-run damage and of coordination among the violent actors. (Cowboys from rival outfits, for example, sometimes played cards, but shifted to shootouts when games went bad.)

Villagers' retaliation against landlords takes place mostly in the zone of scattered attack, but now and then veers into opportunism, violent ritual, or broken negotiations. James Scott has, in fact, spent much of his career examining what causes alternation between passive resistance and active rebellion. Rwanda's complex conflicts centered on coordinated destruction, but violent ritual, opportunism, and scattered attack all occurred at the edges of Rwanda's organized genocide. (Chapter 6 examines in detail the opportunistic overflow of Rwanda's genocide.) That genocide took place in the context of decades-long Hutu–Tutsi struggles for control of the Rwandan state.

Figure 1.1 also specifies what phenomena the present book seeks to describe, differentiate, and explain – and therefore what possibly relevant phenomena it downplays. For the most part, chapters to come neglect individual aggression and the least coordinated forms of brawls. They concentrate instead on common mechanisms and systematic variation among violent rituals, coordinated destruction, opportunism, brawls, scattered attacks, and broken negotiations. The oval containing individual aggression creeps across the threshold into collective violence to accommodate those cases where a lone assassin or terrorist strikes in the name of some dissident group but without visible support from that group.

Similarly, the oval for brawls dips below the collective–individual border to signal that, in the course of some such events, all significant interpersonal coordination disappears. This distinction of individual from collective violence will not satisfy anyone who believes that all violence springs from the same deep individual propensities. (Nor, for that matter, will it please anyone who thinks that crowds obliterate individuality and develop minds of their own.) But it does greatly facilitate the integration of violence into the study of politics at large. Because political analysts have commonly considered violent interaction as marginal (or even antithetical) to politics, that is no small advantage.

Knowledgeable students of collective violence will notice that the salience–coordination typology omits some standard terms. Interstate war, civil war, revolution, and rebellion fail to figure as separate types. Whether authorities and observers label an episode as interstate war, civil war, revolution, or rebellion does make a difference, because each label invokes a different set of legal conventions and calls up a different set of historical analogies. Furthermore, participants in some cases of collective violence organize their actions around existing models, for example of a coup d'état, a lynching, a gang rumble, or an attack on a dishonored house; the model lends coherence and predictability to interaction among the participants. Later chapters will present many episodes of model-based collective violence.

Nevertheless, I argue against thinking of each of these kinds of episodes as constituting a distinct causal realm with its own laws. I advocate recognizing multiple varieties of collective violence – coordinated destruction, broken negotiations, opportunism, and more – in different phases and segments of wars or revolutions. I urge (and practice) identification of analogies (including analogies in the adoption of culturally available models) among the causes of coups, lynching, rumbles, and attacks on dishonored houses.

I have omitted the widely used term "riot" from the typology for a different reason: because it embodies a political judgment rather than an analytical distinction. Authorities and observers label as riots the damage-doing gatherings of which they disapprove, but they use terms like demonstration, protest, resistance, or retaliation for essentially similar events of which they approve. In cataloging thousands of violent events – many of them called riots (or the local-language equivalent) by authorities and observers – from multiple countries over several centuries, I have not once found an instance in which the participants called the event a riot or identified themselves as rioters.

For both sorts of reasons, the word "terror" appears nowhere in the typology. Many violent incidents that people call terroristic show up in later chapters but usually under other terms. Terror always refers to someone else's behavior and actually names episodes ranging from coordinated destruction (simultaneous attacks on multiple buildings) to scattered attacks (furtive killings of police). Deeply ingrained assumptions about the causation of social processes by unified intentions – for example, that revolutions occur because revolutionaries want them, or that terrorism occurs because crazy terrorists exist – will make my analytical choices jarring for many. I ask only that readers bear with me long enough to see how this book's approach helps explain features of collective violence with which intentional accounts have trouble.

Let us not confuse violence with crime or with illegal behavior more generally. At both the individual and the collective level, governments generally distinguish approximately among behaviors that they prescribe, others they tolerate, and still others they forbid. Crime consists of (a) those legally defined behaviors (mostly individual) that governments not only forbid but also detect and punish, plus (b) detected and punished failures to perform behaviors prescribed by governments. Everywhere a great deal of behavior forbidden by one law or another escapes detection and punishment. Many legally forbidden behaviors, furthermore, fall outside the range of crime in any strong sense of the word; traffic violations, nonconformity to building codes, failures to meet tax deadlines, and similar violations offer cases in point. The vast bulk of crime and of noncriminal illegal behavior occurs without a trace of violence. Crime, illegal behavior, and violence overlap, but they do not coincide.

Moreover, a good deal of violent behavior occurs under the cover of law. Government agents and allies regularly employ violence as they pursue their own ends. Soldiers, sailors, police, jailers, and guards enjoy legal rights – even legal obligations – to use violent means on behalf of governments. Within the purviews of most historical governments, multiple parties have exercised some control over violent means with varying degrees of authorization by governments, and their relations to governments have shifted rapidly. Pirates, privateers, paramilitaries, bandits, mercenaries, mafiosi, militias, posses, guerrilla forces, vigilante groups, company police, and bodyguards all operate in a middle ground between (on one side) the full authorization of a national army and (on the other) the private employment of violence by parents, lovers, or feuding clans. We will eventually have to examine how different forms and uses of violence relate to established governmental institutions. Governmental sponsorship and governmental repression strongly affect the character and intensity of collective violence in any regime.

Mechanisms, Processes, and Explanations

If we were idea people, we would no doubt concentrate on how different governments and cultures incorporate different conceptions of violence and its permissibility, then show how variations in prevailing forms of violence correspond to distinctly different shared understandings. When examining different types of violence and the regimes in which they occur, we will pay some attention to variations in ideas but mainly seek explanations elsewhere. If we were behavior people, we would no doubt emphasize how motives, incentives, opportunities, and controls that promote or inhibit damaging acts alter from one social setting to another, again seeking to show how such alterations affect the character and intensity of collective violence. Motives, incentives, opportunities, and controls receive more attention than ideas in the following pages, but still do not constitute the nubs of the explanations to come. As relation people, we will focus our attention on interpersonal processes that promote, inhibit, or channel collective violence and connect it with nonviolent politics.

We are looking for explanations of variability: not general laws or total explanations of violent events, but accounts of what causes major variations among times, places, and social circumstances in the character of collective violence. We search for robust mechanisms and processes that cause change and variation. Mechanisms are causes on the small scale: similar events that produce essentially the same immediate effects across a wide range of circumstances. Analysts often refer to large-scale causes (poverty, widespread frustration, extremism, resource competition, and so on), proposing them as necessary or sufficient conditions for whole episodes of collective violence. Here, in contrast, we search for recurrent small-scale mechanisms that produce identical immediate effects in many different circumstances yet combine variously to generate very different outcomes on the large scale. Relevant mechanisms come in three flavors: environmental, cognitive, and relational.

Environmental mechanisms alter relations between the social circumstances in question and their external environment, as for example when drought depletes the agriculture on which guerrillas depend for their day-to-day survival. *Cognitive* mechanisms operate through alterations of individual and collective perceptions, as when members of a fighting group decide collectively that they have mistaken an enemy for a friend. *Relational* mechanisms change connections among social units, as when a gang leader makes a deal with a cocaine wholesaler and thus converts petty protection rackets into high-risk drug merchandising.

Analyses to follow call on all three varieties of mechanism, but stress relational mechanisms. The mechanism of *boundary activation* will, for example, make appearances time after time in later explanations of collective violence. It consists of a shift in social interactions such that they increasingly (a) organize around a single us–them boundary and (b) differentiate between within-boundary and cross-boundary interactions. (Boundary deactivation denotes the opposite shift, toward new or multiple boundaries and toward decreased difference between within-boundary and cross-boundary interactions.) Hence us–them boundaries such as male–female, Hutu–Tutsi, cowboy outfit A versus cowboy outfit B, or landlord–peasant, although always available in certain settings, shift from being relatively insignificant to absolutely dominant for current interaction.

Again, in pages to come we will often encounter the relational mechanism of *brokerage*. Brokerage operates uniformly by definition, always connecting at least two social sites more directly than they were previously connected. Yet the activation of brokerage does not in itself guarantee more effective coordination of action at the connected sites; that depends on initial conditions and combinations with other mechanisms. For example, if brokerage connects factions on each side of an us–them boundary without establishing new connections across the boundary, then it facilitates polarization of the two sides and thus reduces overall coordination of their actions. If, on the other hand, brokers compete for control on the same side of a boundary, then fragmentation results – at least until one broker eliminates the others.

In some circumstances, then, one mechanism activates another mechanism. Brokerage commonly stimulates boundary activation, as local disputes between individuals or households that happen to occur across an available but not currently salient boundary become large categorical confrontations through the intervention of third parties who connect disputants with other members of their categories. In Rwanda's genocide, brokerage by Hutu activists activated the Hutu–Tutsi boundary among people who had previously lived, however uneasily, in peaceful coexistence.

Processes are combinations and sequences of mechanisms that produce similar effects across a wide range of circumstances. Without the name, we have already encountered the process of *polarization*. Polarization involves widening of political and social space between claimants in a contentious episode and gravitation of previously uncommitted or moderate actors toward one, the other, or both extremes. Polarization combines mechanisms of opportunity–threat spirals, competition, category formation, and the omnipresent brokerage. Polarization generally promotes collective violence because it makes the us–them boundary more salient, hollows out the uncommitted middle, intensifies conflict across the boundary, raises the stakes of winning or losing, and enhances opportunities for leaders to initiate action against their enemies.

Close readers of later chapters will catch me blurring the distinction between mechanisms and processes. Sometimes, for example, I call brokerage a mechanism and sometimes I call it a process. That depends mainly on the scale of analysis: when watching how a single actor produces a precise link between two other clearly defined and previously unconnected actors, I will speak of brokerage as a mechanism. When speaking more broadly about how a whole category of actors (for example, Hutu Power leaders in Rwanda) produce previously missing links, I will generally speak of brokerage as a process. Looked at closely, every mechanism compounds smaller-scale mechanisms – environmental, cognitive, and relational. We may call an invariant and widely applicable cause a mechanism when *at the current level of observation* its components are invisible and its immediate effects indistinguishable.

Mechanisms and processes give us another way of thinking about this book's rationale. The provisional typology of brawls, scattered attacks, broken negotiations, and so on distinguishes locations within the coordination–salience space where similar bundles of mechanisms are operating. Boundary activation and brokerage appear together more frequently, for example, in the high-coordination–high-salience zone called coordinated destruction than in the low-coordination–low-salience zone called scattered attacks. At least so goes the book's argument.

What's Coming

Where are we going? This book pursues three objectives. First, it maps variations in forms of collective violence to clarify what we must explain. Second, within each variety of collective violence it searches for recurrent cause–effect links that operate in similar ways across a wide range of times and places – cause–effect links, for example, that appear in scattered attacks whenever and wherever they occur. Third, it identifies causes that work similarly in diverse types of collective violence and thus affect the likelihood and character of violence at large. For instance, we will see eventually that brokerage – intervention establishing new connections among previously unconnected persons and groups – regularly promotes moves toward more highly coordinated forms of collective violence. The point is not to establish general laws for all sorts of violence but rather to identify crucial causal processes: those that operate similarly in the short run across a wide range of circumstances yet produce dramatically different forms of collective violence depending on their settings, combinations, and sequences.

If successful, such an approach will not produce total explanations of all violent episodes. It will not even provide complete explanations of single events. It will, however, yield several valuable results. It will explain significant variations in violence – in its quantity, intensity, and character – across time, place, and social setting. It will explain critical differences among violent episodes. It will explain shifts in the character of collective violence within particular places and populations. It will pinpoint processes that translate generally favorable conditions for collective violence (e.g., the presence of many unsupervised young men) into actual violent interactions. It will, finally, explain puzzling features of particular episodes: why, for example, otherwise peaceable Rwandans mobilized by the tens of thousands to massacre their neighbors in April 1994.

If successful, the effort will eventually dissolve the classification of collective violence into coordinated destruction, violent rituals, opportunism, brawls, scattered attacks, and broken negotiations. These types will turn out to represent different combinations of settings and causal processes but not distinct species of social interaction. The types will continue to guide comparisons and searches for causes, but they will not require separate kinds of explanation. Furthermore, recognizing the porosity of boundaries among types will make it easier to understand mutations – for example, how a coup d'état escalates into a large-scale massacre or how mass confrontation disintegrates into scattered sabotage. In each case, transition from type to type depends on the activation or cessation of crucial causal processes. The point of this book is to identify those crucial processes and show how they work.

Despite its concentration on collective processes, the book eventually helps explain individual violence as well. It makes four contributions to that difficult enterprise.

First, by showing how the dynamics of interpersonal interaction transform prevailing beliefs, inhibitions, and sentiments in the course of collective violence, it suggests analogues of the same transformations at the individual level.

Second, by identifying social processes that facilitate and constrain large-scale deployment of violent means, it similarly suggests analogous forms of facilitation and constraint at the small scale.

Third, it clarifies where the categories of difference that often activate violence at the small scale – categories of race, gender, ethnicity, religion, or class – come from, and how individuals justify attacks on others who fall on the wrong side of a categorical boundary.

Finally, it sheds light on how violent means and practices become available to individuals and pairs of individuals – not only ordinary people who turn from nonviolent to violent forms of interaction but also the specialists in violence who will figure prominently as we proceed through violent rituals, coordinated destruction, opportunism, brawls, scattered attack, and broken negotiations.

Even if it accomplishes these ambitious aims, the book does not do some things readers might expect of it. For neither the violence to be explained nor the proposed explanations does it lay down a neat array of measurable variables, specify appropriate measures for those variables, and perform the measurements – much less use such measurements to demonstrate that violence varies in accordance with the book's main arguments. I admire good measurement and estimation and will frequently draw on other people's in pages to come; in earlier work, I often attempted just such measurement and estimation myself. But this book has a different aim: to develop new lines of explanation that apply across apparently disparate times, places, groups, social settings, and forms of action.

By the same token, the book overflows with examples but never lines up a systematic body of evidence that could, in principle, verify or falsify its main arguments. The next two chapters, for example, make strong claims about the sorts of political regimes and transitions from regime to regime that promote high or low levels of collective violence. They build on and cite previous research indicating that overall intensities of violence rise at regime transitions and between the extremes of low-violence repressive regimes and low-violence democratic regimes, but they provide neither neat comparisons among well-documented regimes that differ in their levels of collective violence nor new data on international variation in those regards. Instead, the book's innumerable examples serve to construct and clarify new explanations of variation in the form, intensity, and incidence of collective violence. Approach the chapters that follow as a preliminary synthesis, a guide to new research and theory.

Despite its synthetic aims, the book remains open to empirical and theoretical challenge. Empirical challenges could occur at two levels: in demonstrating that I have misrepresented particular cases (such as opportunistic violence in Rwanda) and in showing that available data contradict my claims concerning some sort of variation (such as differences in the character and intensity of collective violence between high-capacity democratic and high-capacity undemocratic regimes). Theoretical challenges could identify either logical flaws

in the general arguments or existing theories that explain change and variation in particular types of collective violence more precisely and economically
than do the mechanisms and processes proposed here. Surely some empirical
and theoretical challenges will require repairs to one aspect or another of the
book's arguments. I am claiming, however, that over the terrain they cover the
relational arguments point to better explanations than the ideal and behavioral
accounts now prevailing in analyses of collective violence.

Here, then, is how such an agenda-setting book proceeds. The next chapter
(Chapter 2) looks more extensively at the place of violence in public political
life. Chapter 3 takes up trends and variations in violence during the last few
centuries. Chapters 4 through 9 deal separately with each of our provisional
types: violent rituals, coordinated destruction, opportunism, brawls, scattered
attacks, and broken negotiations. Chapter 10 draws conclusions from the whole
enterprise.

2

Violence as Politics

Violent Governments

With collective violence we enter the terrain of contentious politics, where people make discontinuous, public, collective claims on each other. By no means all contentious politics generates violence; our problem is precisely to explain when contention takes a violent turn. But all collective violence involves contention of one kind or another.

We can conveniently mark our crossing into contentious politics' territory by noticing when governments – more generally, individuals or organizations that control concentrated means of coercion – become parties to discontinuous, public, collective claims. Governments become parties to contention as claimants, objects of claims, or stakeholders. When leaders of two Muslim activist groups compete for recognition as valid interlocutors for all Muslims, for example, the governments to which the interlocutors would speak inevitably figure as stakeholders. Similarly, when miners strike against mine owners, government officials may avoid vigorous intervention (or even visible involvement) in the conflict, but government looms nearby as a setter of rules for collective bargaining, a supplier of police, and a possible mediator. Collective violence, then, is a form of contentious politics. It counts as *contentious* because participants are making claims that affect each other's interests. It counts as *politics* because relations of participants to governments are always at stake.

Nevertheless, violence and government maintain a queasy relationship. Where and when governments are very weak, interpersonal violence commonly proliferates in the populations under the nominal jurisdictions of those governments. Where and when governments grow very strong, violence among civilians usually declines. Politicians and political philosophers often advocate good, strong government as a bulwark against violent victimization. But all governments maintain control over concentrated means of violence in the form of arms, troops, guards, and jails. Most governments use those means extensively to maintain what their rulers define as public order.

In all governments, furthermore, some rulers also use violent means to further their own power and material advantage. When large-scale collective violence occurs, government forces of one sort or another almost always play significant parts as attackers, objects of attack, competitors, or intervening agents. International war is simply the extreme case – but, on the whole, the most lethal – of governmental involvement in violence. For these reasons, collective violence and nonviolent politics intersect incessantly.

Rulers, police, philosophers, and historians often distinguish between force and violence. Force, in this view, consists of legitimate short-run damage and seizure – which typically means that the persons who administer damage enjoy legal protection for their actions. Force might therefore include legitimate self-defense but not unprovoked aggression. In such a perspective, violence refers to damage that does not enjoy legal protection.

Will the distinction between force and violence serve our purposes? As citizens, all of us want to make some such distinction; we want to draw lines between right and wrong uses of governmental authority to seize and damage persons or their property. To varying degrees and with competing definitions of propriety, we also want governments to deploy their concentrated coercive means against improper uses of violence. For purposes of explaining violent interactions, however, the distinction between (legitimate) force and (illegitimate) violence faces three insuperable objections.

First, the precise boundary of legitimate force remains a matter of fierce dispute in all political systems. Just think of debates about what does or doesn't constitute proper police behavior in pursuing a suspect, about the rights and wrongs of capital punishment, or about permissible military actions against civilians in wartime. In the very course of initially peaceful demonstrations that turn violent, demonstrators and police are almost always contesting the boundary between legitimate and illegitimate uses of coercive means.

Second, in practical experience a long continuum runs from (1) duly licensed governmental actions whose propriety almost everyone accepts through (2) derelictions by governmental agents to (3) damage wrought with secret support or encouragement from some segment of some government. Consider FBI infiltration of violence-wielding black nationalist groups during the 1960s, American support for paramilitary forces in Guatemala, El Salvador, and Nicaragua during the 1980s, or Muslim activists' attacks on New York's World Trade Center in 1993 and 2001; in all these cases, collective violence depended in part on the collusion of governmental officials, domestic or foreign. Exactly where along that continuum could we reasonably locate a firm boundary between legitimate force and illegitimate violence? From whose perspective?

Third – and most important for this book's purpose – a large share of the collective violence in the episodes that people call riots, rebellions, or revolutions directly involves governmental agents as purveyors or objects of damage. Without including deaths inflicted or suffered by police and troops, we would have no way of explaining variation in the deadliness of different sorts of collective encounters. In the Paris Commune of 1871, for example, one set of estimates tells us that about 16,000 rebels died in street fighting with French national troops, the conquering national army executed another 3,500 rebels after street fighting ended, and in the process 880 members of the national army died (Chesnais 1976: 168). In evaluating the Commune's ferocity, we would surely want to include the estimated 16,880 deaths on both sides in street fighting, and might want to include the 3,500 executions as well. For purposes of explanation, it would be odd indeed to call one set of deaths an outcome of violence and another an outcome of legitimate force. If the rebels had won, would their violent acts have converted retroactively to legitimate force?

Not all collective violence, to be sure, consists of confrontations between authorities and citizens. Enough does, however, to require careful examination of authority–citizen interactions. No student of collective violence can afford to exclude actions of governmental authorities or interactions between governmental agents and nongovernmental actors. Indeed, we must eventually explain why regimes differ so greatly with respect to which forms and agents of violence they sponsor, legitimate, tolerate, or forbid.

This chapter identifies the political context for that great variation. After a brief introduction to regimes, it reviews the constitution of political actors, the special place of political entrepreneurs as connectors and organizers of collective violence, and the significance of specialists in violence such as police and bandits. It then turns to comparisons of broad types of regime, characterizes broad patterns of political interaction in different sorts of regime, and looks more closely at variation in kinds and intensities of collective violence in different types of regime. This review of political contexts should make it easier to understand how the organization of political life in general shapes the character of collective violence as well as how closely violent and nonviolent forms of political life interact.

Let us therefore adopt a simple set of conceptual tools for the work at hand. Once we have identified a government, we can search around that government for organized political actors that sometimes interact with the government. The whole set of their interactions with each other and with the government constitutes a *political regime*. Within a regime, we can distinguish:

agents of government;
polity members (constituted political actors enjoying routine access to government agents and resources);
challengers (constituted political actors lacking that routine access);
subjects (persons and groups not currently organized into constituted political actors); and
outside political actors, including other governments.

These are, of course, whole categories of actors rather than single actors. Government-backed categorical boundaries separate them at two levels: overall, and then again within categories. Overall, for example, any government makes some distinctions between its own agents and polity members, typically putting governmental resources directly at the disposition of agents but requiring polity members to follow established procedures (formal applications, petitions, contracts, hearings, and the like) in order to gain access to similar resources.

Governments also sometimes accept or reinforce boundaries separating challengers from polity members by bargaining out who belongs to them and who has the right to speak for the challengers even while denying them routine access to governmental resources. During early stages of the 1960s civil rights movement, for example, U.S. government agents began talking with leaders of civil rights organizations without by any means recognizing them as speaking for African Americans at large. Later, organizations such as the National Association for the Advancement of Colored People acquired a regular place in government-backed discussions of race relations, while the government continued to harass a number of black nationalist groups. Thus the distinctions among governmental agents, polity members, challengers, subjects, and outside political actors acquire legal standing.

Category formation is itself a crucial political process. Category formation creates identities. A social category consists of a set of sites that share a boundary distinguishing all of them from (and relating all of them to) at least one set of sites visibly excluded by the boundary. Category formation occurs by means of three different mechanisms: invention, borrowing, and encounter. *Invention* involves authoritative drawing of a boundary and prescription of relations across that boundary, as when Bosnian Serb leaders decree who in Bosnia-Herzegovina is a Serb and who not, then regulate how Serbs interact with non-Serbs. *Borrowing* involves importation of a boundary *cum* relations package already existing elsewhere and its installation in the local setting, as when rural French Revolutionaries divided along the lines of Patriot versus Aristocrat that had already split Paris and other major French cities. *Encounter* involves initial contact between previously separate (but internally well-connected) networks in the course of which members of one network begin competing for resources with members of the other, interactively generating definitions of the boundary and relations across it.

But categorical boundaries appear within the major clumps of actors as well. Any particular government may, for example, have dealings with different polity members organized as local communities, religious congregations, military units, and categories of property holders. Furthermore, we will soon have to single out two overlapping sorts of political actors that figure prominently in collective violence: (i) political entrepreneurs whose specialty consists of organizing, linking, dividing, and representing constituencies; and (ii) specialists in deployment of violent means such as soldiers, police, thugs, and gang leaders. Distinctions among agents of government, polity members, challengers, subjects, and outside political actors simply start the analysis. They say that a significant divide separates those actors having routine access to government agents and resources from others (e.g., protesting national minorities) lacking that access.

Transactions among agents of government, polity members, challengers, and subjects constitute a *regime*. Public politics within a regime consists of claim-making interactions among agents, polity members, challengers, and outside political actors as well. Public politics includes tax collection, military conscription, individual voting, application for pensions, and many other transactions to which governments are parties.

Contentious politics consists of that (large) subset of public politics in which the claims are collective and would, if realized, affect their objects' interests. Contentious politics therefore excludes routine tax collection, reporting for military service, voting, and application for pensions. But any of these can become contentious if people mount collective resistance to them. In Old Regime Europe, for example, a significant share of all popular rebellions began with royal attempts to impose new or augmented taxes (Tilly 1993).

Some forms of public politics, furthermore, almost always involve collective contention; rebellions, revolutions, social movements, demonstrations, general strikes, and contested electoral campaigns illustrate the irreducibly contentious forms of public politics. Some contentious claim making, finally, takes the form of damage to persons or objects; rebels kill rulers, revolutionaries sack palaces, and so on. That is the subset of contentious politics whose variation we are trying to explain.

In Rwanda of early 1994, President Habyarimana's government based itself in the capital (Kigali) and exercised its contested jurisdiction through the rest of the country. Polity members included Hutu groups loyal to Habyarimana's faction, while challengers included both some dissident Hutu groups and fragmented Tutsi networks, some of them armed. On the boundary of challengers and outside political actors stood Tutsi militias that operated along the Rwandan border with Uganda. The Ugandan government itself, host to Tutsi militias and base for their raids into Rwanda, figured as a significant outside political actor.

The contention in question centered on competing claims for control of the Rwandan state and territory. In this case, the claims rapidly turned violent. Our task is to explain how and why such processes occur. In particular, it is to explain why violence varies so much in salience and coordination. Rwanda gives us a terrifying example of high salience and coordination together. But elsewhere – and even in Rwanda, most of the time before 1994 – collective violence occurs mostly in less salient and less coordinated versions. What accounts for that enormous variability?

Political Actors and Identities

The word "regime" summarizes interactions among governmental agents, polity members, challengers, and subjects. More precisely, it clumps myriad transactions among people into those categories and then abstracts mightily from them. As we will soon see abundantly, it matters whether people organize their interactions as aggrieved citizens, advocates of special interests, religious congregations, local communities, ethnic groups, suppressed nations, women, gays, veterans, or something else. The available array of political identities makes a difference.

Who acts? What sorts of people are likely to engage in contentious politics? What sorts of people, that is, are likely to make concerted public claims that involve governments as objects or third parties and that, if realized, would visibly affect interests of persons outside their own number? In principle, any connected set of persons (within a given regime) to whom a definition of shared stakes in that polity's operation is available would qualify. In practice, beyond a very small scale, every actor that engages in claim making includes at least one cluster of previously connected persons among whom have circulated widely accepted stories concerning their strategic situation: opportunities, threats, available means of action, likely consequences of those actions, evaluations of those consequences, capacities to act, memories of previous contention, and inventories of other likely parties to any action. Many of the Hutu activists who spurred Rwandan massacres of Tutsi and nonconforming Hutu during the spring and summer of 1994 belonged, for example, to a well-connected militia run by the president whose death prompted the bloodletting (Mamdani 2001).

In practice, furthermore, such actors have generally established previous relations – contentious or not – to other collective actors; those relations have shaped internal structures of the actors and helped generate their stories. In practice, finally, constituent units of claim-making actors often consist not of living, breathing individuals but of groups, organizations, bundles of social relations, and social sites such as occupations and neighborhoods. Actors consist of networks deploying partially shared histories, cultures, and collective connections with other actors. Note once again the centrality of Hutu militias as connectors in the Rwandan genocide of 1994.

Such actors, however, almost never describe themselves as composite networks. Instead, they offer collective nouns: they call themselves workers, women, residents of X, or United Front Against Y. Such *political identities* offer public, collective answers to the questions "Who are you?", "Who are we?", and "Who are they?". As such, they are subject to constant challenge and negotiation. Who spoke for the Hutu, and who spoke for Rwandans at large, became questions of life and death in 1994.

Political identities assemble the following crucial elements:

boundaries separating "us" from "them" – for example, dividing Hutu from Tutsi;

shared *stories* about those boundaries – for example, Hutu stories about distinctive characteristics of Hutu and Tutsi, as well as origins of their differences;

social relations across the boundaries – for example, forms of address governing transactions between Hutu and Tutsi;

social relations *within* the boundaries – for example, signals among Hutu to indicate their common membership.

Political identities serve as springboards for claim making, but they do far more political work than that. To put a complicated process very simply, governmental agents sort political identities into legitimate and illegitimate, recognized and unrecognized. Some regimes tolerate special-interest associations such as Greenpeace or Boy Scouts as legitimate political actors, while others do not tolerate public nongovernmental associations of any kind. Even where organizations speaking for ethnic, religious, or racial categories have a legitimate right to exist, some organizations gain recognition as valid representatives of their ethnic, religious, or racial category while others gain no such recognition.

Political rights come into existence through struggles for recognition (Fower-aker & Landman 1997; Tilly 1998a).

The rise of nationalism strongly affected the character of such recognition struggles. Before the American and French Revolutions, people rarely de-manded rights or claimed that others had obligations to them on the grounds of belonging to a distinct nation. People maintained loyalties to religious and cultural traditions, but in most cases they undertook collective action on behalf of those traditions only when someone else proposed to stamp them out or to take away rights attached to them. From the late eighteenth century, however, nationalism gained importance as a political principle: a nation should have its own independent state, and an independent state should have its own nation.

From this principle flowed two antagonistic versions of nationalism. *Top-down* nationalism claimed the right of existing rulers to impose their preferred def-initions of national culture and welfare on subjects of their regimes. *Bottom-up* nationalism claimed the right of distinct nations within heterogeneous states to acquire political independence. Each fed the other; the more rulers tried to im-pose national cultures and obligations, the more distinct minorities clamored for independence. Because people had often organized networks of trust, trade, sociability, and mutual aid around religious and ethnic ties, top-down nation-alism did not simply wound minority self-esteem; it threatened their means of day-to-day survival.

From the American Revolution onward, leaders of powerful states – notably the French Revolutionary and Napoleonic states – used the principle of self-determination to pick apart composite rival powers such as the Habsburg and Ottoman empires. Thus it became advantageous to minorities within all sorts of regimes to designate themselves as nations in the making, to create histories and practices validating that designation, and to ask for outside help in achieving in-dependence. Enterprising ethnic leaders were quick to see that they could gain power by gaining recognition as representatives of valid nations and could easily lose power if someone else got there first. Since World War II, most large-scale violent conflicts across the world have involved some such claims.

Similar recognition struggles occur at a smaller scale on behalf of a wide range of other identities. As American gay and lesbian activists have learned, gaining legitimacy as a category of political actor entails significant costs and benefits (Bernstein 1997). Presenting your constituency as an unjustly excluded minority, for instance, requires stressing analogies with formerly excluded mi-norities; if successful, this gives the new minority access to already established rights. As competition among different would-be spokespersons for gay and les-bian interests illustrates, the stakes of recognition are also serious for particular organizations and leaders: does ACT UP, for instance, speak for all American gays?

Much of what people loosely call "identity politics" consists of struggles over legitimation and recognition. The struggles take place within boundaries, across boundaries, over the placement and character of boundaries, around stories attached to those boundaries, and about relations between people sharing a common answer to the question "Who are you?" on one side and other political actors, including agents of government, on the other (Tilly 2002).

Political Entrepreneurs and Specialists in Violence

The mention of contemporary social movements should remind us of political actors whose voices have remained muted so far. Like their economic counterparts, *political entrepreneurs* engage in various forms of brokerage: creating new connections between previously unconnected social sites. But they do more than link sites. They specialize in activation, connection, coordination, and representation. They specialize in activating (and sometimes deactivating) boundaries, stories, and relations, as when Bosnian Serb leaders sharpened boundaries between Serbs and their Muslim or Croatian neighbors with whom Bosnians of Serbian lineage had long mingled, married, traded, and collaborated. They specialize in connecting (and sometimes disconnecting) distinct groups and networks, as when those same leaders integrated armed Serbian gangs into larger nationalist coalitions. They specialize in coordination, as when those leaders organized joint action on the part of those coalitions.

Political entrepreneurs specialize, finally, in representation, as when Bosnian Serb leaders claimed to speak for all Bosnians of Serbian lineage while demanding aid from Serbia in establishing Serbian political entities within Bosnia. In these ways, political entrepreneurs wield significant influence over the presence, absence, form, loci, and intensity of collective violence. When they promote violence, they do so by activating boundaries, stories, and relations that have already accumulated histories of violence; by connecting already violent actors with previously nonviolent allies; by coordinating destructive campaigns; and by representing their constituencies through threats of violence. After the fact, both participants and observers speak of deeply felt identities and age-old hatreds. But before and during contention, political entrepreneurs play critical parts in activating, connecting, coordinating, and representing participants in violent encounters.

By means of activation, connection, coordination, and representation, political entrepreneurs necessarily engage in inequality-generating opportunity hoarding. They often engage in exploitation as well. They organize opportunity hoarding as they construct or activate us–them boundaries between their networks and outsiders, fend off rival claimants to coordinate and represent some or all of the same networks, draw necessary resources from those networks, and deploy those resources in ways that simultaneously forward collective claims, reproduce the structures they have built, and sustain their own power. Of course they often fail in one regard or another. If that happens, the failure often generates collective violence inside the coalition's boundaries as rival entrepreneurs and their factions battle for control of activation, connection, coordination, and representation.

When political entrepreneurs coordinate the efforts of a large coalition to the advantage of a smaller set within that coalition, their opportunity hoarding becomes a form of exploitation. These well-known risks of contentious politics deserve emphasis because they help explain why political entrepreneurs often promote collective violence when a cool reading of their whole constituency's interest prescribes disbanding, escaping, or lying low. They become specialists in activating boundaries that serve their own readings of collective advantage.

Political entrepreneurs complement and overlap with another significant type of political actor, the *violent specialist*. Every government includes specialists in violence, people who control means of inflicting damage on persons and objects. The cast of characters varies considerably by type of government but commonly includes military personnel, police, guards, jailers, executioners, and judicial officers. In my youth I served a term in the U.S. Navy as paymaster of an eight-ship amphibious squadron. When my staff and I went out to pay the troops, we strapped on loaded .45-caliber pistols to protect the cash we carried as we moved from ship to ship. Although we were far from crack shots, for those hours we became petty specialists in violence. (In fact, an unpleasant interchange with a naval base sentry during which I displayed my gun too prominently almost got me court-martialed. Even cowards like me become dangerous when supplied with heavy weapons.) Most governmental specialists in violence command greater coercive means and more extensive skills in using them than did my little band. They range from sharpshooters to bombardiers to executioners.

Plenty of specialists in violence, however, work outside of government. Some athletes – boxers, gladiators, bullfighters, and rugby players are obvious examples – specialize in doing damage. Armed guards, private police, paramilitary forces, guerrilla warriors, terrorists, thugs, bandits, kidnappers, enforcers, members of fighting gangs, and automobile wreckers sometimes enjoy governmental protection, but usually operate outside of government, even in defiance of government. Before the rise of centralized states on the European model during the seventeenth and eighteenth centuries, indeed, innumerable specialists in violence exercised their trades in at least partial independence of governmental control through most of the world. Even powerful Chinese dynasties lived with warlords and bandits in their midst as well as with armed and predatory nomadic peoples along their edges. In Europe itself, private armies, mercenaries, local militias, bandits, and pirates all competed at some times and collaborated at other times with nominally national armies (Thomson 1994).

Lest we slip into thinking of violent specialists as driven by bloodlust, we should recognize that for most of them most of the time the ideal outcome of a political interaction is to manipulate others without damaging anything. The genuinely effective specialist deploys *threats* of violence so persuasively that others comply before the damage begins (Blok 2001; Cohn 1993). To be sure, an occasional demonstration of ruthlessness solidifies a specialist's reputation, and backing away from visible challenges damages a specialist's credibility. Real-life mafiosi (as distinguished from their cinematic simulacra) know this well; by threatening violence for noncompliance, they provide guarantees for contracts where courts and kin fail to guarantee them, but now and then mafiosi also display the requisite readiness to kill, maim, and steal (Blok 1974, 2001; Gambetta 1993; Varese 2001; Volkov 2002). For government-backed armies, precision parades and displays of weapons produce some of the same effects. Visible ability to inflict damage promotes power over and above anything that damage itself might accomplish.

The category of political entrepreneurs therefore overlaps with the category of violent specialists. At the intersection of the two we find leaders of mercenaries, international weapons merchants, regional warlords, military rulers, and many a political figure who disposes of his or her own armed force. Over the long run of human history, indeed, most important political figures have combined entrepreneurship with control of coercive means. Only during the last few centuries has the unarmed power holder become a common political actor.

Contemporary India provides striking examples of specialists in violence, some of whom are also political entrepreneurs. Psychiatric ethnographer Sudhir Kakar describes a *pehlwan* (wrestler–enforcer) he met through a Muslim political boss in Hyderabad. Akbar, the *pehlwan*, has a long police record, beginning with petty crimes when he was 20. He also joined the police for a while, only to end in prison for assaulting a police inspector. He now owns a hotel and three wrestling gymnasiums, but he makes most of his money from the "land business":

Baldly stated, "land business" is one of the outcomes of India's crumbling legal system. Since landlord and tenant disputes as well as other disputes about land and property can take well over a decade to be sorted out if a redress of grievances is sought through the courts, the *pehlwan* is approached by one of the parties to the dispute to evict or otherwise intimidate the opposing party. The dispute being thus "settled," the *pehlwan* receives a large fee for his services. In the case of well-known *pehlwans* with [gymnasiums] and thus a large supply of young toughs as students and all-purpose assistants, land business can be very profitable. (Kakar 1996: 60)

When both sides in a dispute hire their own *pehlwans*, the two enforcers usually get together and reach a settlement without open fighting; their joint forces then make it difficult for the aggrieved parties to resist the settlement. But when Hindus and Muslims take to the streets in Hyderabad, Akbar's athletes join the front lines on behalf of Muslim power. As Akbar boasts:

The impression is false that in every riot more Muslims than Hindus are killed. I can say with complete confidence that at least in Hyderabad this is not true. Here the Muslims are very strong and completely united. More Hindus than Muslims are killed in every riot. (Kakar 1996: 64)

Akbar is, of course, a certain sort of political entrepreneur who specializes in activation, connection, coordination, and representation. But Akbar and his young men are also specialists in violence. Studying India in the 1980s and 1990s, Paul Brass speaks of an "institutionalized riot system" including a wide array of violent specialists who operate under loose control of party leaders (Brass 1997: 13–20). Outside of riots, they act as guards and enforcers of various kinds. Within riots, they serve as coordinators and shock troops.

Vadim Volkov describes a Russian variant of specialists in violence who eerily echo their Indian counterparts. As markets opened up in Ekaterinburg during the late 1980s, members of sports clubs took to offering protection to merchants for regular fees. They specialized in exploitation with a vengeance; their control over violent means allowed them to draw tribute from shopkeepers' efforts. The founders of the Uralmashevskaya gang were "brothers Grigorii and Konstantin Tsyganov, the wrestler Sergei Vorobiev, the skier Alexander Khabarov, and boxers Sergei Terentiev and Sergei Kurdiumov" (Volkov 2000: 734; see also Volkov 2002, chap. 4).

Fending off other gangs, Uralmashevskaya fought its way to a position of economic and political power in the Ekaterinburg region. Its leaders became active political entrepreneurs. In 1996, for example, Khabarov organized the regional Worker's Movement in Support of Boris Yeltsin; for his services, he received a personal letter of thanks from reelected president Yeltsin and an engraved watch from the regional governor.

Local citizens, Volkov reports, still regard the association as a criminal gang. Yet he summarizes its career:

Uralmashevskaya racketeer gang has thus undergone the following evolution: Specialists in violence – former sportsmen – create an organization, a violence-managing agency that allows them to extract tribute from the local business by offering protection. Having established a kind of territorial control, the agency wages a war with competing violence-managing agencies. It survives and wins the elimination contest, expanding both in terms of territory and commercial opportunities. Having attained the monopoly position among informal enforcers, *uralmashevskaya* makes a conscious choice of economic policy of reasonable taxation and reliable protection of property, thus creating a relatively secure environment and competitive advantages for its business partners. (Volkov 2000: 741)

We see a criminal gang forming strong ties to the regional government; indeed, we see it becoming something like a government agency. Although organizations like Uralmashevskaya continue to carry on technically illegal activities, they engage increasingly in the provision of services that businesses themselves demand – protective services, contract enforcement, debt collection, and the like. Although they continue to recruit lower-level operatives from the worlds of thugs and thieves that formed in the prisons of the defunct Soviet regime and sometimes supply services to organizations mainly involved in theft or extortion, they differentiate increasingly from those worlds. Like governments engaged in nuclear deterrence, they specialize in the strategic *non*use of their control over violent means (Volkov 2002, chap. 3).

The Ekaterinburg adventure may seem an odd case, a peculiar product of Russia's troubles during the 1990s. But, as Volkov says, it recapitulates a common historical process. Over and over again, effective nongovernmental specialists in violence have made alliances with governments, become parts of governments, taken over existing governments, or become governments on their own. Where (unlike Akbar's troops) Indian enforcers align themselves with regional ruling parties, they occupy positions broadly similar to that of Uralmashevskaya. The story of Robin Hood's bandits joining the English king's forces offers a parable of the same kind. In fact, the historical exceptions are the cases where the line between government and nongovernment specialists in violence has become well defined and impermeable.

Close observer Bill Berkeley views African collective violence as an extreme instance of the same phenomenon.

Ethnic conflict in Africa is a form of organized crime. The "culture" driving Africa's conflicts is akin to that of the Sicilian Mafia, or of the Crips and Bloods in Los Angeles, with the same imperatives of blood and family that bind such gangs together. Africa's warring factions are best understood not as "tribes" but as racketeering enterprises, their leaders calculating strategy after the time-honored logic of Don Vito Corleone.

It is the stakes in Africa that are different – multiplied exponentially in circumstances where the state itself is a gang and the law doesn't exist. It is as if men like Vito Corleone seized control of not just "turf" on the margins of society, but of the state itself and all of its organs: police and army, secret police, the courts, the central bank, the civil service, the press, TV, and radio. (Berkeley 2001: 15)

Berkeley overstates the uniformity of ethnic conflict in Africa. As the case of Rwanda has already shown us, militias, guerrillas, and self-armed citizens sometimes play critical parts in Africa's collective violence in defiance of those who nominally run the state. Mercenaries such as the ruthlessly efficient South Africa–based Executive Outcomes have intervened with lethal effect in Sierra Leone and elsewhere (Shannon 2002). Yet, as Berkeley says, plenty of predatory violence occurs across Africa. Violent specialists – many of them noncitizens of the countries in which they operate, and some of them European mercenaries or adventurers – join Africa's organized crime syndicates without becoming their obedient servants.

In Latin America as well, specialists in violence have repeatedly seized or tipped the balance of power in whole countries. Central America has suffered especially from the frequent availability of external allies – including drug dealers, arms runners, and the U.S. government – for newly forming armed units, however unsavory. William Stanley describes the terrible year of 1980 in El Salvador, when assassins struck Attorney General Mario Zamora Rivas, Archbishop Oscar Romero, and many other opponents of paramilitary violence. Those killings were only the most visible:

These deaths were accompanied by almost twelve thousand others. Most were either captured and executed by the death squads or killed in wholesale massacres carried out by government forces in rural areas. With each major demonstration or labor strike, the popular movement lost dozens of supporters and key leaders. In a sense, the repression worked. Demonstrations grew smaller, and fewer people would outwardly identify themselves as being affiliated with leftist organizations. Yet the repressive state paid a high price: though the demonstrations and strikes gradually became smaller, there was a concomitant shift within the leftist opposition toward a military strategy. In May, the left began to move its militants into rural areas to develop a military structure; by September, this process was well advanced, though the groups still lacked arms; and by November, the left, now united as the Farabundo Martí Liberation Front (FMLN) had begun obtaining sufficient weapons to form an army. (Stanley 1996: 178)

The chilling experience of El Salvador makes several important new points about specialists in violence: they vary systematically in their proximity to (and sponsorship by) governments; they sometimes organize in opposition to existing organizations of violent specialists; and no sharp line separates their politics from those of armed forces belonging to established governments. These points apply in South Asia, Russia, and Africa as well.

All over the world – for example, in Colombia, the Caucasus, Palestine, Liberia, Sri Lanka, and Indonesia – specialists in violence figure importantly in the larger-scale versions of collective violence. To be sure, violent specialists sometimes include or become fanatics, even suicide bombers. They also include many obedient servants of lawful states. But in any of their many guises, they often initiate violent political interaction, sometimes cause nonviolent political interaction to turn violent, and frequently determine the outcome of political interaction, violent or otherwise.

The complex but central position of violent specialists has three major implications for the study of collective violence. First, although it will help to start with distinctions among agents of government, polity members, challengers, and outside political actors, in closer looks at actual regimes and episodes we will have to recognize mobile and intermediate actors – political entrepreneurs and violent specialists prominent among them. No simple distinction between "insurgents" and "forces of order" can possibly capture the complex social interactions that generate collective violence.

Second, specialists in violence do not simply serve the interests of the larger entities (governments, parties, communities, ethnic groups, or others) with which they are currently aligned. They follow dynamics of their own. They regularly engage in exploitation and opportunity hoarding, sometimes at the expense of their own nominal employers or constituencies. At a minimum, any explanation of variations in collective violence will have to account for the acquisition and control of coercive means and skills by those specialists. Regimes differ significantly, furthermore, in the opportunities they offer and the places they assign to specialists in violence. We have no choice but to consider the care and feeding of violent means: recruitment and organization of military forces, supplies of weapons, ties between illicit trades and arms flows, taxation for war, hostage taking as a source of revenue, and employment of violent specialists by established political actors.

Third, the character of relations between governments and specialists in violence strongly affects the extent and locus of collective violence within a regime. Overall, collective violence rises with the extent that organizations specializing in deployment of coercive means – armies, police forces, coordinated banditry, pirate confederations, mercenary enterprises, protection rackets, and the like – increase in size, geographic scope, resources, and coherence. But democratic civilian control over violent specialists mutes those effects. Conversely, collective violence rises to the extent that the specialists escape democratic civilian control. (A valuable rule of thumb follows: if a regime's police force reports directly to the military rather than to civilian authorities, that regime is almost certainly undemocratic.)

When it comes to government-led deployment of coercion against challengers, collective violence increases further to the extent that violent specialists' organization offers opportunities for private vengeance and incentives to predation. Where participation in organized violence opens paths to political and economic power, collective violence multiplies. Most notably, power seeking by violent specialists promotes the types of violent interaction I have called coordinated destruction and opportunism. Specialists in violence do not simply deploy damage for the pleasure of it or for the profit it brings them; they use violence and threats of violence to pursue projects of their own.

Over a wide range of collective violence, the interaction of violent specialists and political entrepreneurs with other political actors and with each other therefore deeply affects the extent, character, and objects of damage done. But the places of violent specialists and political entrepreneurs in public politics vary systematically by type of regime.

Variation in Regimes

Regimes vary in two ways that significantly affect the character and intensity of collective violence within them: in terms of governmental capacity and democracy. *Governmental capacity* means the extent to which governmental agents control resources, activities, and populations within the government's territory. It varies in principle from almost no such control (low) to nearly absolute control (high). As a practical matter, however, governments that do not exercise significant control over resources do not survive long. Instead, they collapse from internal pressures or adjacent governments overrun them. At the other extreme, no regime has ever come close to absolute control; even Hitler and Stalin at their heights fell far short of commanding all the resources, activities, and populations that existed somewhere within their regimes.

Democracy means the extent to which members of the population under a government's jurisdiction maintain broad and equal relations with governmental agents, exercise collective control over governmental personnel and resources, and enjoy protection from arbitrary action by governmental agents. Like their nondemocratic counterparts, the governments of democratic regimes engage in opportunity hoarding and exploitation; for example, every real democratic regime expends a significant part of its effort on keeping noncitizens away from its citizens' benefits. But the proportion of a democratic regime's population that actually shares the benefits of opportunity hoarding and exploitation is much larger than in nondemocratic regimes.

Over the five thousand years that governments at a larger scale than villages have run major parts of the world, in any case, the vast majority of regimes have operated with little or no democracy. Only over the last two centuries have any significant number of democratic regimes appeared. Even today, only a minority of the world's regimes combine relatively broad and equal relations of citizens with governmental agents, collective popular control over governmental personnel and resources, and substantial protection of citizens from arbitrary action by governmental agents.

Like governmental capacity, then, democracy is a matter of degree. Figure 2.1 sketches variation of regimes with regard to capacity and democracy. It shows both capacity and democracy as varying from 0 to 1; in each dimension, 0 represents the lowest level ever observed in history, 1 the highest. The diagram's lower left-hand corner combines low governmental capacity with little democracy. We can call that zone Fragmented Tyranny because in such a regime warlords, bandits, and other political predators typically work their ways in collusion with or in defiance of nominal rulers.

The diagram's upper left includes a zone of Authoritarianism: very high governmental capacity combined with little or no democracy. The upper right-hand corner contains Citizenship, in which governmental agents bind to whole categories of the population through relatively broad and equal rights and obligations. Citizenship overlaps with Authoritarianism, however, because in some regimes broad and equal citizenship rights and obligations couple with little or no effective popular control over the government as well as minimal protection against arbitrary governmental action. Those regimes establish not democracy but authoritarian citizenship.

On the whole, the proportion of all collective violence in which governmental agents are directly involved rises with governmental capacity; it is higher near the top than the bottom of Figure 2.1. (I am not speaking of the sheer quantity of collective violence – for example, the death rate from violent encounters – but rather of the share of all violent encounters directly engaging troops, police, officials, and other governmental agents. More on overall levels of violence later.) The proportion rises for several reasons:

- because higher-capacity governments monitor larger proportions of all claim-making interactions and then intervene (with sometimes violent consequences) in those interactions of which their agents disapprove;

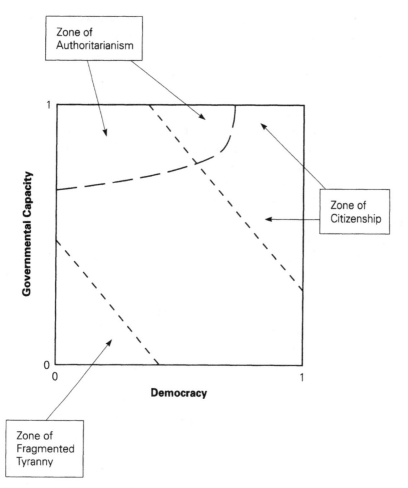

Figure 2.1 Types of Regime.

- because higher-capacity regimes monitor with particular closeness those political interactions in which nongovernmental specialists in violence engage;
- because higher-capacity regimes increase the likely costs to nongovernmental actors of using violent means to make their claims;
- because higher-capacity governments expand their shares of all existing violent means and attack independent concentrations of such means; and
- because higher-capacity regimes make extensive demands on others and back those demands with threats of damage.

A small current flows in the opposite direction: the forms of violence authorities call terrorism also concentrate in high-capacity regimes. When organized but excluded political actors face high-capacity regimes, they often choose some combination of underground communication with clandestine physical attacks on persons and property of their rulers or enemies. This countercurrent does not come close to reversing the overall correlation of governmental capacity with direct involvement of governmental agents in collective violence.

What about democracy? With two major qualifications, collective violence generally declines with democratization. Democratic regimes, on the average, harbor less collective violence than undemocratic regimes. Broadening of political participation, extension and equalization of political rights, regularization of nonviolent means for making claims, and increasing readiness of third parties to intervene against violent resolution of disputes over claims all dampen the processes that generate violent contention.

Here come the qualifications. First, democratic governments themselves often employ violence against their external enemies as well as against excluded political actors and population categories within their jurisdictions. Although interstate war, punitive detention, and selective police brutality might wither away in ideally complete democracy, none of them disappears with really existing democratization (Chevigny 1999; Davenport 2000; Geller & Singer 1998; Gowa 1999; Huggins 1998; della Porta & Reiter 1998). The democratic United States, after all, herded Japanese-Americans into concentration camps during World War II (Kotek & Rigoulot 2000).

Second, along the way to democratization, struggles often become *more* violent for a while as the stakes rise with regard to who will win or lose from democratic institutions. Surges of democratization often follow violent interstate wars, civil wars, and revolutions; cases in point include the partial democratization of Switzerland after the Sonderbund civil war of 1847, of the United States after the Civil War, of France after the Commune of 1871, and of Japan and Germany after World War II. Struggle both precedes and accompanies democratization.

Political Interaction under Different Types of Regimes

Regime control over claim making affects collective violence strongly, even if indirectly. Governmental agents, polity members, challengers, and subjects interact in many different ways, most of which do not involve making of claims. People pay taxes, buy services, perform military duties, reply to censuses, draw pensions, and otherwise interact with governments most of the time without engaging in contention – without making discontinuous, public, collective claims. But sometimes political actors do make contentious claims on each other. Sometimes those claims include inflicting damage on persons or property. At that point, the interactions become part of what we are trying to explain.

We might think of collective claim making as an interactive performance; like veteran members of a theatrical troupe, political actors follow rough scripts to uncertain outcomes as they negotiate demonstrations, humble petitions, electoral campaigns, expulsions of enemies, hostage taking, urban uprisings, and other forms of contention. Such performances link pairs or larger sets of actors, the simplest pair being one claimant and one object of claims. The actors in question often include governmental agents, polity members, and challengers as well, with challengers sometimes newly mobilizing from the regime's previously unmobilized subject population. In any particular regime, pairs of actors have only a limited number of performances at their disposal. We can conveniently call that set of performances their *repertoire of contention.*

In Great Britain of the 1750s, for example, the contentious repertoire widely available to ordinary people included

Attacks on coercive authorities: liberation of prisoners; resistance to police intervention in gatherings and entertainments; resistance to press gangs; fights between hunters and gamekeepers; battles between smugglers and royal officers; forcible opposition to evictions; military mutinies.

Attacks on popularly designated offenses and offenders: Rough Music; ridicule and/or destruction of symbols, effigies, and/or property of public figures and moral offenders; verbal and physical attacks on malefactors seen in public places; pulling down and/or sacking of dangerous or offensive houses, including workhouses and brothels; smashing of shops and bars whose proprietors are accused of unfair dealing or of violating public morality; collective seizures of food, often coupled with sacking the merchant's premises and/or public sale of the food below current market price; blockage or diversion of food shipments; destruction of tollgates; collective invasions of enclosed land, often including destruction of fences or hedges.

Celebrations and other popularly initiated gatherings: collective cheering, jeering, or stoning of public figures or their conveyances; popularly initiated public celebrations of major events (e.g., John Wilkes's elections of the 1760s) with cheering, drinking, display of partisan symbols, fireworks, and sometimes with forced participation of reluctant persons; forced illuminations, including attacks on windows of householders who fail to illuminate; faction fights (e.g., Irish vs. English, rival groups of military).

Workers' sanctions over members of their trades: turnouts by workers in multiple shops of a local trade; workers' marches to public authorities in trade

disputes; donkeying, or otherwise humiliating, workers who violated collective agreements; destroying goods (e.g., silk in looms and/or the looms
themselves) of workers or masters who violate collective agreements.

Claim making within authorized public assemblies (e.g., Lord Mayor's Day): taking of positions by means of cheers, jeers, attacks, and displays of symbols; attacks on supporters of electoral candidates; parading and chairing
of candidates; taking sides at public executions; attacks or professions of
support for pilloried prisoners; salutation or deprecation of public figures
(e.g., royalty) at theater; collective response to lines and characters in plays
or other entertainments; breaking up of theaters at unsatisfactory performances (Tilly 1995).

Not all British claim makers, to be sure, had access to all these performances;
some of the performances linked workers to masters, others linked market reg-
ulars to local merchants, and so on. In any case, the repertoire available to
ordinary Britons during the 1750s did not include electoral campaigns, formal
public meetings, street marches, demonstrations, petition drives, or the formation of special-interest associations, all of which became quite common ways of
pressing claims during the nineteenth century. As these newer performances
became common, the older ones disappeared.

How do repertoires shape contentious politics? Most obviously, they provide
approximate scenarios – and choices among scenarios – for political interactions.
With scenarios available, participants on all sides can generally coordinate their
actions more effectively, anticipate likely consequences of various responses, and
construct agreed-upon meanings for contentious episodes. They can construct
those meanings both as episodes unfold and after the fact: although this episode
began as an attack on a moral offender (the employer), it ended up as a turnout;
this other episode began as a public celebration and ended as a faction fight, and
so on.

The possibility of switching alerts us to the fact that performances vary in
adjacency to each other – adjacency in terms of locales, participants, and types
of action. During the eighteenth century, British collective seizures of food
could mutate into turnouts only with great difficulty, but they easily turned into
popular attacks on moral offenders such as price-gouging bakers and hoarding
merchants. (Women frequently played leading parts in such episodes; they specialized in activating morally charged boundaries, stories, and relations.) Repertoires therefore provide templates for interaction, bases for collective memory,
and switchpoints for collective struggle.

Interactions among claimants, including governmental agents, produce major alterations in contentious repertoires. At any given time, however, governments themselves react differently to the various claim-making performances currently available to claimants. We can make a rough distinction among performances that governments prescribe, those they tolerate, and those they forbid. *Prescribed* performances typically include ceremonies of allegiance (e.g., singing of national anthems) and transfers of resources (e.g., tax money and conscripts) to governmental control. *Tolerated* performances vary enormously from regime to regime, but they typically include filing of legal claims and organized responses to moral offenders. *Forbidden* performances likewise vary significantly among regimes, but always include violent attacks on rulers and governmental resources. The map of prescription, toleration, and interdiction differs among political actors as well; powerful actors can usually get away with performances that would land lesser actors in serious trouble.

Using these rough distinctions, Figure 2.2 lays out an argument concerning the relation between regime reactions and contentious politics as a function of variation in governmental capacity and degree of democracy. Remember that capacity and democracy refer to the regime defined by a country's national government rather than other subgovernments within it. Examples of each type in the figure might then include:

high-capacity undemocratic – China, Iran;
low-capacity undemocratic – Somalia, Congo (Kinshasa, formerly Zaïre);
high-capacity democratic – Germany, Japan;
low-capacity democratic – Belgium, Jamaica.

In each case, the large oval in Figure 2.2 represents all the interactions – claim-making or otherwise, violent or nonviolent – in which any pair of political actors within a government's jurisdiction ever engages. It then guesses at the range of interactions prescribed by governments, representing the likelihood that authoritarian (high-capacity undemocratic) regimes compel a wider array of performances than other regimes. It argues that the range of tolerated performances rises with democracy but declines with governmental capacity.

Democracy enlarges the range of acceptable interactions among political actors. It does so mainly because each newly established political actor brings into the political arena its own particular set of social connections and maintains at least some of them. High-capacity regimes, however, channel interactions into a narrower range than low-capacity regimes – both because government agents have more control of all interactions and because dominant constituencies

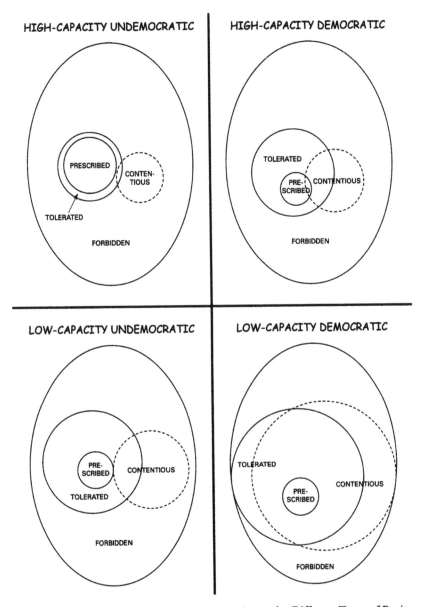

Figure 2.2 Configurations of Political Interaction under Different Types of Regime.

collaborate with governments in putting their stamp on acceptable and unacceptable ways of interacting in public. In Great Britain, we can date incorporation of the industrial bourgeoisie into the public politics of that increasingly high-capacity regime roughly at the Reform Act of 1832. Empowerment of the bourgeoisie increased the importance of their favored means of collective action – through special-purpose associations and campaigns based on them – in British public politics, while rendering the older forms of direct action riskier and less effective. A wide variety of political performances moved from tolerated to forbidden.

Figure 2.2 continues by relating *contentious* interaction to other forms. It incorporates the idea that, in any actual regime, the repertoire of contentious performances is significantly narrower than the full range of interactions among political actors and usually smaller than the range of tolerated interactions; a number of interactions acceptable to the government occur without discontinuous, public, collective making of claims. But this varies by type of regime. Low-capacity regimes experience wider arrays of contentious interactions because their governmental agents lack means to control claim-making performances and also because their public politics includes more variable and particular relations among actors.

Undemocratic regimes make it difficult for anyone to make contentious claims in the course of prescribed performances, where people act directly under the eyes of authorities; the occasional assassination or seditious shout that happens during a solemn royal ceremony provides an exception proving the rule. (The exception proves the rule because in undemocratic regimes the rare claim-making violators of prescribed performances hardly ever escape unscathed.) Under democratic regimes, contentious claims sometimes appear in the course of prescribed performances, take shape in a wide range of tolerated performances, and spill over into forbidden performances, including major forms of collective violence.

What does this mean for individual types of regime? *Low-capacity undemocratic regimes,* Figure 2.2 declares, tolerate a relatively wide range of performances for lack of ability to police them; they concentrate control on prescribed performances and on showy public punishment of forbidden performances – when they can catch the performers. As a consequence, runs the argument, contentious politics in such regimes takes place mainly outside of prescribed performances but extends through a limited range of tolerated and forbidden performances, many of them oriented to partly autonomous centers of power within the regime's nominal jurisdiction. These generalizations are supposed to fit Congo-Kinshasa, Somalia, and regimes like them.

Low-capacity democratic regimes, in contrast, tolerate an even wider range of performances and forbid relatively few. In such regimes, according to Figure 2.2, contention occurs in the course of prescribed performances (e.g., in resistance to taxes and conscription), over most of the tolerated range, and well into the zone of forbidden forms of claim making. Without government means to defend rights, enforce obligations, and contain conflicts, runs the argument, a wide variety of actors involve themselves in collective efforts to pursue interests by their own means. These generalizations are supposed to fit Belgium, Jamaica, and regimes like them.

High-capacity democratic regimes operate quite differently. They impose a relatively small number of prescribed performances but enforce them rigorously. They channel claim making energetically into a modest array of tolerated performances and forbid a wide range of technically possible forms of claim making. As a consequence, I suggest, contentious politics occasionally enters prescribed performances (e.g., via draft resistance), commonly occurs by means of tolerated performances (e.g., in public demonstrations), but sometimes borrows forbidden forms (e.g., clandestine attacks on government property). These generalizations are supposed to fit Germany, Japan, and regimes like them.

Finally, *high-capacity undemocratic regimes* prescribe an exceptionally wide range of claim-making performances, leave only a narrow range of tolerated performances, and forbid many (if not most) technically possible performances. The result of extensive monitoring and repression is to minimize the scope of contentious politics but also to push most of it into the forbidden range. The few tolerated performances receive extensive use, but collective claimants constantly run the risk of interdiction and/or retaliation. These generalizations are supposed to fit China, Iran, and regimes like them.

Regimes and Violence

Let us take a large leap: Assume that these arguments about contentious politics in general are correct. How can we stretch from them to explanations of variations in collective violence? From four strands we can fashion a makeshift bridge. First, the pattern of prescribed and tolerated performances within a regime significantly affects loci of violent claim making. In all sorts of regimes, a significant share of all collective violence occurs as an outcome of claim making that does not begin with violence; soldiers shoot down peaceful petitioners, nonviolent demonstrators start to break windows, participants in rival religious processions begin to rough each other up, and so on. Hence there is a rough correspondence between the occasions of nonviolent and violent claim making. In high-capacity *undemocratic* regimes, for example, we should expect to find a high proportion of collective violence beginning with forbidden performances. In high-capacity *democratic* regimes, in contrast, we should expect to find most violence originating in tolerated performances.

Second, in many regimes certain performances in the tolerated repertoire – most obviously violent rituals and some forms of coordinated destruction – directly entail inflicting damage on persons or objects. A significant share of the 1750-era British performances reviewed earlier had small-scale violence built into them.

Third, regimes that radically narrow the range of tolerated performances – which means especially high-capacity undemocratic regimes – drive claimants that have retained their own capacity to act collectively toward forbidden performances and thus toward encounters likely to have violent outcomes.

Fourth, differing configurations of prescribed, tolerated, and forbidden performances affect the likely prevalence of conditions promoting forms of violence in which damaging acts are salient rather than peripheral, high levels of coordination exist among violent actors, or both. As later chapters will show in detail, *salience* generally increases when (a) participants in political interaction are themselves specialists in violence, (b) uncertainty about an interaction's outcome increases, (c) stakes of the outcome for the parties increase, and (d) third parties to which the participants have stable relations are absent. Activation and suppression of different political identities (i.e., of bundled boundaries, stories, and social relations) directly affect conditions (a) to (d). But the ease of activation and suppression of various political identities depends in turn on the regime's array of prescribed, tolerated, and forbidden performances. Some regimes, for example, make it easy for representatives of lineages (including female representatives of lineages) to act publicly as such but almost impossible for women to act publicly as representatives of women.

The *extent of coordination* among violent actors increases as (e) political entrepreneurs create connections among previously independent individuals and groups, (f) authorities control the stakes – both rewards and punishments – of outcomes for participants, (g) categories dividing major blocs of participants (e.g., gender, race, or nationality) figure widely in routine social life, and (h) major participants organize and drill outside of violent encounters. Incorporation and separation strongly affect conditions (e) through (h).

Processes (a) to (h) do not map neatly into regimes; for example, though on average uncertainty runs higher in low-capacity regimes, even that generalization ignores the way that disasters and military losses make high-capacity regimes vulnerable to attack. But the configuration of prescribed, tolerated, and forbidden performances does affect processes (a) to (h); the tendency of low-capacity undemocratic regimes to repress forbidden performances incompletely and unpredictably, for instance, increases the salience of violence in their contentious interactions. Both forbidden performers and violent special-ists reach out to damage each other more immediately than under other regimes.

The argument of Figure 2.2 therefore has significant implications for a regime's extent of collective violence, and for who gets involved in it. Leaving aside government-initiated warfare, we should expect overall levels of violence to be higher in low-capacity regimes, whether undemocratic or democratic. We should also expect democracy to depress violence within domestic politics, if not necessarily in relations among governments. Thus the overall implications for levels of collective violence within polities look like this:

high violence – low-capacity undemocratic regimes;

medium violence – high-capacity undemocratic *and* low-capacity democratic regimes;

low violence – high-capacity democratic regimes.

If substantial shifts from type to type occur in the world, we should expect them to affect overall levels of collective violence. If high-capacity undemocratic regimes lose capacity – as happened widely in the disintegrating Soviet Union after 1985 – we should expect levels of violence to increase. If many regimes democratize without losing capacity, we might expect short-run increases in col-lective violence as struggles for control intensify, followed by long-term declines in violent encounters.

Type by type, we have some further expectations. In *low-capacity undemocratic* regimes such as Congo-Kinshasa and Somalia, we expect petty tyrants to use coercion freely, governmental officials to deploy violent punishments when they can catch their enemies, and means of violence to be widely distributed across other political actors. In *low-capacity democratic* regimes such as Belgium and Jamaica, we expect less involvement of governmental officials in violent repres-sion but widespread spiraling of initially nonviolent conflicts into violence – because government agents do not serve as effective third-party enforcers of agreements, much less as inhibitors of escalation.

When it comes to *high-capacity democratic* regimes such as Germany and Japan, we expect low levels of violence in routine claim making as well as highly selec-tive – and hence relatively rare – deployment of violent means by governmental agents. But in such regimes we also expect extensive involvement of govern-ment agents (as initiators, objects, or peacemakers) in the collective violence that does occur. Ironically, the net effect is to magnify the political impact of violence when it happens; each bit of damage dramatizes the significant politi-cal stakes over which participants are contending, and more so than in regimes where collective violence occurs every day.

Finally, *high-capacity undemocratic* regimes such as China and Iran should have widespread threats of violence by governmental agents, frequent involvement of governmental agents in collective violence when it occurs, but great variability in the actual frequency of collective violence, depending on the opening and closing of opportunities for dissent. In such regimes, as in the case of high-capacity democratic regimes, visible violence tends to broadcast the high political stakes of contention. Chapter 3 will by no means prove all these points, but at least it will show that collective violence does vary among regimes in ways that these arguments help explain.

Questions Recast

Our expedition into contentious politics leaves us with valuable results. We can now refine the questions about collective violence posed in the previous chapter. In principle, we are seeking answers to these large questions.

1. *Under what conditions, how, and why do people make collective claims on each other?* The remainder of the book draws on available answers to this big question, but it does not propose new answers except with regard to violent claim making. This chapter has offered a first look at how variations in political regimes and actors affect the character of collective claim making. It has also identified the construction and activation of different sorts of political identities as a crucial element in the forms taken by contentious politics.

2. *What causes different forms of political claim making to include or exclude violence?* Later chapters uncover no crisp general laws in this regard. In fact, they identify a middle ground where the difference between violence and nonviolence depends on unpredictable combinations of small causes. But the analysis does provide guidance for distinguishing between high-violence and low-violence social processes. This chapter has drawn special attention to the importance of political entrepreneurs, violent specialists, and regime controls over different forms of claim making. It has thereby raised further questions about how political actors acquire (or fail to acquire) coercive means and the skill to use them.

3. *When violent claim making does occur, what explains variation in the form, salience, and coordination of outright damage to persons and objects?* Here we arrive at the book's central problem. Building on the general ideas about claim making, regimes, and political actors laid out in this chapter, later sections look hard at change and variation in violent episodes in order to identify recurrent mechanisms and processes that in various combinations, sequences, and settings promote particular forms of violent claim making and inhibit others.

These three pressing questions will guide the next chapter's inquiry into trends and variations in collective violence. After that, they will help us round the spiral of violent rituals, coordinated destruction, opportunism, brawls, scattered attack, and broken negotiations. Eventually they will clarify how activation, suppression, incorporation, and separation interact to generate or inhibit violent contention.

3

Trends, Variations, and Explanations

A Violent Century

In absolute terms – and probably per capita as well – the twentieth century visited more collective violence on the world than any century of the previous ten thousand years. Although historians rightly describe China's Warring States period, Sargon of Akkad's conquests, Mongol expansion, and Europe's Thirty Years War as times of terrible destruction, earlier wars deployed nothing like the death-dealing armaments, much less the state-backed extermination of civilians, that twentieth-century conflicts brought with them. Between 1900 and 1999, the world produced about 250 new wars, international or civil, in which battle deaths averaged at least a thousand per year. That means two or three big, new wars per year. Those wars caused about a million deaths per year.

Assuming midcentury world populations of 0.8 billion, 1.2 billion, and 2.5 billion, the world death rate for large-scale war ran around 90 per million population per year during the eighteenth century, 150 per million during the nineteenth century, and over 400 per million during the twentieth (Holsti 1996; Tilly et al. 1995). Altogether, about 100 million people died as a direct result of action by organized military units backed by one government or another over the course of the twentieth century. Most likely a comparable number of civilians died of war-induced disease and other indirect effects.

To be sure, two world wars contributed mightily to twentieth-century totals; battle deaths in World War I amounted to about 10 million across all theaters, and battle deaths in World War II ran close to 15 million. But the 1990s alone brought virulent violence to the Caucasus, former Yugoslavia, Liberia, Sierra Leone, Angola, Rwanda, Congo-Kinshasa, Haiti, Colombia, Iraq, Algeria, Lebanon, Palestine, Yemen, India, Afghanistan, Sri Lanka, the Philippines, Indonesia, Papua New Guinea, and Laos. As we have seen, by itself

Rwanda produced close to a million deaths through collective violence during the 1990s.

During the first half of the twentieth century, massive interstate wars produced most of the world's political deaths, although deliberate efforts of state authorities to eliminate, displace, or control subordinate populations also accounted for significant numbers of fatalities (Chesnais 1981; Rummel 1994; Tilly et al. 1995). During the century's second half, civil war, guerrilla, separatist struggles, and conflicts between ethnically or religiously divided populations increasingly dominated the landscape of bloodletting (Creveld 1989, 1991; Holsti 1991, 1996; Kaldor 1999; Luard 1987). Between 1950 and 2000, civil wars killing half a million people or more occurred in Nigeria, Afghanistan, Sudan, Mozambique, Cambodia, Angola, Indonesia, and Rwanda (Echeverry, Salazar, & Navas 2001: 116). Over the century as a whole, the proportion of war deaths suffered by civilians rose startlingly: 5 percent in World War I, 50 percent in World War II, up to 90 percent in wars of the 1990s (Chesterman 2001: 2). War burrowed inside regimes.

At first, decolonization and the Cold War combined to implicate the major Western powers heavily in new states' domestic conflicts. For the French and the Americans, Indochina provides the most pungent memories of that time. But the Netherlands faced similar crises in Indonesia (1945–1949), as did Great Britain in Malaya (1948–1960). Most former European colonies began their independence as nominal democracies, then rapidly moved either to single-party oligarchies, military rule, or both at once. Military coups multiplied during the 1960s, as segments of national armed forces bid for their shares of state power.

Coups became less common and less effective from the 1970s onward (Tilly et al. 1995). With backing from great powers, however, existing rulers began to consolidate their holds on the governmental apparatus, to use it for their own benefit, and to exclude their rivals from power. In the process, dissident specialists in violence (often backed by international rivals of the power that patronized the existing rulers) turned increasingly to armed rebellion; they sought either to seize national power or to carve out autonomous territories of their own. Civil war became more and more prevalent.

Figure 3.1 gives an idea of trends between 1960 and 1999 (for a similar series covering 1950–1995, see Echeverry et al. 2001: 89; for greater detail on 1990–2000, see Sollenberg & Wallensteen 2001). It represents the number of large civil wars (combats between governmental and rebel units generating at least a thousand battle deaths, each side sustaining at least 5 percent of the casualties) being waged in any given year. The number of civil wars expanded much more rapidly than the number of independent states, which rose from about 100 in 1960 to 161 in

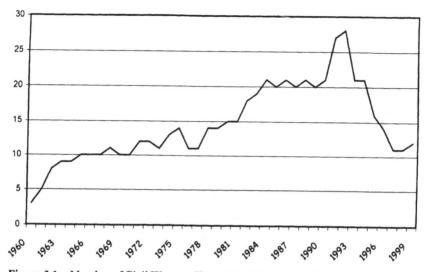

Figure 3.1 Number of Civil Wars per Year, 1960–1999. *Source:* Computed from Collier & Hoeffler (2001, Table 1).

1999. An early peak arrived in 1975, when substantial civil wars were going on in Angola, Burma, Cambodia, Ethiopia, Indonesia, Iran, Iraq, Lebanon, Morocco, Mozambique, Pakistan, the Philippines, Vietnam, and Zimbabwe. But civil wars continued to multiply until they reached their height in 1992, when a full 28 internal military conflicts were raging across the world. The number of civil wars fell off during the later 1990s, but internecine killing continued at much higher levels than had prevailed during the 1960s.

Postwar increases likewise occurred in genocide (state-directed or state-authorized killing of populations identified by race, ethnicity, and/or religion) and politicide (wholesale killing of populations identified by political affiliation); as our earlier look at Hutu–Tutsi conflict revealed, genocide and politicide overlap. Large postwar waves of genocide and politicide occurred before 1980 in the Soviet Union (1943–1947), China (1950–1951), Indonesia (1965–1966), again China (1966–1975), Pakistan (1971), Uganda (1971–1979), and Cambodia (1975–1979). During the 1980s they continued on substantial scales in Afghanistan, Uganda, El Salvador, Iran, Syria, Sri Lanka, Ethiopia, and probably Iraq (Gurr & Harff 1994: 26–7).

For a moment in 1989 it looked as though the aging century might be contemplating retirement from the business of mass destruction. Genocide and politicide seemed to be diminishing. From a peak of 27 wars (both civil and interstate) underway two years earlier, twelve had ended, only fifteen were continuing, and not one new war above the thousand-death threshold began that year.

War-sized conflicts in Angola, Colombia, East Timor, El Salvador, Guatemala, Iran, Lebanon, Ethiopia, Mozambique, Peru, the Philippines, Sri Lanka, and Sudan, were, on the whole, winding down. Even in Afghanistan, where war had killed a million of the country's 17 million people since the 1978 military coup, the carnage was declining as Soviet troops withdrew. The revolutions of 1989 in Eastern Europe were momentous but relatively bloodless; only in Romania did the struggle approach civil war.

The downward trend did not last long. In 1990–1991, the splintering of Yugoslavia and the Persian Gulf War reversed it, Somalia broke into even more intense factional violence, and civil wars began to sunder Georgia and Azerbaijan. New or renewed conflicts in India, Kuwait, Liberia, Somalia, South Africa, and Tibet all thrust above the thousand-death threshold in 1990. In every instance (except perhaps Kuwait), organized armed men killed large numbers of unarmed civilians on the basis of their group identification; they committed, that is, genocide or politicide. World War II seems to have set the process in motion, but it accelerated thereafter.

There lies paradox: a war that became famous for immense armies, elaborate technologies, centralized planning, and eventually atomic weapons generated a shift away from the efficiently segregated military activity that Carl von Clausewitz analyzed and advocated as the essence of rational modern warfare (Clausewitz 1968). Since World War II, increasingly prevalent military practices go by such names as guerrilla, massacre, low-intensity conflict, genocide, politicide, democide, and ethnic cleansing. Recent decades have brought increased deployment of violence not by officially constituted national armed forces but by paramilitary forces, guerrilleros, death squads, secret police, and other irregulars. They have also brought increased direction of state-sponsored and state-seeking violence against civilians, especially whole categories of the population stigmatized for their religious, ethnic, and/or political identities.

Since 1945, then, the world as a whole has taken decisive, frightening steps away from its painfully achieved segregations between armies and civilian populations, between war and peace, between international and civil war, between lethal and nonlethal applications of force. It has moved toward armed struggle within existing states and toward state-sponsored killing, deprivation, or expulsion of whole population categories. These trends greatly exceed population growth and the multiplication of independent states; they constitute an enormous increase per capita and per state.

Such momentous shifts in the character of collective violence reverse trends that had lasted several centuries. From the seventeenth century to World War II, violence generally moved in two directions across the world: toward increasing deadliness of international war but also toward increasing pacification of domestic life, including declines in both large-scale and small-scale killing. Both trends resulted from states' increasing monopolization and perfection of coercive means. Yes, Western powers continued their forceful conquest of non-Western areas through most of the period, and usually put down resistance to their rule ruthlessly. Yes, in times of war the distinction between international and domestic killing often blurred. Yes, if we include the effects of state actions on famine and disease, the reversal will look earlier and less dramatic. Yet even with these qualifications, the period since World War II stands out for the rising prevalence of civil war, genocide, and politicide.

How and why did these dramatic changes occur? Some of the reasons are fairly clear.

- With international backing, decolonization and separatist movements roughly doubled the number of formally independent countries and hence the number of governments over which dissidents and opportunists could try to seize control.
- Throughout the Cold War, both the Soviet Union and the United States often subsidized domestic opponents of those regimes that aligned against them.
- Both Western countries and members of the Soviet bloc greatly increased their shipments – legal and illegal – of arms to the rest of the world.
- Enormous expansion of international trade in contraband such as cocaine, heroin, sexual services, illegal migrants, dirty money, rubber, oil, diamonds, and other minerals provided sources of support for rebels, intervening forces from adjacent countries, and merchants who profited from weak and corrupt governments (note that markets for the contraband in rich countries, notably the United States, sustained the trade).
- In a time of improved communications and relatively inexpensive travel, increasing numbers of emigrants maintained contact with their home countries and either supported opposition movements, provided outlets for contraband, or both.

We who study such grisly processes are still trying to work out the interplay and relative weight of these reasonably well-documented changes.

The Western Experience of Violence

Except occasionally to wring their hands at other people's barbarity, residents of rich Western countries have not much noticed. Outside of two brutal world wars, they have managed mostly to export or individualize their violence. It was not always so. Up to the great eighteenth-century consolidation of Western states, individual and collective violence beset everyday life. Marauding mercenaries, bandits, private armies, town militias, and armed rebels repeatedly brought large-scale collective violence home throughout Western Europe. On a smaller scale, robbers and armed avengers ravaged local life (Blok 1974, 2001; Hanagan 1999).

In Great Britain, two major civil wars plus a number of rebellions and regional struggles filled the seventeenth century with political violence. As we have already seen, well into the eighteenth century Great Britain's everyday routines of contentious politics included a number of violent acts (see also Brewer & Styles 1980; Charlesworth 1983; Charlesworth et al. 1996; Hay et al. 1975). Elsewhere in Europe, furthermore, mass rebellions and bloody repression still occurred from time to time through the seventeenth century. If something called "Western culture" explains the relative civility of domestic political life in today's Western Europe, the crucial features of that culture must have developed since the seventeenth century.

From the eighteenth century onward, however, widespread domestic pacification occurred. Both rising governmental capacity and democratization deeply altered the conditions for domestic collective violence. Four currents of change flowed together.

1. Built up by preparations for war, states began disarming their civilian populations, imposing tighter control over routine social life, and installing specialized police to contain both criminal activity and small-scale interpersonal violence (Chittolini 1994; Emsley 1983; Liang 1992; Palmer 1988; Raeff 1983; Storch 1976; Tilly 1986).

2. Contentious repertoires shifted away from direct retaliation and toward nonviolent displays of political potential (Tilly 1989).

3. Ordinary people began turning to courts and police for protection from small-scale assaults on persons and privacy (Beattie 1986; Feeley & Little 1991; Lis & Soly 1996; Samaha 1974).

4. Instead of confronting each other in quasi-military fashion, local authorities (notably including police) began bargaining out agreements on nonviolent political uses of public space (Bayley 1985; Brewer et al. 1988; Emsley & Weinberger 1991; Fillieule 1997a,b; Lindenberger 1995; Lüdtke 1989, 1992; della Porta 1995; della Porta & Reiter 1998; Robert 1996; Sommier 1993; Tilly 2000).

As a consequence, murder, assault, and other small-scale interpersonal violence sank rapidly (Chesnais 1976, 1981; Cockburn 1991; Hair 1971; Rousseaux 1995; Ylikangas, Karonen, & Lehti 2001; Zwaan 2001). Compared with Western

Europeans of 1700, Westerners now live with about ten times less chance of being physically attacked by other local people.

This massive domestic pacification does not mean, however, that violence has disappeared from Western countries. The same countries that so effectively brought down frequencies of homicide, assault, and violent struggles for local political power also built the world's greatest and most destructive military forces. They visited violence on the rest of the world. Their young men suffered much less risk from domestic homicide and much more risk from death in combat. In addition, accidental deaths rose precipitously, especially deaths from motor vehicles and other means of transportation.

During the twentieth century, for rich Western countries the sources of violent death switched dramatically between war and peace. In times of war, military action caused deaths through combat, bombardment, and militarily mediated transmission of disease. (The influenza pandemic of 1918, which killed around 40 million people worldwide, gained much of its scope from troop movements. Within the United States itself, military units were major sources of infection for the country's 700,000 deaths: Crosby 1989; Kolata 1999.) During major wars, the rank order of violent mortality – not including disease – typically ran (1) deaths in combat or bombardment, (2) accidents, (3) suicide, (4) homicide, and far behind, (5) collective violence. In the absence of international war, even during extensive civil strife, the usual order remained (1) accidents, (2) suicide, (3) homicide, and (4) collective violence. Since the seventeenth century, both individual homicide and domestic collective violence have dramatically diminished in importance as causes of death in the richer Western countries.

Consider what all these changes meant for one of the better documented countries, France. Russian statistician Boris Urlanis estimated French battle deaths during the seventeenth century at 500,000, during the eighteenth century at 1.4 million, and during the Napoleonic Wars alone at 226,000 (Urlanis 1960: 44, 63, 91). Over the period from 1816 to 1980, Melvin Small and J. David Singer identify France as the world's most frequent participant in large-scale warfare: 22 wars, at war 31 percent of the time, and almost 2 million battle deaths (Small & Singer 1982: 276). During the nineteenth and twentieth centuries, France's war deaths fluctuated greatly from year to year, depending on the country's external involvements. So did deaths from collective violence. But France still lost many more people to homicide, suicide, and (especially) accidents than to war. Any of these numbers, furthermore, generally dwarfed the count of deaths through domestic collective violence. On the 14th of July 1789, great day of the Bastille's fall, after all, a total of about 110 people died in all of France's violent political encounters.

During the decade of revolution (1789–1799), the balance shifted temporarily. Urlanis estimates France's military deaths in that period's external wars at 120,000 (Urlanis 1960: 52). This time domestic political killing exceeded external wars. Executions under the Terror (which mostly occurred one at a time, but could reasonably qualify as outcomes of collective violence) included about 17,000 legal events and a likely 23,000 more from unauthorized but still revolutionary executions (Greer 1935). Controversy still swirls around the number of deaths in the great Vendée civil wars of 1793–1796, but estimates are settling down in the range of 140,000–190,000 troops and civilians of all political persuasions (Guenniffey 2000: 234–5).

Other rebellions and civil wars during the Revolution probably push the total number of deaths attributable to domestic struggles above 200,000, or about 1 person in 140 over the French population as a whole. As sources of mortality, no French domestic struggles since that time have come close. For that very reason, critics and defenders of the Revolution – still astonishingly polarized more than two centuries after the facts – continue to battle over the quantity, character, propriety, and meaning of revolutionary violence (Furet 1995; Kaplan 1993; Mayer 2000).

In 1830 – a year of conquest in Algeria, of no interstate war, but of revolution at home – 400-plus French troops (and uncounted numbers of Algerians) died in Algeria, some 1,000 French people died in popular contention (650 in the Parisian rising of 27–29 July), and 4,478 more died accidental deaths somewhere in France. War shifted the balance: in the Crimean War (1854–1856), 10,000 French troops lost their lives in battle while another 85,000 died from cholera, typhus, or lingering wounds. During those same years, French statisticians reported 28,500 accidental deaths but no one died in collective violence within France. Even the revolutions of 1871 produced only about 21,000 deaths, as compared with the 77,000 dead in the Franco-Prussian War of 1870. Both war and domestic collective violence fluctuated much more dramatically than small-scale accidents and assaults; as a killer, however, war far overshadowed other forms of collective violence.

The twentieth century brought France two bloody world wars and further pacification of popular contention. Between 1930 and 1960, about 600,000 French people died in accidents, some 200,000 died as a direct result of war, and only a hundred or so died from domestic collective violence. Despite high levels of popular mobilization, furthermore, French death rates from collective violence declined after World War II.

Let the turbulent year of 1968 make the point. Millions of students and workers mobilized against the de Gaulle government that year, striking widely,

Table 3.1. *Violent Deaths in France, 1968*

Cause	Male	Female	Total
Homicide	211	150	361
Suicide	5,467	2,162	7,629
Road Accidents	10,503	3,775	14,278
Other Accidents	11,273	11,134	22,407
Collective Violence	6	0	6
Total	27,460	17,221	44,681

Sources: Chesnais (1976: 298–331); Delale & Ragache (1978: 230).

occupying factories and schools, setting up street barricades, and battling police all over France. Yet no more than half a dozen persons died in the course of France's mighty confrontations during the year, while another half dozen met death along the edges of embattled areas (Delale & Ragache 1978: 230).

Table 3.1 shows the result. Of the estimated 44,681 French people who died violent deaths in 1968, fewer than 1 in 5,000 lost their lives in collective violence. The few deaths in domestic collective violence, it is true, had much more immediate political impact than killing through suicide, homicide, accidents, or even external war. But by the twentieth century, France's mortality from collective violence occurred almost exclusively in wars and colonial struggles. That was generally the case with Western democracies. As the growth of high-capacity democratic regimes brought down the frequency of homicide, it depressed deaths in domestic politics even more.

Catalogs of Collective Violence

After all the careful typologizing in previous chapters, astute readers have already noticed how much my description of twentieth-century violence mixes different sorts of conflict. For the whole world, no one has done comprehensive century-long counts of collective violence, much less sorted it out into violent rituals, coordinated destruction, broken negotiations, and the like. By and large, available catalogs of violent events follow different, narrower principles. They count large interstate wars, civil wars, organized genocides, or something else. Nevertheless, they converge on a picture of unprecedented twentieth-century violence – and of shifts from interstate to intrastate concentrations of large-scale killing.

Ted Robert Gurr's catalogs of violence involving ethnically defined minorities between 1945 and 1999 provide an important baseline for comparison (Gurr

1993, 2000). Gurr's earlier study followed 233 "nonstate communal groups that were politically salient" from 1945 to 1989. His second study expanded the range to 275 such groups for the period 1986–1998. The list included Turks in Germany, Afro-Brazilians, Chinese in Malaysia, Kurds in Iran, Iraq, Syria, and Turkey, Egyptian Copts, indigenous Bolivians and Ecuadorians, Hutu and Tutsi in Burundi and Rwanda, Tibetans under Chinese hegemony, and India's Muslims. It also featured self-identified Russians in Ukraine and Estonia, the Gagauz of Moldova, Roma in East Central Europe, Kazakhs in China, Germans in Kazakhstan, Chechens in Russia, and many other majority–minority combinations in the zones dominated by state socialism before 1989.

Gurr's method, as it happens, mixes violence inflicted by governmental agents and allies with that delivered by dissident groups. In fact, state-backed armies, police forces, militias, vigilantes, and other specialists in coercion inflicted a substantial but unknown share of all the damage summed up in Gurr's scores for violent protest and open rebellion. Groups included were publicly identified ethnopolitical minorities having at least 100,000 members in countries of at least 500,000 total population when, according to standard reports, members of those minorities both (a) received systematic differential treatment and (b) had movements, parties, committees, and/or militias that claimed to speak on their behalf. Gurr's studies by no means covered all ethnic conflicts wherever those conflicts occurred; they singled out big, politically identified minorities in relatively large countries.

Gurr's group used case reports to grade the presence or absence of certain kinds of activity involving such groups over five-year periods, locating each case at the highest value reached during the period. Their scale for rebellion comes closest to estimating the level of collective violence in ethnopolitical conflicts. The scale runs:

0 – none reported;
1 – political banditry, sporadic terrorism, unsuccessful coups by or on behalf of the group;
2 – campaigns of terrorism, successful coups by or on behalf of the group;
3 – small-scale guerrilla activity, or other forms of conflict;
4 – guerrilla activity involving more than 1,000 armed fighters carrying out frequent armed attacks over a substantial area, or group involvement in civil, revolutionary, or international warfare that is not specifically or mainly concerned with group issues;
5 – protracted civil war, fought by military units with base areas.

My eagle-eyed students have a field day criticizing both the basic definitions and the crudity of these measures, but generally curb their contempt when they start trying to do better on their own. (For a less sympathetic critique, see Horowitz 2001: 28.)

Through the period from 1945 to 1999, groups on the scale of Gurr's populations rarely mobilized without declaring themselves ethnically distinctive; either they claimed the right to rule an existing state on the basis of nationality or they demanded autonomy in the name of a distinct nation. As a consequence, Gurr's enumeration captures trends in large-scale conflict within regimes fairly well. Over the entire set, Gurr's catalogs show substantial increases in nonviolent protest, violent protest, and open rebellion for almost every five-year period from 1945 through 1994, then a slight drop after 1994. By Gurr's rough measures, the frequency of violent conflicts tripled from start to finish. After 1989, the increase from 233 to 275 groups occurred mainly because of rising ethnopolitical conflict in Eastern Europe and the former Soviet Union. Over the world as a whole, according to Gurr's measures, the frequency of open rebellion around ethnically defined issues declined from the mid-1980s. Protest activities up to the level of strikes and riots reached their world peak during the early 1990s but declined slightly after then.

The Central Intelligence Agency's count of international terrorist incidents from 1968 through 2000 bears a broad resemblance to Gurr's catalog (Johnson 2001; U.S. Department of State 2001). The international terrorist incidents in the count include only those in which a group based outside a given country attacked targets within that country. They therefore exclude relatively contained civil wars such as that of Sri Lanka, but they emphatically include Arab and Israeli attacks on each other as well as the work of such groups as the Red Army Faction, the Red Brigade, and the Japanese Red Army. Year-to-year variation in the frequency of such events depended especially on fluctuations in bombing.

Minor spurts occurred during the 1970s, which included the Munich Olympic Village attack of 1972. But the high point came in the five years from 1984 through 1988. During those years, CIA counts averaged 615 per year, as compared with 489 in 1981 and 473 in 2000. After 1988, terrorist attacks fell off irregularly but substantially. Bombing, armed attacks, and hostage taking all became more common during the peak years. Then all – especially bombing – declined. National liberation movements played an increasingly prominent part in terrorism as the overall frequency of incidents decreased. (I wrote these words in Manhattan, ten kilometers or so north of the World Trade Center's still-smoking ruins, on the day after suicide squads steered two passenger-packed aircraft into the

Center's twin towers. No one should read me as saying that the age of terrorism has ended.)

For the period of their overlap, Gurr's worldwide catalogs also correspond well with Mark Beissinger's counts of "protest events" in the Soviet Union and its successor states from 1987 to 1992. Taking sheer number of events rather than number of participants, Beissinger's evidence shows a dramatic increase in nonviolent protest demonstrations from 1987 through 1990, leveling off in 1991 and then declining in 1992. Mass violent events, in contrast, generally remained infrequent from 1987 through 1990 except for a minor peak in mid-1989, but then rose dramatically through 1991 and 1992. Nonviolent demonstrations emphasized nationalist and ethnic issues – generally demands for rights based on nationality or ethnicity. Violent events, however, centered on claims concerning the borders of republics. In such events, organized armed forces – including guerrilla forces, paramilitary groups, and militias – often performed much of the killing, wounding, and damaging.

During the six-year period, then, a broad shift occurred from peaceful demands for recognition to violent struggles over the fruits of recognition, the territories to be dominated by one titular nationality or another. Extended past 1992, Beissinger's series would most likely show a decline in the sheer number of nationalist and ethnic claims as republics both inside and outside the Russian federation worked out settlements with each other. (In an impressive parallel, struggles among Russia's criminal syndicates and protection agencies for shares of their markets were likewise rising during the early 1990s, peaking around 1994, then settling into a more stable pattern of control during the later 1990s: Volkov 2002, chap. 3.) In such regions as Georgia, Tajikistan, Chechnya, and Northern Ossetia, however, we would witness an intensification of the remaining conflicts. Broadly speaking, nonetheless, the experience of the former Soviet Union matches that of Ted Gurr's international array.

What can we conclude from these diverse catalogs of collective violence? Behind recent short-term fluctuations loom two long-term trends: (i) reduction of violence in the domestic contentious politics of high-capacity democratic countries; and (ii) shift of warfare on a world scale from interstate violence by means of nationally controlled armed forces to action by a much wider range of violent specialists *within* regimes. Increasingly, high-capacity democratic regimes participate in warfare not as declared belligerents but as suppliers of arms, purchasers of contraband, and peacekeepers. (At the start of the twenty-first century, for example, as the United States was becoming an increasingly reluctant peacekeeper, it was also supplying just under half of the entire world's international arms shipments and providing the world's premier market for illegal drugs.) Meanwhile, outside the charmed circle of high-capacity democratic regimes, struggles intensify over who is to rule and thus to benefit from salable resources.

As the twentieth century wound down, the struggles producing the bulk of large-scale collective violence over the world as a whole centered on demands for political autonomy in the names of unjustly subordinated nations, similar demands for control of existing governments on the part of excluded or subjugated populations, or (more rarely) demands that tyrannical rulers step down in favor of opponents claiming to speak for the people at large. Brawls, opportunism, scattered attacks, and violent rituals continue to occur, but they produce only small shares of total damage from collective violence.

Broken negotiations and coordinated destruction fluctuate and interact as sources of most immediate damage to persons and objects. Those are the forms of collective violence in which control over governments is at stake; they are also the ones in which political entrepreneurs and violent specialists play the most prominent parts. In broken negotiations and coordinated destruction, availability of outside support – in the form of arms, money, military training, and markets for contraband – make large differences to the relative success of armed factions. These days, broken negotiations and coordinated destruction concentrate in low-capacity undemocratic regimes.

That concentration is at once ironic and tragic. It is ironic because one might have thought the governments of such regimes were less attractive targets for takeover bids than the governments of high-capacity regimes, with their command of much more extensive resources. Other things equal, low-capacity regimes are less effective at opportunity hoarding and exploitation, hence produce fewer advantages for those who run them. But high-capacity regimes, whether democratic or authoritarian, generally leave little space for disloyal oppositions to accumulate military power. They monitor, contain, co-opt, or destroy nongovernmental specialists in violence while effectively driving almost all public claim making into prescribed or tolerated performances. In low-capacity undemocratic regimes, governments that lack extensive external backing typically also lack the means of suppressing armed opposition. Because they are vulnerable to seizure by well-organized petty tyrants, they actually lend themselves to exploitation of what governmental power exists for the advantage of a small faction.

When the country exports substantial natural resources such as oil, drugs, timber, or diamonds, and when a large diaspora provides support for rebellious activity and/or the export of contraband, the opportunities and incentives for exploitation and opportunity hoarding increase (Collier & Hoeffler 2001). So do the attractions of secession – or at least political autonomy – for power holders in resource-rich regions. In such regimes, disparities between the advantages of those who currently hold governmental power and those who do not sharpen fiercely. A tragic pattern of rent seeking, exclusion, and armed rebellion results.

If we were public health sleuths tracking down and exterminating violent viruses, the concentration of collective violence in low-capacity undemocratic regimes would no doubt lead us to ignore other sorts of regimes. That, however, is not my plan. On the contrary, mapping and explaining high concentrations of collective violence only begins the project. Beyond that point, we must ask how and why violence – whether frequent or infrequent, small or large in scale – connects differently with nonviolent politics in different kinds of regimes, and what causes shifts from one pattern to another.

Collective Violence in 1989

To escape grim comparisons of casualties across the whole world, let us take a quick look at the remarkable year of 1989. As the *New York Times* headlines in Table 3.2 remind us, 1989 provided a historical hinge, swinging a door open to a new era. Although Chinese troops crushed a student–worker uprising in Beijing and other cities, Russia completed its withdrawal of troops from Afghanistan, relatively free elections brought in or confirmed new regimes in the Soviet Union, Poland, Hungary, Czechoslovakia, and elsewhere in the Soviet bloc, Romanians started open battles with their regime, Germans began tearing down the Berlin Wall, and the United States made gestures signaling an end to the Cold War.

To be sure, during 1989 civil wars continued or restarted in Afghanistan, Angola, Burma, Cambodia, Colombia, El Salvador, Ethiopia, Guatemala, India, Indonesia, Iran, Iraq, Lebanon, Liberia, Morocco, Mozambique, Nicaragua, Peru, the Philippines, Somalia, Sri Lanka, and Sudan. In the next few years' uncertainty, as we have seen, civil wars actually multiplied across the world. Yet an era was ending: the time when potential rebels could usually find backers in either the socialist or the capitalist camp. A few high-capacity undemocratic regimes were edging toward democracy, while many more were losing capacity with little or no democratization. The map of regimes was shifting fast, and with it the map of collective violence.

Carol Mueller describes one of the crucial moments of that year:

November 9, 1989. The Berlin Wall. At the end of a long and rambling press conference, Gunter Schabowski, spokesman for the recently defunct Politburo of the East German Social Unity Party (SED), announced in an offhand manner that provisional travel regulations would be in effect until a new law was passed; namely, East Germans could now

Table 3.2. *Selected Headlines from the* New York Times, *1989*

2/15	(Moscow): Last Soviet Soldiers Leave Afghanistan After 9 Years, 15,000 Dead and Great Cost
2/19	(Warsaw): Solidarity May Win 40 Percent of Parliament
3/17	(Moscow): Soviets Savor Vote in Freest Election Since '17 Revolution
5/4	(Beijing): Urging Chinese Democracy, 100,000 Surge Past Police
5/17	(Beijing): A Million Chinese March, Adding Pressure for Change
6/4	(Beijing): Troops Attack and Crush Beijing Protest; Thousands Fight Back, Scores are Killed
6/8	(Warsaw): Warsaw Accepts Solidarity Sweep and Humiliating Losses by [Communist] Party
6/16	(Budapest): Hungarian Who Led '56 Revolt is Buried as a Hero
10/1	(Hof, West Germany): More Than 6,000 East Germans Swell Tide of Refugees to the West
10/25	(Helsinki): Gorbachev in Finland, Disavows Any Right of Regional Intervention
11/10	(Berlin): The Border Is Open; Joyous East Germans Pour Through Wall; Party Pledges Freedoms, and City Exults
11/10	(Sofia): Bulgarian Chief Quits After 35 Years of Rigid Rule
11/15	(Prague): Unease in Prague; A Soviet Warning on Foot-Dragging is Given to Prague
11/20	(Prague): 200,000 March in Prague as Calls for Change Mount
11/25	(Prague): Prague Party Leaders Resign; New Chief, 48, Surprise Choice; 350,000 at Rally Cheer Dubcek
11/26	(Budapest): Hungarians Hold First Free Vote in 42 Years, Shunning a Boycott
11/28	(London): Unease Fills Western Allies over Rapid Changes in East
12/3	(Valletta, Malta): Bush and Gorbachev Proclaim a New Era for U.S.–Soviet Ties
12/7	(Moscow): Lithuania Legalizes Rival Parties, Removing Communists' Monopoly
12/8	(Mexico City): Castro Says He'll Resist Changes Like Those Sweeping Soviet Bloc
12/24	(Bucharest): Rumanian Army Gains in Capital but Battle Goes On
12/29	(Prague): Czechoslovakia: Havel, Long Prague's Prisoner, Elected President

Source: Gwertzman & Kaufman (1991).

travel to the West without the usual restrictions on visas. Apparently, neither Schabowski nor the remaining Krenz government had intended to open the Berlin Wall, but East Germans who saw the press conference on television decided to see for themselves. Arriving at the checkpoints, crowds of East Berliners found that the exits were still barred and guarded as they had been for 28 years. Instead of going home to clarify the meaning of Schabowski's strange press conference the next day, they stood their ground shouting,

"Open the gate! Open the gate!" to badly outnumbered guards. With television cameras feeding graphic images back to GDR audiences via West German stations, the standoff continued for three hours while the size of the crowds continued to grow.

As taunts and shoving broke out at points of contact, the guards still had no instructions. Finally, at 10:30 P.M., the ranking East German border guards at Bornholmer Strasse and three other crossing points in the center of the city took matters into their own hands and opened the gates. Thirty minutes later, the Interior Minister ratified their decision with an official order. By this time, one of the great celebrations of the century was underway at the Brandenburg Gate as tens of thousands poured through the checkpoints, and Berliners of East and West joined in toasting an historic moment. (Mueller 1999: 698)

Little violence occurred in Berlin that day – some pushing and shoving, some destruction of the hated Wall, not much more. But the November rush took place against the backdrop of street fighting in Dresden and demonstrations provoking scuffles with police in Leipzig, as well as massive peaceful demonstrations in Berlin itself. (On Monday 6 November alone, a full 750,000 demonstrators had turned out in half a dozen East German cities.) After a series of governmental improvisations and cabinet shuffles, the entire Politburo and Central Committee resigned on 3 December. The high-capacity East German regime was collapsing as the claim-making performances of neighboring West Germany proliferated in its ruins.

Over the year 1989 as a whole, German-speaking people massively repudiated socialist regimes. Roughly 350,000 people moved from East to West Germany, and a similar number of ethnic Germans settled in the West from elsewhere in the Soviet bloc (*Annual Register* 1989: 150). By year's end, East and West Germans were organizing the demise of the German Democratic Republic and its integration into a reunited Germany. A year later, the GDR had disappeared.

Within West Germany (that is, the Federal Republic of Germany, or FRG), most of the year's contention passed without violence. For example, Green activists successfully concluded a long campaign against construction of a nuclear reprocessing plant in Bavaria. Nevertheless, two outlawed terrorist groups worked in the forbidden zones of German contentious politics. Contingents of the Irish Republican Army attacked British military personnel stationed in the FRG at least three times in July and August, killing the German wife of a British soldier. The left-wing Red Army Faction assassinated Alfred Herrhausen, head of the Deutsche Bank, in November. Left-wing activists also deliberately challenged Berlin police, wounding more than 300 of them, during the year's May Day festivities (Koopmans 1995: 33).

Even during the extraordinary year of 1989, however, the bulk of FRG contention conformed to the model of high-capacity democratic regimes: low levels of violence in routine claim making as well as highly selective (and hence relatively rare) deployment of violent means by governmental agents, but also extensive involvement of government agents (as initiators, objects, or peacemakers) in such collective violence as did occur. Over the period 1965–1989 as a whole, Ruud Koopmans's sample of 1,767 "protest events" in West Germany included 8.4 percent police–demonstrator clashes, 4.2 percent "light" violence such as window breaking, 5.5 percent "heavy" violence such as fire bombing, and 1.6 percent violence against persons including murders and kidnappings (Koopmans 1995: 82). Koopmans's figures mean, of course, that more than 80 percent of all protest events proceeded without collective violence.

What of *low-capacity* democratic regimes? There we expect less involvement of governmental officials in violent repression but also widespread spiraling of initially nonviolent conflicts into violence – because government agents do not serve as effective third-party enforcers of agreements and can do little to inhibit escalation. In 1989, Jamaica can stand as our exemplar. During the campaign for the general election of 9 February, activists of the People's National Party (PNP) and the Jamaica Labor Party (JLP) frequently attacked each other, with a toll of 13 deaths and 108 injuries (*Annual Register* 1989: 83; in that election, the PNP won 45 seats to the JLP's 15). Years later, Jamaica-born Harvard sociologist Orlando Patterson explained the Jamaican organizational background:

A politician's political survival depends entirely on his or her ability to win repeatedly at the local level. One sure method of ensuring repeated victory is to create what is called a garrison constituency: a pocket of housing erected with public funds, with carefully screened residents who will constitute the unbeatable core of the politician's voters.

These began with Edward Seaga, now the leader of the Jamaica Labor Party, when he was in office during the 1960s and 80s. The leading politicians of the other main party soon followed his lead. There are now about 15 hard-core garrison constituencies, and political fights between them during elections have spilled over into broader, ongoing turf wars. The resulting gangs, initially formed for political purposes, now also serve the drug trade. During the 80s, many of these gangs migrated to America, where they became known as posses and soon forged a reputation for violence.

These gangs have increasingly worked to generate unrest as a political tactic. This may have been a cause of the recent violence, which was as much a police riot as a counterattack by political thugs against police. The violence took place in garrison constituencies loyal to the opposition party, and many commentators here see it as an attempt by the opposition to pressure the government to call an early election. (Patterson 2001: 1)

Even outside of electoral campaigns, however, Kingston's armed gangs frequently shoot each other up, contributing to Jamaica's unenviable position as possessor of the Caribbean's highest murder rate. Jamaica serves as an important transit point for Colombian cocaine on its way to the United Kingdom and the

United States, which helps explain the intensity of turf wars and the heavy armament of politically aligned gangs (Grimal 2000: 175). The power of drug-based gangs threatens to diminish hard-won and long-established Jamaican democracy (Sheller 2000).

Still, the politics of *low-capacity undemocratic regimes* differs markedly from that of today's (or 1989's) relatively democratic Jamaica. In such regimes, you will remember, we expect petty tyrants to use coercion freely, governmental officials to deploy violent punishments when they can catch their enemies, and means of violence to be widely distributed across other political actors.

Somalia offers a terrifying case in point. Perhaps Africa's most homogeneous country from an ethnic point of view, Somalia openly contradicts the idea that homogeneity minimizes conflict. Rival (yet closely related) clans have fought for governmental control since the country's independence in 1960. Somalia's President Siyad Barre seized the government in a 1969 coup. Barre kept his Darood clan in power first by buying off heads of rival clans with patronage, then by pitting one clan against another. The second tactic worked well until Barre responded to Soviet tilting toward Somali neighbor and enemy Ethiopia by terminating his pact with the Soviet Union. Barre's attempt to wrest the Ogaden region from Ethiopia in a disastrous war of 1977–1978 further alienated foreign donors. After the war, nevertheless, Italy, Germany, China, and the United States provided military aid as a way of establishing their own presence in the region, holding off the possible influence of revolutionary Iran, and matching Soviet support for Ethiopia. Emboldened neighboring powers began to supply arms to various segments of Barre's opposition. As internal and external threats multiplied, Barre adopted ever more repressive policies. Segmented civil war ensued, with incessant shifts of coalitions among clans. In addition to many battle deaths, Somalia then experienced lethal famines and epidemics as a direct consequence of interruptions to food distribution and preventive medicine.

By the beginning of 1989, Barre's forces controlled the Somalian capital of Mogadishu and its region but not much more of the country. Even in Mogadishu their control faltered. As the *Annual Register* summarized:

On 14 July major disturbances broke out in Mogadishu, in response to government measures following the assassination of the Catholic bishop, Salvatore Colombo, an Italian. The Government arrested several leading Muslim imams, and over the next few days more than 400 people were killed, the great majority of them by government forces; nearly 50 were summarily executed. The upheavals were reportedly coordinated by the United Somalia Congress, an opposition movement formed by the southern Hawiye clans. The third congress of the ruling Somali Revolutionary Socialist Party was held in early July, shortly before the disturbances. Although it reiterated the SRSP's role as the sole permitted political organization, President Siyad announced in August that multi-party elections would be held in 1990. Disaffection also appeared among members of the Ogaden clan, which had provided the President with much of his support, and was well-represented in the army; an Ogadeni garrison at Kismayu near the Kenya border mutinied in March, and many of the soldiers defected to another opposition movement, the Somali Patriotic Front. (*Annual Register* 1989: 245)

Barre did not last much longer; after rebel forces overran Mogadishu, he fled the country in January 1991. The militia competition and protection rackets that accompanied the Barre regime's collapse first caused one of Africa's great twentieth-century famines, incited a series of partially successful international interventions, then finally produced a new round of militia competition and protection rackets based on the inflow of international aid (de Waal 1997, chaps. 8 & 9). Although the intensity of civil war declined in 1992, since then Somalia has lived with constant fighting among warlords and criminal gangs.

China stands as an exemplary *high-capacity undemocratic regime*. Such regimes, according to the argument laid out in Chapter 2, should have widespread threats of violence by governmental agents, frequent involvement of governmental agents in collective violence when it occurs, but great variability in the actual frequency of collective violence – depending on the opening and closing of opportunities for dissent. In such regimes, as in the case of high-capacity democratic regimes, visible violence tends to broadcast the high political stakes of contention. In 1989, China certainly fulfilled these expectations.

The high (or low) point came in the confrontations of May–June 1989. Table 3.3 offers an abbreviated summary of events in Beijing alone; in fact, by June students and workers all over the country were participating in one version or another of the Beijing events. When connected dissidents face authoritarian regimes, they commonly have three choices: bide their time in silence, engage in forbidden and clandestine acts of destruction, or overload the narrow range of tolerated occasions for assembly and expression. In the third case, criticism of regimes often occurs in the course of public holidays and ceremonies – Mardi Gras, inaugurations, funerals, royal weddings, and the like – when authorities tolerate larger and more public assemblies than usual. The Beijing events started exactly that way, with student memorials to the dead Hu Yaobang, a former secretary general of the Chinese Communist Party reputed to have been sacked in 1987 for his excessive sympathy with student demands.

When the government held a state funeral for Hu in Tiananmen's Great Hall of the People on 22 April, some 50,000 students arrived in the square for the ceremonies. Some of them reenacted old regime rituals by kneeling on the Great

Table 3.3. *Chronology of the Beijing Student Movement, 1989*

4/16	At death of Hu Yaobang, former secretary general of Chinese Communist Party, students post wreaths and elegiac couplets in Tiananmen Square and many Beijing colleges.
4/17	Students march to Tiananmen to memorialize Hu Yaobang.
4/20	Skirmishes between police and students at Xinhua Gate; some students begin class boycott.
4/22	Hu's funeral in Great Hall of the People; about 50,000 students march to Tiananmen to participate; numerous student actions include kneeling on the Great Hall's steps to deliver a petition and request a meeting with premier Li Peng.
4/23	Students form Beijing Student Autonomous Union Provisional Committee.
4/26	*People's Daily* editorial calls student mobilization "planned conspiracy" and "turmoil".
4/27	About 100,000 students march to Tiananmen and protest the editorial. State Council announces willingness to meet with students.
4/29	Senior government officials meet with 45 selected students from 16 Beijing universities, but other students challenge both the dialogue and the student representatives.
5/4	Students march in commemoration of the May 4th Movement (of 1919).
5/5	Students form Beijing Student Dialogue Delegation. Most students end class boycott.
5/13	300 students start a hunger strike at Tiananmen, with numbers eventually rising to about 3,000 plus thousands more as spectators and supporters.
5/14	High-level state delegation meets student activists, chaotic discussion ensues because of student divisions, students withdraw from the talks.
5/15	Mikhail Gorbachev arrives for a state visit; because of Tiananmen's occupation, government holds its official reception at the Beijing airport.
5/17	More than a million Beijing residents march in support of students and hunger strikers.
5/19	Government declares martial law, but residents and students block the troops. Students from outside Beijing continue to arrive in the city.
6/3	Military repression begins, with hundreds of people killed by government troops.
6/4	Troops encircle remaining 4,000 students at Tiananmen; students leave the square.

Source: Adapted from Zhao (2001: xxv–xxvi).

Hall's steps to present a petition and ask humbly for a meeting with premier Li Peng. Over the whole period from mid-April to the beginning of June, groups of students played cat and mouse with the government's armed forces, marching despite prohibitions against assemblies, chanting slogans, staging hunger strikes, resisting orders to evacuate public spaces, tossing bottles or shoes at the police, eventually blocking the 100,000 troops sent to clear Tiananmen the night of 19–20 May. By that time, thousands of nonstudents had joined student activists in open challenges to the regime. Students at the square consisted increasingly of recent arrivals from outside of Beijing.

As martial law forces assembled in and around Beijing, residents often insulted and attacked the soldiers. But when troops began their assault on Tiananmen the night of 3 June, they brought in overwhelming force. On their way to retaking the city, they killed about 250 people and suffered a half dozen deaths of their own men. Between 4:30 and 6:30 A.M. on the 4th, the remaining students marched out of Tiananmen through columns opened by the military (Zhao 2001: 203–7).

Explaining Trends and Variations

During 1989, then, patterns of collective violence in Germany, Jamaica, Somalia, and China corresponded broadly to the arguments of Chapter 2. Variations in governmental capacity and democracy seem to have made large differences to intensities, loci, and forms of large-scale violent interaction. We find the most extensive violence in the low-capacity undemocratic regime (Somalia), the least extensive in the high-capacity democratic regime (Germany), with the others (Jamaica and China) in between. We also find violent specialists enjoying much more autonomy from government in the low-capacity regimes (Somalia and Jamaica) than in the high-capacity regimes (China and Germany). As a result, government-backed specialists wrought much more of the damage done in China and Germany. By no means do these deliberately chosen examples of a single year's events prove my arguments. But at least they show that the capacity–democracy scheme has some power to differentiate and illuminate national styles of violent incidents.

Notice one feature of the trends and variations that we have reviewed: A significant share of collective violence involves activation and reinforcement of boundaries. Claims to be or represent a certain "we" always identify a boundary separating us from "them," whoever they are. Any individual or population, however, always has multiple identities – and thus multiple boundaries – available. In India, many of the very same people can on different occasions act together as workers, women, Hindus, Gujaratis, villagers, or members of certain castes. Boundary activation singles out one of these shared identities and its opposition to other identities. As the Rwandan massacre suggests, activation of us–them boundaries often promotes damaging interaction where social relations previously went on in a generally peaceful fashion. As the mass killing of nonconforming Hutu by Hutu activists indicates, furthermore, violence sometimes occurs in the course of power struggles *within* categories and for control over public representation of those categories. The stronger the emphasis on a single us–them boundary, in general, the greater the salience of damage in all interactions and the more extensive the coordination among all violent actors.

Which sorts of boundaries are present and available for activation varies systematically by type of regime. High-capacity regimes limit drastically the range of categorical pairs – hence boundaries – in terms of which people can make claims. In the high-capacity undemocratic Soviet Union, for example, members of religious sects, women, ethnic groups outside the privileged number of titular nationalities, and even the informal mutual aid networks through which people actually conducted their daily affairs had no public standing as political actors and little opportunity to gain that standing. In high-capacity democratic Canada, members of categories that can present themselves as certain kinds of citizens (including categories currently deprived of their proper citizenship rights) have a much greater chance of being heard than do kinship groups or religious sects. Yet in general democratic regimes erect fewer barriers to formation of new bounded groupings so long as they model themselves on existing political actors. Thus, boundaries of sexual preference become more available for public political action in democracies than in nondemocracies, in so far as the people involved make their claims as categories of citizens deprived of equal rights rather than as separatist communities.

What about activation of boundaries in collective violence? When violence swells rapidly from a small to a large scale, three processes are usually at work, although in varying sequences and combinations. Political entrepreneurs are engaged in their work of activation, connection, coordination, and representation. Polarization – the widening of political and social space between claimants in a contentious episode and the gravitation of previously uncommitted or moderate actors toward one or both extremes – commonly accompanies or results from the work of entrepreneurs. Finally, and often as a result of political brokerage and polarization, uncertainty rises across the boundary as actors on each side have less reliable information (and hence more exaggerated estimates) concerning the likely actions on the other side.

Violence generally increases and becomes more salient in situations of rising uncertainty across the boundary. It increases because people respond to threats against weighty social arrangements they have built on such boundaries – arrangements such as exploitation of others, property rights, in-group marriage, and power over local government. Violence becomes more salient among all interactions because existing nonviolent routines lose their guarantees of pay-off. Uncertainty over identity boundaries can rise through a number of different processes.

- Overarching political authorities lose their ability to enforce previously con-straining agreements that would bind actors on both sides of the boundary.
- Those same authorities take actions that threaten survival of crucial connect-ing structures within populations on one side of the boundary while appearing to spare or even benefit those on the other side.
- The declining capacity of authorities to police existing boundaries, control use of weapons, and contain individual aggression facilitates cross-boundary opportunism, including retaliation for earlier slights and injustices.
- Leaders on either side of the boundary face resistance or competition from well-organized segments of their previous followers.
- External parties change, increase, or decrease their material, moral, and po-litical support for actors on one side of the boundary or the other.

Such processes affect not only boundaries but also the stories and social rela-tions attached to them. Change and variation in these circumstances help explain the surge in violence over nationality issues that occurred in Eurasia between 1986 and 1995. During those years, major powers (including the United States and the United Nations) responded to the weakening of central authority in the Warsaw Pact, the Soviet Union, and Yugoslavia by signaling increased support for claims of leaders to represent distinct nations currently under alien control. That signaling encouraged leaders to emphasize ethnic boundaries, compete for recognition as valid interlocutors for oppressed nations, attack their ostensi-ble enemies, suppress their competitors for leadership, and make alliances with others who would supply them with resources to support their mobilization.

All those moves in turn generated what observers saw as ethnopolitical vio-lence. International authorities then grew less receptive to new claims for au-tonomy and independence as they saw how much violence attended those claims and how little formal autonomy reduced the violence. But by that time arms dealers, mercenaries, drug runners, diamond merchants, oil brokers, and others who benefited from weak central political control had moved in to take advan-tage of supposedly ethnic conflicts – and even to promote them.

In summary: What explains variation in the presence, salience, coordination, personnel, identity relevance, and political impact of violent claim making? An-swers to these questions will eventually fall into two clusters that we can call *activation–suppression* and *incorporation–separation*. In the activation–suppression cluster we will find mechanisms that activate or deactivate existing boundaries, ties, and stories. In a friendly cowboy card game that turns into a shooting match, for example, someone activates the boundary between workers from two different outfits and thereby raises the stakes of the interaction. Political entrepreneurs often loom large in activation and suppression on the larger scale.

In the incorporation–separation cluster we will find mechanisms that create new connections, or sever old connections, among social sites. Political entrepreneurs, violent specialists, and both together often play critical roles in incorporation and separation. In Hyderabad, for example, Akbar brings his wrestlers into street fighting as forces on the Muslim (anti-Hindu) side. He connects tough Muslim enforcers with normally peaceable Muslims.

Activation and suppression have especially strong effects on the *salience* of violence within political interactions. Salience generally increases when participants in political interaction are themselves specialists in violence, when uncertainty about an interaction's outcome increases, when stakes of the outcome for the parties increase, and/or when third parties to which the participants have stable relations are absent. Activation of different political identities (i.e., of bundled boundaries, stories, and social relations) directly promotes those conditions. To the extent that just one pair of political identities – Hutu–Tutsi, landlord–tenant, rival cowboy outfits, and so on – orients all interactions among participants in claim making, we can say that, in general: violent specialists more readily join the action; uncertainty about outcomes increases; stakes rise; and third parties flee, detach themselves, or lose relevance. Conversely, suppression of prevailing political identities (e.g., through reaction to disasters shared across identity boundaries) reduces the salience of violence and increases the importance of nonviolent interactions.

The ease of activation and suppression of various political identities depends in turn on the regime's array of prescribed, tolerated, and forbidden performances. Some regimes, for example, make it easy for representatives of lineages to act publicly as such but almost impossible for women as such to do so. Within limits set by regimes, activation or deactivation of different boundaries, stories, and relations greatly alters incentives and opportunities to inflict damage. Volkov's Russian gangs do not use violence indiscriminately; they distinguish with exquisite care between those they protect and those they destroy.

Incorporation and separation have their most notable effects on *coordination* of violence. Incorporation promotes coordination on a large scale, whereas separation promotes coordination on a small scale. Akbar's toughs switch between small-scale bullying and large-scale killing not chiefly as a result of their own mood swings but because political entrepreneurs like Akbar sometimes link them with other like-minded specialists in violence. The extent of coordination among violent actors increases as political entrepreneurs create connections among previously independent individuals and groups, as authorities control the stakes – both rewards and punishment – of outcomes for participants, as categories dividing major blocs of participants (e.g., gender, race, or nationality) also figure widely in routine social life, and/or as major participants organize and drill outside of violent encounters. Incorporation and separation strongly affect these conditions.

In turn, configurations of prescribed, tolerated, and forbidden performances limit incorporation and separation. Some regimes tolerate vengeance at a local scale but step in immediately (and vengefully) if someone begins connecting dissidents across regions. In 1989, the Chinese government closed in rapidly when high officials saw local Beijing student activism becoming a national movement. More generally, high-capacity regimes block incorporation except when it corresponds to established divisions within the polity and supports major holders of power.

The explanations we are seeking do not take the form of general laws for collective violence as a whole or even particular laws governing one type of violence or another. Nor do they center on reconstructing the propensities of violent actors – whether we consider those propensities to be motives, mentalities, urges, or programs. They do not consist of identifying the functions that violence may serve for large systems of power or production. The explanations at issue single out violent transactions among social sites, map variation in the character and intensity of violent transactions across time, space, and social settings, then look for the recurrent causal mechanisms and processes that cause variation in the character and intensity of collective violence.

Where to now? The following chapters follow our established spiral, looking more closely in turn at violent rituals, coordinated destruction, opportunism, brawls, scattered attack, and broken negotiations before reexamining relations and transitions among different types of collective violence. In each case we will not only discover regimes affecting the character of violent interactions but also will notice political entrepreneurs, violent specialists, contentious repertoires, salient political identities, and political boundaries behaving differently from one sort of regime to another.

In chapters to come, we will watch exploitation and opportunity hoarding as they give political actors means and incentives to activate certain boundaries at the expense of others, thereby altering the intensity, character, and locus of collective violence. We will observe mechanisms of activation and suppression affecting the identities around which people organize violent interactions as mechanisms of incorporation and separation affect the coordination (or lack of coordination) of violent action across social settings. Rather than complete explanations of violent episodes wherever they occur, we will be seeking explanations of *variations* in violent incidents among political circumstances and settings.

4

―――――――――――――――――――――――――――――――

Violent Rituals

Scripted Damage

A sports fan I'm not. Somehow I was absent when the gods implanted the res-
onators that start New York males vibrating at a victory of the city's Knicks,
Yankees, Giants, Jets, or Rangers and reciting endless streams of information
about past and present stars of basketball, baseball, football, and hockey. Yet
during the baseball season I rarely resist a glance at the daily newspaper's sports
pages to see whether the hapless Chicago Cubs are doing better than in the half
century since they last won a National League pennant and the near century
since they last won a World Series. Growing up in the Chicago area implanted
one reed of a resonator – not enough to capture emanations from the Chicago
Bulls, White Sox, Bears, or Black Hawks, but sufficient to sound a plaintive note
of sports chauvinism when I least expect it.

Pursuing the classic question "Why is there no soccer in the United States?",
Andrei Markovits and Steven Hellerman remark that working-class males
throughout the Western world generally grow up attached to the professional
sports teams they followed as children. In that way, they acquire one of the few
national cultural idioms that put them on easy speaking terms with fellow nationals from different classes, callings, and cultures. Nor is the attachment to
teams politically innocent:

If anything, nationalism plays an even greater role in team sports than it does in individual sports. Whereas it could be argued in the case of the former that the contestant
represents him or herself as much – if not more – than their countries, in the case of the
team's collective entity and very being, the collective in the form of the country, city,
or region most definitely supersedes any identification with the individual. Indeed, any
placement of individual loyalties and achievements over those of the collective are seen
as selfish, wrong, detrimental to the collective good – and often unpatriotic.

Because soccer is the world's most widely performed team sport played internationally by more nations than are represented in the United Nations, nationalism has enjoyed a greater presence in this game than in perhaps any other sport. In most cases, this has been benign. In many, however, it has led to ugly riots, furthered nationalist excesses, spawned national hatreds and prejudice, while appealing to hostility and contempt toward opponents. In the case of El Salvador and Honduras in the 1970s, a disputed soccer game exacerbated the already present hostilities between these two Central American neighbors, leading to a brief "soccer war" between them. (Markovits & Hellerman 2001: 37)

No subsequent soccer match has spiraled into an international war, but soccer fans continued to engage in violent confrontations after the 1970s. Table 4.1 lists a few of the many incidents from 1999 through 2001; they range from Buenos Aires to Dhaka. Clearly soccer violence has become an international phenomenon.

Unlike American football, soccer involves little outright violence on the field, most of it accidental and almost all of it punished as fouls. When soccer matches generate serious damage, spectators and supporters have usually started the trouble. More often than not the violent performers consist of young male fans who have arrived in clusters; fortunately for the death rate, they rarely use weapons more lethal than clubs, broken bottles, and knives (Bromberger 1998, chap. 3; Buford 1991). Deaths become frequent chiefly when police battle unruly fans (Giulianotti, Bonney, & Hepworth 1994). Gary Armstrong describes the strong-arm supporters of Sheffield United, the Blades, with whom he hung around for years:

One scenario would involve an individual Blade, in a company of up to 200 similar Blades, journeying to another city, where their equivalents would await their arrival. Upon recognition the two groups would be prepared to fight, despite having never met and being unlikely ever to see each other again. As a parallel to the match they had traveled to watch, Blades could decide if they (as a parallel team) had won, lost, or drawn their competitive engagement. Not that this mattered too much, for future weeks would bring other groups of lads and similar scenarios in a repetitive process. (Armstrong 1998: 6)

Across the world similar groups of violent specialists have formed in parallel to professional soccer teams. Both on and off the field, team sports provide spectacular illustrations of the organized us–them boundary activation, separation of spectators from participants, channeling by well-defined repertoires, and stylized enactments of more wide-ranging political identities that characterize violent rituals.

In violent rituals, at least one relatively well-defined and coordinated group follows a known interaction script entailing the infliction of damage on themselves or others as they compete for priority within a recognized arena. We can

Table 4.1. *Some Violent Soccer Incidents, 1999–2001*

Buenos Aires, Argentina, March 1999: A friendly match between Boca Juniors and Chacarita ended when men with clubs and knives (alleged to be Boca fans) attacked rivals at the Boca stadium.

Leipzig, Germany, May 1999: Supporters of both teams invaded the pitch of a match between VfB and Sachsen after VfB opened the scoring, attacking each other and police.

Ho Chi Minh City, Vietnam, August 1999: "Four people were killed and 150 injured when street celebrations marking Vietnam's win over Myanmar in a regional soccer game turned ugly."

Turkish border, Iraq, October 2000: Following a brawl between players from the two teams, Dahuk supporters attacked Zakhu fans, who then burned cars and looted shops.

Johannesburg, South Africa, November 2000: Fans spilled onto the field of a women's match between South Africa and Nigeria, breaking up the game before it could end.

Nikosia, Cyprus, January 2001: Nine people were injured and the main stadium extensively damaged in "crowd trouble" at a match between Omonia and Olympiakos.

Lubumbashi, Democratic Republic of the Congo, April 2001: At least ten people were killed and 51 injured during a football match.

Melbourne, Australia, May 2001: After a 0–0 match, supporters of the Melbourne Knights attacked a coach and players of Perth Glory plus a Soccer Australia official and a security guard, knocking the guard unconscious, as the teams left the stadium.

Zagreb, Croatia, May 2001: As the match between Dinamo Zagreb and Hajduk Split was ending with Split behind 2–0, hundreds of Hajduk supporters rushed the field; police eventually used clubs and tear gas to remove them, with hundreds of spectators and 30 policemen injured.

Accra, Ghana, May 2001: After Kumasi Asante Kotoko lost 2–1 to Hearts of Oak, Kumasi supporters began tearing up stadium seats; police fired tear gas. In the rush to escape, about 120 people died and another 150 were injured.

Richmond, U.K., June 2001: Minutes after England lost a match to Portugal, five "football thugs" punched and kicked three Londoners, one of whom was wearing a Portugal jersey.

Dhaka, Bangladesh, August 2001: As a match between Rahmatganj and Dhaka Mohammedan Sporting Club was ending in a 1–1 tie, fans began torching stadium seats and damaging cars in nearby streets; police used tear gas and a baton charge to break up the crowd, arresting three people.

make a rough distinction between those rituals (like team matches) in which at least two of the parties enjoy rough equality of standing and those (like shaming ceremonies) in which one party begins with far greater force than the other(s). Coalition making can convert one into the other, as when spectators at the placing of a supposed wrongdoer in the stocks cheer and reward the object of punishment. In either case, however, participants activate a certain boundary, maintain it zealously, and direct their violence across it.

Violent rituals provide the extreme case of coordination among violent actors. Thus violent rituals simultaneously exaggerate and discipline features that are visible in other forms of collective violence. They form their own distinctive versions of political entrepreneurs and violent specialists. They give unusually sharp definition to the identities in play: boundaries between the parties, stories about those boundaries, relations across those boundaries, and relations within those boundaries. By the same token, they mute the effects of previously existing relations among participants except where they correspond precisely to the boundaries of identities activated by the rituals. Participants in violent rituals ordinarily tolerate a very limited range of damaging actions, punishing or excluding participants who violate those limits. They establish unusually clear criteria for success and failure, with victors frequently celebrating their triumphs immediately, boastfully, even cruelly. Those who organize violent rituals also dramatize differences among categories of participants by such devices as assigning them distinctive costumes. In all these regards, damage-dealing sports events clearly qualify.

Although violent rituals share causal processes with adjacent forms of collective violence, their organization gives special prominence to certain mechanisms and processes. To an exceptional degree, those mechanisms *activate* relevant boundaries, stories, and relations to the exclusion of most others as they *incorporate* all the relevant actors and social sites into a single connected set of performances. Activation produces high salience of violent means, while incorporation produces high coordination of violent actors and actions. In the cases at hand, we will see the following mechanisms and processes recurrently at work.

> *Boundary activation/deactivation* – a shift in social interactions such that they increasingly (a) organize around a single us–them boundary and (b) differentiate between within-boundary and cross-boundary interactions. (Boundary deactivation denotes the opposite shift, toward new or multiple boundaries and toward diminished difference between within-boundary and cross-boundary interactions.)
>
> *Polarization* – widening of political and social space between claimants in a contentious episode and gravitation of previously uncommitted or moderate actors toward one, the other, or both extremes.
>
> *Competitive display* – simultaneous or consecutive signaling of capacity by two or more actors within the same arena.

Monitoring – exercise of continuous surveillance over actions within a social site.

Containment – placement of a relatively impermeable perimeter around an actor, set of actors, place, or other social site.

Certification/decertification – validation of actors, their performances, and their claims by external authorities; decertification is the withdrawal of such validation by certifying agents.

In the simple example of sports teams, individual players who may well be good friends off the court separate into rival teams, eliminate any straddling of the boundary between them, and engage in ostentatious displays of prowess. Meanwhile, referees monitor their interaction, maintain the boundary between legitimate players and others, and either ratify, reject, or punish different performances. These obvious elements of soccer matches reappear in a wide range of violent rituals. Speaking of nineteenth-century Ireland, Carolyn Conley points out that judges frequently distinguished sharply between fair fights – one of the time's most frequent violent rituals – and ganging up on someone:

In keeping with the recreational aspect of fighting there were rules of combat even in brawls. Though supporting one's comrades was expected, in most cases justice required roughly even sides. Justice Murphy was indignant when he heard a case in which six members of the Callaghan family had assaulted and beaten Bernard Faddin outside a pub on Christmas day. Faddin had been alone except for his sister, and the uneven sides offended the judge who sentenced the Callaghans to sixteen months each. In another case, the quarter sessions chairman laid out the rules as he saw them: "If the fight had been left between Whelan and the prosecutor who at first struck each other, the law would take a very lenient view of the case." But, ganging up was not acceptable. Nor was continuing to pummel a defeated opponent. When John Delany came to the assistance of a friend who was already winning a fight the judge was incensed. "The fact of Delany coming to the other's assistance, and then, as proved, they both kicking him while down rendered the case a very treacherous one." For his treachery Delany was sentenced to twelve months, while his friend who had started the fight was sentenced to only six months. (Conley 1999b: 61; "prosecutor" here = plaintiff)

Violent rituals obviously go beyond contact sports. They include chivalric and gladiatorial combat, courtly duels, blood feuds, shaming ceremonies, and stylized battles between supporters of rival sports teams, entertainers, warlords, or electoral candidates. In eighteenth-century Europe, rival groups of journeymen, of students, of soldiers, and of local youths often attacked each other in violent rituals that left dead and wounded on the ground. Although outsiders often described such events as brawls, their stylized organization belied that label. Violent rituals' scripting, containment, and deliberate deployment of coercive means make them the extreme case of coordination and salience combined. Students of violence and of contentious politics have generally avoided violent rituals as something outside their fields – sport, initiation, consumption, or display, perhaps, but not serious politics.

Ritual does matter politically, however. Some time ago, Richard Trexler pointed out the high political stakes of Florentine public rituals about the same time that Karen and Jeffery Paige were making a more general case for coming-of-age rituals as political contests (Paige & Paige 1981; Trexler 1981). In both cases, failures to bring out adequate followings reduce future credibility and alliance value of the principals. Even when such ceremonies begin decorously, challenges to ritual performances often render them violent. Rebels, furthermore, sometimes adopt symbol-charged ritual violence to dramatize their opposition to regimes and holders of power (Davis 1975; Le Roy Ladurie 1979; Nirenberg 1996; Thompson 1991).

David Kertzer has underlined the frequent channeling of conflict by ritual.

For as long as intergroup hostilities have existed, rituals have been used to express them. These rites assume a wide variety of forms around the world, sometimes limiting physical aggression, but often, simultaneously, keeping tensions alive. The occasions for these rites are themselves varied. Many such rites involve symbolic forms of intergroup combat. These range from mock battles between rival clans and rival age groups within a society to mock skirmishes between rival tribes. Indeed, in many parts of the world, warfare itself is highly ritualized, with a special permanent site for the hostilities, special bodily adornment, special songs and verbal insults, and rules about the actual conduct of combat. In many of these cases, as soon as an individual is seriously wounded, hostilities cease and a round of post-battle ritual begins. (Kertzer 1988: 130)

In the contemporary United States, football matches, gang fights, tag-team wrestling, and reenactments of famous battles all match Kertzer's description.

Most such rituals, to be sure, proceed with no more than virtual violence; despite threats and simulations, no actual seizure or damage occurs. But a subset of them either incorporate violent practices into their scripts or frequently generate violent encounters as an outcome of struggles for precedence and for public acknowledgment of precedence (Ruff 2001; Smith 1999). By-product encounters (e.g., battles between volunteer fire companies or between youths of adjacent villages) veer into our categories of scattered attack and broken negotiations when participants deviate significantly from available scripts.

Scripted violent practices (e.g., contact sports) look something like coordinated destruction, like contained versions of war. Yet it is worth giving the zone of elaborate scripting its own name – violent rituals – and separate attention. In our coordination–salience space, violent rituals occupy the upper right-hand corner: extremely high on coordination, and extremely high as well on the salience of violence within all relevant social interactions. They offer an important exception to the overall tendency of violence to rise with coordination and salience; except when they burst their containment barriers, violent rituals generally produce less total damage than does coordinated destruction.

Violent rituals ordinarily reflect and reinforce existing systems of inequality. One-sided rituals such as public executions and shaming ceremonies victimize people who have contravened the existing order. That is precisely why they occasionally precipitate resistance and rebellion on the part of other people who share the punished persons' victimization by exploitation or opportunity hoarding. Forms of violent ritual involving two or more established contenders do not regularly pit exploiters against victims, but they do involve struggles for precedence within hierarchies and do generally confirm the overall systems of inequality within which precedence operates: we challenge the priority that the goldsmiths claim over us silversmiths, but by so doing we actually affirm the principles that a hierarchy of guilds should run our city's public affairs and that members of higher-ranking guilds should garner greater rewards.

Potlatch, Flagellation, and Hanging

Consider three very different examples: potlatches of Canadian-American Northwest Coast populations, flagellant confraternities of Renaissance Italy, and ceremonious London executions of the eighteenth century. Because Franz Boas founded a whole school of anthropology on the study of Northwest Coast populations, anthropologists have frequently reasoned about the potlatch. In the form that crystallized after 1849 among the people Boas called Kwakiutl, potlatch designated great public displays and giveaways of wealth. In particular, performers of potlatch gave away large numbers of blankets bought from the Hudson's Bay Company and bestowed or destroyed copper shields or "coppers" worth a currently known number of blankets in the Kwakiutl exchange system. Potlatch may have developed from pre-1849 routines of slave trading and warfare along the Northwest Coast (Wolf 1999: 121). In any case, the scale of potlatch escalated up to 1921, when the Canadian government stepped in to ban such a destructive procedure.

In his review of the ceremonial practice, Eric Wolf linked escalation of potlatch to a survival crisis doubled with increased competition for high standing among kin groups. Coppers were rising rapidly in value, partly as a result of intensifying competition and partly as a consequence of inflation; as Kwakiutl adults moved increasingly into capitalist markets, more and more bought

Hudson's Bay blankets, and the ratio of blankets to coppers increased. Destruction and reconstitution of any particular copper made it even more valuable. (If this seems strange, consider that, in today's world of art collectors, prices for the work of some artists rise rapidly as a result of promotion and competition, but absolute prices of sculptures and paintings hardly ever decline.)

As suggested by the analyses of Trexler and of Paige and Paige, potlatches definitely marked ritual transitions and especially marriages between members of high-ranking kinship groups. Most dramatic was the ritual destruction of copper shields:

These shields were equated with hundreds and thousands of blankets in distributive events, but they reached an evaluative climax when they were ritually destroyed or thrown into the sea. Throwing a copper into the sea transferred vital force to the fish-people. Melting down a copper in fire conveyed vital energy to the sky spirits. "Killing" a copper by breaking it up simulated the death of the vitality contained in it; riveting the pieces together once more, however, was understood as a transformation that multiplied its power to redistribute vital forces among human beings. (Wolf 1999: 121)

In the Kwakiutl potlatch, violent rituals unquestionably partook of contentious politics. They connected, indeed, with a very general political phenomenon: the politics of reputation, in which successful or unsuccessful public defense of perquisites, precedence, and honor affects the readiness of witnesses, patrons, and clients to commit future enterprises to one or another of the contestants.

Italy's flagellant confraternities seem a far cry from Kwakiutl potlatches. Still, the two phenomena not only belong to the world of violent rituals but also share some political properties. Religious confraternities proliferated in Italy during the later Middle Ages. Chiefly restricted to relatively high-ranking males, they combined devotion, service, and public display in varying degrees. From 1260 onward, a flagellant movement accelerated. Whatever other devotion, service, and public display they engaged in, these men undertook penitential public self-flagellation as part of their regular activity.

The Genoese *casacce*, for example, formed in the thirteenth century, continued their activity unabated into the eighteenth century, and did not disappear definitively until the nineteenth. (In 1890, the Italian government finally banned confraternities throughout the country as a mere "spectacle of religious ceremonies" that spread "fanaticism and ignorance": Wisch & Ahl 2000: 3.) During the fifteenth and sixteenth centuries:

According to the chronicler Giustianiani, their principal collaborative ritual was the Good Friday procession. Five thousand confratelli clothed in sackcloth traversed the streets in

total silence calling at churches and beating themselves until the blood ran in a spectacle which moved the sinful and the pious alike.... The success of the Eucharistic cult in
the fifteenth century had led the flagellant confraternities to move their main public ritual from Good Friday to Holy Thursday. The visit to the sepulchre in San Lorenzo led
to bouts of fierce competition among the casacce, which centered not only on the rival
displays of coffers, vestments, singing and crucifixes, but often ended in fighting which
led to violent assault and even on occasion murder. (Bernardi 2000: 238)

Thus Genoa's violent rituals neighbored on broken negotiations, perhaps
sometimes on coordinated destruction as well. Although no one would mistake
a penitential procession for a potlatch, they had in common circumscribed sites
for competition, clear distinctions between the performers and their knowledgeable audiences, heavy scripting, reinforcement of solidarity within each
performing group, competitive public display of standing, and significant consequences for that standing. In these regards they also bear resemblances to contact
sports, violent election battles, gang rivalries, and some struggles among supporters of sporting teams or entertainment stars. The mechanisms they involve
include such familiar ones as competitive display, polarization, and activation of
us–them categories.

Many of Europe's eighteenth-century rulers ran states of increasing capacity, but their repressive agents lacked the capacity to capture most criminals.
By and large, victims of thieves and robbers who could afford it posted rewards
and gave bounties to thief catchers when those specialists in the underworld
tracked down perpetrators or retrieved the lost goods. When authorities did
catch a felon, however, they often organized public violent rituals to advertise their success and deter future wrongdoers. Depending on the offense, they
paraded offenders through streets in humiliating garb with denigrating plac-
ards or symbols, exhibited them in stocks where spectators could pelt them and
curse them, broke them on the wheel, hacked off their hands, hanged them ostentatiously, or (if they were nobles) decapitated them. When members of the
audience considered the sentence unjust, the victim's category worth defending,
or the punishment itself badly performed, they sometimes attacked the execu-
tioner, rescued the intended victim, retrieved a body to give it proper burial, or
at least cheered those who took their punishment bravely. They participated in
one-sided violent rituals.

In 1768, London reached the peak of its eighteenth-century struggles between
capital and labor (Rudé 1971: 191–2). Groups of weavers attacked merchants and
cut cloth from the looms of other weavers who worked below the prevailing
wage, as striking coal heavers attacked masters, nonstrikers, coal dealers, ship
captains, and their dwellings. On the 26th of May, reported *Gentleman's Magazine*,

numerous coal heavers "assembled in a riotous manner in Wapping, went on board the colliers, and obliged the men who were at work to leave off; so that the business of delivering ships, in the river, is wholly at a stand .... This riot was attended with much blood shed, the rioters having met with opposition fought desperately, and several lives were lost" (*GM* 1768: 197).

Many street struggles of 1768 intertwined with popular support for the rebellious gentleman John Wilkes, whom supporters seized from his guards as he proceeded to prison on 27 April. Mass marches of weavers and sailors to parliament on behalf of their rights to just wages added to the atmosphere of incessant conflict. London magistrates extended to local attacks on property those laws (the Black Acts) passed in the 1740s authorizing capital punishment for certain rural property offenses, successfully prosecuting coal heavers under that new reading of the law. In consequence:

Seven coal-heavers received the "cramp jaw" at the Old Bailey only after a new interpretation was placed upon the Waltham Black Act. The seven danced "a new jig without music" on 26 July 1768. This particular "crack neck assembly" was located in Sun Tavern Fields, Shadwell, where the river people had held their mass meeting a few months before. The move from Tyburn was designed to terrify the poor and working people of the river parishes. The "breath stopper" was witnessed by 50,000 spectators, perhaps the largest crowd at such a scene since the hanging of the Earl of Ferrers eight years earlier. The Government anticipated disorders, if not rescue attempts, when these seven were to dance "tuxt de ert and de skies". From 6 A.M. more than 600 soldiers patrolled the streets of Wapping and Shadwell. The Sheriff ordered all the constables of the Tower and Holborn divisions to assemble at the hanging site and to come armed with their staves. (Linebaugh 1992: 321–2)

This time sheriff and hangman succeeded; the crowd dispersed without impeding the execution. The following year, however, the government set out to hang cutters who had struck cloth from looms, beaten renegade workers, and battled troops. They staged the executions in Bethnal Green, site of the violence. Although the workers who came *en masse* to the execution were unable to save the lives of their fellows, they stoned the executioners and burned the gallows. Violent rituals did not always stay within prescribed bounds.

Ritualized as these interactions may be, they belong at least in part to the world of contentious politics. Indeed, they overlap with the quintessentially contentious encounters of coordinated destruction; at the edge of their scripted contests they often generate violent conflicts among participants, among spectators, or between participants and spectators. Genoa's overflow from ostentatious self-flagellation to murderous assault illustrates precisely that deviation from the main script into coordinated destruction.

Outside their area of obvious overlap, violent rituals and coordinated destruction differ in four important regards. First, the stakes of the contest in full-fledged violent ritual remain relatively fixed and finite, whereas the stakes in coordinated destruction often increase, decrease, or shift as participants and available resources change. Second, violent ritual takes place within a fairly well-defined perimeter outside of which third parties inhibit continuation of the conflict, whereas coordinated destruction easily spills out beyond its initial territory and shifts bases. Third, the scripts of violent rituals distinguish between proper and improper participants, objects of attack, and means of inflicting damage; all these elements are more negotiable and contingent in coordinated destruction.

Finally, violent ritual imposes a distinction between participants, on one side, and monitors or spectators, on the other, while coordinated destruction typically either absorbs or expels both monitors and spectators. Peacekeepers who intervene in coordinated destruction usually try to push it back toward violent (or, better yet, nonviolent) ritual.

Sudhir Venkatesh begins his ethnography of a Chicago housing project by describing just such an effort at containment in 1992. In the 20,000-resident Robert Taylor Homes, ritualized fights between youth gangs had long since mutated into struggles for control of drug sales, protection rackets, and other profitable activities. "Several days before the meeting," reports Venkatesh,

the first gang war of the year had commenced in the Robert Taylor Homes. The Sharks had conducted drive-by shootings and injured two members of the enemy Black Kings gang. To retaliate, Prince [Williams, leader of the Black Kings] declared "war" against the Sharks, and for the next thirty-six hours, there was an intermittent exchange of gunfire between the two gang families. After the injury of the two Black Kings members, a twelve-year-old girl was fatally shot, and her friend critically injured, while playing in an open concrete expanse that surrounded the housing development's high-rise buildings. A community already in shock from the injuries to the two youths now grieved for the family of the young girl and for her friend, who lay in critical condition at a local hospital. (Venkatesh 2000: 1–2)

The leader of an agency called No More Wars attended that June 1992 meeting at Robert Taylor, hoping precisely to help residents find ways of creating restraints on gang activity. Their shared agenda was essentially fixing the stakes of competition, drawing sharp perimeters around the conflict, distinguishing sharply between proper and improper participants, objects, and means, establishing clear distinctions among spectators, monitors, and participants, generally reducing the uncertainty that promotes cross-boundary violence. Rather than seeking to eliminate the gangs entirely (as much as some residents would have preferred that solution), they sought to drive gangs back toward ritualized and preferably nonviolent interaction.

Regimes and Rituals

Violent rituals vary significantly from one type of regime to another. High-capacity regimes draw sharper lines between prescribed and tolerated claim-making performances, on one side, and forbidden performances, on the other. As a consequence, the violent rituals of high-capacity regimes take place either in secret or within perimeters imposed by authorities. In low-capacity regimes, a wider variety of locales, participants, and occasions generate violent rituals, and such rituals flow more easily to or from coordinated destruction, broken negotiations, or opportunism.

Democratic regimes (governmental capacity held constant) generally host fewer violent rituals than undemocratic regimes because they shelter fewer privileged political enclaves and offer a wider range of opportunities for nonviolent claim making. On the way to democracy, however, violent rituals often surge temporarily as competing groups use established tests of strength to challenge each other's claims for priority within the democratizing polity. Once again, the reasoning leads us to expect the greatest variety and frequency of violent rituals to appear in low-capacity undemocratic regimes, the least in high-capacity democratic regimes.

With no claim to have assembled sufficient evidence for verification or falsification of these arguments, let me illustrate each quadrant of the capacity–democracy space with a well-documented case. The order runs as follows:

> *high-capacity undemocratic* – registered revenge in Tokugawa Japan;
> *low-capacity undemocratic* – Balkan blood feuds;
> *low-capacity democratic* – election fights in the nineteenth-century United States;
> *high-capacity democratic* – gang battles in the United States after World War II.

The interplay between violent rituals and their host regimes poses a nicely complex problem. On one hand, violent rituals necessarily draw deeply on the particular histories of the settings in which they occur. They stem from the previous practices of governments, from major nongovernmental institutions, from folk traditions, and from the history of struggle itself. On the other hand, they display family resemblances among regimes having little or no historical contact with each other. Across a wide range of low-capacity undemocratic regimes, for instance, bands of males from established kin groups follow well-known scripts as they use violence to avenge offenses by members of similar kin groups – with authorities rarely intervening unless the violence begins to threaten their own control of local affairs.

Registered Revenge

As governments gain capacity, they typically impose greater controls over collective private vengeance by either suppressing disputes or drawing them into government-backed judicial institutions. But even high-capacity undemocratic regimes often leave space for special violent rituals such as the duel, blood sports, and public executions. The expanding state of Tokugawa Japan supplies a memorable case in point: registered revenge. Like their European counterparts, prior to the seventeenth century, samurai warriors not only served their current masters in regional struggles for power but also regularly fought each other individually or collectively over affronts to honor and interest. Most often, samurai who were not serving as military vassals acted with and on behalf of their own kinsmen. From the Tokugawa shogunate (1603) onward, however, national and regional power holders undertook the slow work of subordinating and containing the samurai. The samurai fought to retain their autonomy but lost an unequal battle.

Even so, a contained, ritualized, and still deadly form of vengeance survived. "Survived" does not quite describe the case, since the institution of registered revenge formed under governmental auspices after the Tokugawa takeover. In principle, the Tokugawa regime forbade private vengeance. The regime nevertheless made three exceptions for samurai: killing a commoner who showed disrespect to a samurai's honored standing; killing an unfaithful wife and her lover; and registered revenge (Ikegami 1995: 244). Registered revenge could occur when someone had killed a samurai's lineage elder, especially his father, and then fled the jurisdiction in which the murder occurred. (If no son survived, a wife or daughter could register as an avenger.) The avenger applied to a town or national (i.e., shogunate) magistrate for inscription on the list of authorized avengers and then received a copy of the authorization.

Properly pursued, the ritual allowed the avenger and helpers to kill without public retribution.

In 1701, when Akabori Mizunosuke murdered Ishii Uemon, a vassal of Lord Inaba and the father of Ishii Genzo and Ishii Hanzo, he left town immediately. The brothers thereupon registered their names as avengers at the shogunate magistrate's office. During his escape, Akabori found employment at the house of Lord Ikatura and changed his name. Having procured this information, the Ishii brothers went to the castle town of the Itakura family and waited for an opportunity to kill their foe while working as servants for one of Itakura's vassals. When they finally succeeded in killing Akabori near the castle gate, the brothers placed a letter addressed to Lord Itakura beside the body. The letter explained that Akabori had murdered their father; it went on to claim that they "had received permission from the Edo public office granting [them] the right to conduct a vendetta anywhere." Lord Itakura did not attempt to punish the Ishii brothers who had killed his vassal. (Ikegami 1995: 249)

The Ishii brothers followed up with an official report to the Edo magistrate. That ended the affair; Tokugawa authorities did not countenance second-round revenge in such conflicts.

As in other acts of honor-based revenge, the samurai lost face if he performed the required acts in a cowardly or incompetent way, failed to avenge the wrong his house had received, or did so outside of accepted procedures. In such cases, kinsmen and lords sometimes drove the shamed samurai into another violent ritual: ceremonious suicide by sword, or *seppuku*. Such violent rituals differ greatly from sporting events, potlatches, and flagellants' bloodletting, but they share the following common properties: public scripts, known scorecards, fixed and finite stakes, defined perimeters, stylized enactment of us–them boundaries, clear delineation of proper participants and targets, and sharp distinction between those participants from either monitors or spectators. In high-capacity undemocratic regimes, however, such rituals generally occur either in secret or within limits monitored closely by governmental agents. Tokugawa Japan's registered revenge fell into the category of close governmental monitoring.

Blood Feuds

Governments of low-capacity undemocratic regimes rarely carry out such close monitoring. They tolerate a considerable range of violent rituals carried on in nongovernmental institutions and settings. (Those very facts, of course, help us classify the regimes in question as low-capacity.) Codes of honor take on great importance in low-capacity undemocratic regimes because, in the absence of any certifying authorities or wide-ranging citizens' associations, the credibility of commitments made by individuals or groups depends heavily on reputation. We have already seen reputational arrangements at work in two rather different settings: (i) in violent specialists' use of force to verify their readiness to back up further threats and demands with force; and (ii) in the importance of successfully performed public rituals to the standing of kin groups, confraternities, guilds, and similar organizations.

Under low-capacity undemocratic regimes, indeed, sets of people who are carrying on long-term, high-risk enterprises such as long-distance trade, marriage exchange, and maintenance of forbidden cults commonly build or draw on networks that incorporate their own internal enforcement mechanisms and protect their collective reputations with great care (Besley 1995; Bowles & Gintis 1998; Burt & Knez 1995; Edwards, Foley, & Diani 2001; Gambetta 1993; Granovetter 1995; Greif 1994; Landa 1994; Ledeneva 1998; Levi & Stoker 2000; Muldrew 1993, 1998; Rotberg 1999; Seligman 1997; Shapiro 1987; Woolcock 1998). Most of the time, participants in such trust networks shield them zealously from governmental interference. (The major exceptions occur among networks that happen to run their own governments.) The cult of male honor that long prevailed around the Mediterranean is simply a special case of a very general phenomenon (Blok 2001).

Where the effective units of trust and cooperation build on lineages, blood feuds or their equivalents often arise as means of dispute settlement among distinct kin groups. They deserve attention because outsiders have regularly taken the presence of blood feuds as evidence of barbarism and of primeval rivalries, both of them kept in check only by a strong hand from above. In his history of Bosnia, Noel Malcolm quotes a parliamentary speech by Britain's Prime Minister John Major in 1993:

The biggest single element behind what has happened in Bosnia is the collapse of the Soviet Union and of the discipline that that exerted over the ancient hatreds in the old Yugoslavia. Once that discipline had disappeared, those ancient hatreds reappeared, and we began to see their consequences when the fighting occurred. There were subsidiary elements, but that collapse was by far the greatest. (Malcolm 1996: xx)

Major was invoking a popular image of ethnic conflict: removing the lid from a boiling pot. "It is hard to know," remarks Malcolm, "where to begin in commenting on such a statement" (Malcolm 1996: xx). Stalin had, after all, expelled Tito and his uncooperative regime from the Cominform in 1948. The collapse of the Soviet Union did affect Yugoslavia's disintegration, but quite indirectly, through the increased readiness of European regimes such as Germany to support demands of Yugoslav republics for recognition as independent states. Bosnian hostilities (although they certainly existed) stemmed from recent realignments and current competition for political control rather than from ancient hatreds.

The prevalent misunderstanding gains some of its plausibility from the idea of the Balkans as an inherently violent, lawless, feud-ridden region. Mark Mazower counters that misunderstanding:

"Ethnic cleansing" – whether in the Balkans in 1912–1913, in Anatolia in 1921–1922 or in erstwhile Yugoslavia in 1991–1995 – was not, then, the spontaneous eruption of primeval hatreds but the deliberate use of organized violence against civilians by paramilitary squads and army units; it represented the extreme force required by nationalists to break apart a society that was otherwise capable of ignoring the mundane fractures of class and ethnicity. (Mazower 2000: 148; see also Fearon 1995; Mueller 2000)

In our terms, political entrepreneurs and violent specialists played major parts in activating certain available boundaries, stories, and social relations at the expense of others. Malcolm and Mazower warn us not to read hatred, violence, and retaliation into Balkan character but instead to look at the actual political processes generating collective violence.

In the Balkan blood feud, a forbidden cross-boundary interaction initiates retaliation by members of the wronged party, who seek visible satisfaction for the wrong by means of inflicting some specified kind of harm on people beyond the boundary. The boundary separates lineages, and the acting groups are usually younger males of the same lineage. Feud-triggering interactions include:

- calling a man a liar in the presence of other men;
- killing a man;
- killing a house's guard dog within the house's territory;
- insulting a man's wife;
- taking a man's weapons;
- violating hospitality – for example by stealing from a host (Malcolm 1998: 18–21; see also Allcock 2000: 388–90; Boehm 1987).

Any of these interactions impugns the honor not only of the man but also of his lineage. It puts lineage members "in blood" with a neighboring lineage. Lineage members take on the obligation to hunt down and kill an adult male member of the offending lineage. At that point the killer(s) must announce the feat, then may request a truce between the lineages for some period. At the truce's expiration, a new round may begin as members of the lineage that started the interaction set out to avenge their loss. The ritual opens alternative avenues through conciliation and material compensation.

Powerful third parties sometimes intervene to contain or suppress a feud when killing escalates. But without a firm stopping rule (comparable to the clock's running out in football) and in the absence of Tokugawa-style imperial control, ritual killing can continue for years. Blood feuds once existed widely in other parts of Europe, but starting in the sixteenth and seventeenth centuries European governments either suppressed them or channeled them into judicial proceedings from which rulers could exact significant fines or confiscations of property (Ylikangas et al. 2001). In the Balkans, central governments rarely achieved that kind of control (Tilly 1993, chap. 3).

Lest anyone misunderstand, this does *not* in the least mean that the bloodletting of the 1990s in Bosnia and Kosovo consisted of blood feuds writ large. On the contrary, as Mazower says, the lethal battles that accompanied Yugoslavia's disintegration lacked the containment, scripting, separation of participants from spectators, and close monitoring by third parties that distinguish violent rituals from other forms of collective violence. Some rivalries among lineages surely continued into the struggles of the 1990s, but the intervention of political entrepreneurs and violent specialists moved the bulk of the Balkans' collective violence into coordinated destruction, scattered attack, and opportunism.

American Elections before 1860

Until the Civil War, the American national government qualified as low in capacity but at least moderately democratic for its time (Bensel 1990). Its elections, however, often lacked decorum. Reading widely in archives and published sources, David Grimsted cataloged 1,218 American events from 1828 to 1861 in which "six or more people band[ed] together to enforce their will publicly by threatening or perpetrating physical injury to persons or property extralegally, ostensibly to correct problems or injustices within their society without challenging its basic structures" (Grimsted 1998: xii).

Having myself done a lot of event cataloging along these lines, if this were a public debate on historical methods then I would quarrel with Grimsted's definition, his method, and his labeling of the events as "riots" (see Diani & Eyerman 1992; Franzosi 1998; Gerner et al. 1994; Oliver & Myers 1999; Olzak 1989; Rucht, Koopmans, & Neidhardt 1998; Tilly 1995: 393–418). Still his heroic effort gives us a rich sampling of violent encounters in a turbulent period of American history. Most of Grimsted's events consisted of attacks on stigmatized figures, with anti-black, anti–slave catcher, anti-abolitionist, and anti-anti-abolitionist attacks becoming more frequent over time (see also Brown 1975; Gilje 1996; McKivigan & Harrold 1999). But a significant minority centered on elections.

Grimsted recounts Henry B. Miller's experiences in the August 1838 Missouri elections from a diary preserved at the Historical Society of Missouri. Whigs and Democrats were competing fiercely for public office. St. Louis Democrats had opted for a slow *viva voce* voting method – clerk reads voter's name, voter announces preference – in hopes that they could get their votes inscribed first and so discourage their Whig rivals. By the second day, however, the slow poll had inspired operatives of both parties to charter boats for free trips downriver, where their electors could join shorter queues. At Carondelet, seven or eight miles down the Mississippi, the Democratic boatload arrived to find the polling place surrounded by Whigs. When Democrats approached the polls, Whig activists threw them out.

After the Whigs had voted at Carondelet, however, they relaxed their vigilance; Miller and his companions were able to vote. As the day wore on, Miller reported, Democrats and Whigs fought repeatedly, using

"Dirks, Bowie knives, clubs, handkerchiefs with stones in, with all the other kinds of tools that the occasion might require." Veins of humor as well as blood were opened, as several fighters were too drunk to hit anyone, and as the Whigs, hoisting a 350-pound man on their shoulders as symbol of how they'd carry the state, suddenly dropped him as "a bad job, or wrong calculation." When the steamboat returned to St. Louis in the evening, the Democrats marched in procession to the courthouse, where they were told that the Whigs "drove the Democrats away entirely" after the steamboat left. (Grimsted 1998: 182–3)

In riotous elections, the formal ritual of the poll and the more chaotic ritual *surrounding* the poll interweave even more closely than soccer matches and soccer violence. Soccer fans can occasionally disrupt a match and affect its later interpretation, but violent Whigs and Democrats could actually determine an election's final score. The winner-take-all format of American elections raised the stakes; winners took offices while losers lost jobs. The frequent use of two- or three-day polls with announcement of results at the end of each day, furthermore, almost certainly encouraged competitive mobilization for the later days.

Of his 1,218 violent events, Grimsted classifies only 72 as serious "political riots" (Grimsted 1998: 184). Of those, about half began as nonelectoral political gatherings, the other half as parts of elections. Electoral events produced significantly more violence: 89 deaths, or about 2.5 deaths per event. American election rituals included not only struggles at the polls but also costumed torchlight parades, picnics, and rallies – all with ample supplies of alcohol. Despite increasing participation of women in abolitionist and temperance movements, the restricted suffrage prevailing before the Civil War meant that public election struggles remained overwhelmingly white male affairs.

Not all these events, to be sure, qualified by our strict definition of violent rituals: damage-dealing interactions involving public scripts, known scorecards, fixed and finite stakes, defined perimeters, stylized enactment of us–them boundaries, clear delineation of proper participants and targets, and sharp distinction between those participants from either monitors or spectators. As we might expect under low-capacity democratic regimes, the polling that did qualify by these criteria often mutated into other forms of violence we could better classify as coordinated destruction, opportunism, or brawls. Around elections, nevertheless, Americans built a distinctive set of violent rituals.

Gang Battles

From the Civil War to the 1920s, the United States moved from our low capacity democratic quadrant toward notably higher capacity. The country even democratized to some degree: slavery ended, some blacks acquired political rights and protections, disfranchised immigrants gained citizenship, and female suffrage came into force at a national scale. Relative to other regimes elsewhere, the United States became a high-capacity democratic regime.

Under high-capacity democratic regimes, violent rituals bifurcate. Some go on in secret, shielded from detection by nonmembers and governmental authorities; violent initiation ceremonies and damage-dealing cults illustrate the genre. They remain rare and always run the risk of detection and repression. More occur in public but within a tight perimeter patrolled by authorities who guard against their transformation into coordinated destruction or opportunism. We have already seen sporting matches and soccer violence as cases in point. On American college campuses, pep rallies, competitions among fraternities, raids by fraternities on sororities, and the occasional academic ceremony that produces a scuffle all meet the criteria.

During the years after World War II, however, battles between urban gangs became the country's most lethal and visible violent rituals. They gained a niche in American popular culture through such stylized presentations as Leonard Bernstein's *West Side Story*, which updates Shakespeare's dramatization of a Renaissance feud between the Capulets and Montagues. Although the popular representation sentimentalizes them, gangs did compete fiercely during their heyday. Every large American city produced its own version of gang battles.

Eric Schneider has looked closely at the evolution of New York City's youth gangs between 1940 and 1975. Schneider shows that postwar gangs formed along racial and ethnic lines corresponding broadly to the city's own racial and ethnic segregation. Gangs were classic opportunity hoarders, with bounded networks jealously guarding resources from which the members gained benefits. For many participants, the main benefits were protection and self-respect. Leaders sometimes benefited additionally from payoffs and political power.

Some gangs did little more than seek recreation and sociability together. Gangs that battled frequently divided into two main categories: defensive and fighting. Both of them operated within well-defined turfs, usually a few city blocks. Within those turfs, they claimed priority over all other adolescents and demanded respect from them. (Sometimes adjacent gangs agreed on neutral territories such as churches, schools or, more rarely, stores.) Internally they maintained clear pecking orders – hierarchies maintained, challenged, and occasionally overturned by internal fights, verbal battles, and feats of bravado. The gang's young men often had a well-defined set of girl friends – the debs – whom they defended from all other males. They would also, on occasion, grab non-deb girls for gang rapes.

Like village youth groups in Old Regime Europe, defensive gangs concentrated on making sure that outsiders did not invade their territories or take their girls, but they rarely engaged in offensive actions outside the turf. Fighting gangs (which often started as challengers within someone else's established turf) swaggered out of their territories *en masse* ready to fight with any other youths who issued challenges, conducted raids on persons or property in adjacent territories, and frequently tried to expand the boundaries of their own territories. Both sorts of gangs, however, adopted codes of honor: a young man gained standing by facing down and damaging others, taking serious risks, refusing to betray comrades, and challenging the police; but he lost mightily and soon if he failed visibly in any of these regards.

Youth gangs operated according to impressively elaborate scripts. They typically avoided attacking small children, older people, women, clergy, and even other adolescents ("coolies") who lacked attachments to any gang. They adopted colors, signs, and stylized languages. Even their battles, for the most part, followed well-defined scripts. Battles sometimes took the form of quick raids into hostile territory, or "fair fights" in which one member of each gang would settle a dispute between the gangs in individual combat. But the violent routine that most clearly embodied violent ritual was the rumble, the contained battle between all members of two gangs. Sometimes gangs would show up in formation and regalia at a known fighting spot, such as Coney Island or Brooklyn's Prospect Park, and then challenge each other on the spot.

In the most elaborate form of rumble, however, the leader of one gang would issue a challenge to the leader of another; the two would set time, place, weapons, and combat rules; and the two forces would show up for a fight. Not that they always kept their agreements:

When the Young Stars arranged to fight the Hoods in Crotona Park in the Bronx, the two gangs agreed that combatants would meet at 10:00 P.M. and that clubs, chains, and knives – but no guns – were to be used. Both sides cheated. The Young Stars brought guns, and when they arrived at the park, they found that the Hoods had arrived early and arranged an ambush. (Schneider 1999: 159)

With high stakes and no monitors, participants had strong incentives to cheat. Yet a surprisingly high proportion of rumbles conformed to the agreed-upon script – at least until someone died or received serious injuries.

For years, authorities dealt with New York's youth gangs chiefly by containing them within their territories, repressing them if possible when they started producing serious damage, and opening social exit routes for youngsters who wanted to escape. During the later 1960s, worried city leaders began more extensive and effective efforts to co-opt, pacify, or destroy youth gangs, as civil rights and nationalist groups also began to draw black youths into different forms of political activism. The gangs shrank into their territories, transformed their organizations, and lost much of their popular appeal. During the following decades, expansion of the drug trade produced an entirely new form of turf control, centered on hoarding income from sale of illegal substances. For all their kinship with traditional routines of youth groups in other times and places, the violent rituals of New York's postwar gangs survived for only twenty years or so.

Ritual Violence Reviewed

Violent rituals consist of damage-dealing interactions involving public scripts, known scorecards, fixed and finite stakes, defined perimeters, stylized enactment of us–them boundaries, clear delineation of proper participants and targets, and sharp distinctions between those participants and either monitors or spectators. By now it should be clear that "ritual" does not mean "decorous"; violent rituals can kill. Soccer violence, penitents' processions, executions, gang fights, election disputes, and blood feuds have also shown that, in the absence of monitors and perimeter controls, ritual violence provides opportunities for participants to cheat, for conflict to escalate, and for coordinated destruction or opportunism to emerge from what was originally a circumscribed contest. Regimes vary precisely in the extent to which they impose monitors and police perimeters around dangerous activities. Low-capacity undemocratic regimes may well host the most lethal and varied forms of violent ritual, but each type of regime has its own version of ritualized destruction.

In examining violent rituals we have inescapably seen something of coordinated destruction, in which persons or organizations that specialize in the deployment of coercive means undertake a program of damage to persons and/or objects. Recall how Russian and Indian sportsmen become violent specialists engaged in killing, maiming, and extorting well outside of any sports arena. As we move from violent rituals to coordinated destruction, we follow their path.

5

Coordinated Destruction

Destruction as Conquest

Welsh-born adventurer John Rowlands created a new life and identity for himself as Henry Morton Stanley, American explorer and self-dramatizing rescuer of Dr. Livingstone. In August 1877, Stanley completed the first European expedition from Zanzibar, off the east coast of Africa, to the Congo River's mouth, on the west. He had started that journey down the Congo with 356 people and more than eight tons of weapons, equipment, and trading goods. For Stanley,

continual combat was always part of exploring. He never bothered to count the dead that the expedition left behind it, but the number must have been in the hundreds. Stanley's party carried the latest rifles and an elephant gun with exploding bullets; the unlucky people they fought had spears, bows and arrows, or, at best, ancient muskets bought from slave-traders. "We have attacked and destroyed 28 large towns and three or four score villages," he wrote in his journal.... As he piloted the *Lady Alice* toward a spot on Lake Tanganyika, for instance, "the beach was crowded with infuriates and mockers ... we perceived that we were followed by several canoes in some of which we saw spears shaken at us ... I opened on them with the Winchester Repeating Rifle. Six shots and four deaths were sufficient to quiet the mocking." (Hochschild 1998: 49)

Like many another European colonialist and many an American Indian fighter, the Welsh-American explorer deployed vindictive violence as a matter of right and pride. In his gunsights, hostile natives were fair game. The adventure-hunting *New York Herald* and (London) *Daily Telegraph* sponsored Stanley's exploration and subsequent conquest of the Congo. Then as now, reports of killing sold newspapers.

Stanley's trek from Zanzibar to Boma indirectly initiated the formation of Belgium's prime colony. Ambitious Belgian King Leopold followed reports of Stanley's expedition with rapt attention and soon made himself Stanley's patron.

Belgium's subsequent takeover of the Congo served European greed but continued to employ coordinated destruction (Acemoglu, Johnson, & Robinson 2001). What is more, it stimulated Germany and Italy to join earlier comers Portugal, Spain, Britain, and France in using similar methods to carve out their own pieces of African territory. They, too, carved by means of coordinated destruction. After a trip to Algeria in 1841, after all, no less a figure than Alexis de Tocqueville spoke of French policy in these terms:

I consider big expeditions necessary from time to time, first, to keep showing both the Arabs and our soldiers that no obstacles within the country can stop us; and second, to destroy anything like a permanent concentration of population, any city. I consider it of the greatest importance to let no city survive or arise in the domains of Abd el-Kader. (Le Cour Grandmaison 2001: 12)

Even the great liberal justified coordinated destruction in the cause of European conquest.

Coordinated destruction approaches the upper right-hand corner of our coordination–salience space: high in both overall coordination of violent actors and in the salience of damaging acts within all interactions, although not quite so high as violent rituals in either regard. Coordinated destruction refers to those varieties of collective violence in which persons or organizations specialized in the deployment of coercive means undertake programs of actions that damage persons and/or objects. It results from combined activation of boundaries, stories, and relations, on one side, and incorporation of multiple social actors and sites, on the other. Together, activation and incorporation produce higher levels of damage, on average, than other forms of collective violence. They also override previously existing relations among participants except in so far as those relations correspond to the activated identities.

Coordinated destruction overlaps with broken negotiations because specialists in coercion participate in both and because threats of force sometimes escalate into struggles between coercive organizations. It also overlaps with violent rituals, since at times the parties perform according to elaborate, self-limiting scripts like those of chivalrous combat. Here, though, the organizations' strategies center (however temporarily) on the production of damage. Both salience and coordination of damage production reach high levels. Examples include war, genocide, torture, collective self-destruction, public penance, and government-backed terror.

Parallel to the distinction between relatively symmetrical and asymmetrical violent rituals, a major distinction within coordinated destruction separates (a) lethal contests, (b) campaigns of annihilation, and (c) conspiratorial terror.

(a) In *lethal contests,* at least two organized groups of specialists in coercion confront each other, each one using harm to reduce or contain the others' capacity to inflict harm. War is the most general label for this class of coordinated destruction, but different variants go by the names civil war, guerrilla, low-intensity conflict, and conquest. Although lethal contests of various sorts stretch back as far as humanity's historical record runs, the standard image of two or more disciplined national armies engaged in destroying each other within generally accepted rules of combat applies to only a small historical segment: roughly 1650 to 1950 for Europe, a few much earlier periods for China, and even rarer intervals elsewhere in the world. Outside of those exceptional moments, autonomous raiding parties, temporary feudal levies, mercenary assemblages, bandits, pirates, nomads doubling as cavalry, mobilized villages, and similar conglomerate or part-time forces have fought most historical wars.

(b) Lethal contests shade over into *campaigns of annihilation* when one contestant wields overwhelming force or the object of attack is not an organization specialized in the deployment of coercive means. In recent decades, analysts have employed the term *genocide* for those campaigns in which attackers define their victims in terms of shared heritage and the term *politicide* for those in which victims belong to a common political category; so far, no commonly accepted term has emerged for similar campaigns aimed at members of religious or regional categories. The usual stakes in campaigns of annihilation are collective survival, on one side, and recognition as the sole party with the right to territorial control, on the other. Because of those stakes, such struggles tend to generate vast mobilizations of support extending far beyond the specialists in coercion who initiate them.

(c) In the other direction, lethal contests give way to *conspiratorial terror* when a small but well-organized set of actors begin attacking vastly more powerful targets by clandestine means – assassinations, kidnappings, bombings, and the like. When it has serious political effects, conspiratorial terror simultaneously demonstrates the vulnerability of apparently insuperable powers and the presence of a dangerous, elusive alternative to those powers. It thereby shakes up routine politics, shortens time horizons, and identifies possible allies for dissidents.

Distinctions among lethal contests, campaigns of annihilation, and conspiratorial terror rest on the degree of inequality among the damage-wielding parties. Another way to put it is this: lethal contests constitute the special case of coordinated destruction in which the parties approach parity. The special case looms large because obviously weaker parties usually avoid combat if they can get away, and they often seek allies to equalize forces on either side. Shows of strength, spying on enemies, and negotiations with potential coalition partners therefore figure significantly in the dynamics of lethal contests.

In coordinated destruction, struggles over exploitation and opportunity hoarding come doubly into play: (i) in control of the government; and (ii) in use of political power to establish, maintain, seize, alter, or destroy inequality-generating systems of social relations outside of government. Governments always engage in opportunity hoarding and usually engage in exploitation as well; they always involve members of categorically bounded networks' acquisition of access to resources that are valuable, renewable, subject to monopoly, supportive of network activities, and enhanced by the network's operating routines (opportunity hoarding). But they also commonly involve powerful, connected people's commandeering of resources from which they draw significantly increased returns by coordinating the efforts of outsiders whom they exclude from the full value added by that effort (exploitation).

The sharper the boundary and the greater inequality across that boundary, the weightier are the stakes of control over government for both incumbents and challengers. Coordinated destruction occurs when well-organized incumbents strike down resistance to their demands, when incumbents use force of arms to extend their jurisdictions, and when excluded parties organize on a sufficient scale to challenge incumbents' own armed force. These effects become stronger when the parties on either side of the boundary polarize – when cooperative arrangements and overlapping actors disappear – and/or when uncertainty about the other side's future actions increases on either or both sides. Following Sigmund Freud, Anton Blok (2001: 115–35) stresses the ironic, tragic "narcissism of minor differences" that comes into play as political entrepreneurs fortify the boundaries, empty the middle ground, and increase the uncertainty of fundamentally similar neighbors such as Bosnian Croats and Serbs or Rwandan Hutu and Tutsi.

In Algeria of the mid-1990s, Salafi Islamic purists broke with their more moderate allies in the struggle against the secularist regime. According to the leader of the Groupe Islamique Armé (GIA), Algerians divided opponents of the regime into three categories: (1) true freedom fighters who supported holy war, (2) those supposed Islamists who actually opposed holy war by "force, talk, or with the pen"; and (3) Islamists who supported democracy. Treating members of categories (2) and (3) as traitors, they drew their boundary at (1) versus everyone else, directing their most vicious violence not against the regime itself but against their neighbors in groups (2) and (3). The GIA chief Abu al-Moudhir declared that:

It is clear that there is no indiscriminate killing. Our fighters only kill those who deserve to die. We say to those who accuse of indiscriminate killing that we will fight those traitors who have gone over to the "taghout" [un-Islamic government]. We do no more than carry out the wishes of God and the Prophet. When you hear of killings and throat-slittings in a town or a village, you should know it is a matter of the death of government partisans, or else it is the application of GIA communiqués ordering [us] to do good and combat evil. (Wiktorowicz 2001: 70)

Thus they massacred whole villages of women and children that failed to enlist in their cause. On the whole, when control of governments is at stake, the most savage violence pits close cousins, rather than truly alien peoples, against one another.

Outside the government, under some conditions the struggles over and within systems of exploitation and opportunity hoarding likewise take the form of co-ordinated destruction. Low-capacity regimes, especially undemocratic ones, live with greater vulnerability to coordinated destruction within their domestic politics because they allow greater scope for dissidents and rivals to organize their own violent specialists on a large scale. As Colombia's central state capacity has declined since the 1970s, for example, paramilitary forces have typically formed coalitions with rural landlords while guerrilla forces have typically formed coalitions with enemies of rural landlords. Both, however, have adopted kidnapping and taxes on the cocaine trade as means of support for their lethal activities. (As a result, Colombian kidnappings – which typically ran under 50 per year before 1985 – averaged 1,206 per year for 1990–1997 and then rose from 1,800 to 3,200 to 3,700 between 1998 and 2000; Ramirez 2001: 175.) Both sides have formed their own protection rackets and their own systems of exploitation; their private systems feed on existing nongovernmental systems of exploitation and opportunity hoarding (Echeverry et al. 2001; Walker 1999).

In a different version of a similar process, disintegration of central government control in the former Soviet Union has generated warlike contests for precedence within a number of different regions. From Stalin onward, the Soviet Union had established a dual policy of (a) awarding political preference to a single titular nationality within each of the Union's subdivisions while (b) assigning Russians and the Russian language privileged status as connectors among regions (Barrington 1995; Beissinger 1993; Nahaylo & Swoboda 1990; Smith et al. 1998; Suny 1993, 1995). Both within and outside the surviving Russian Federation, that heritage has promoted a number of three-way struggles: political entrepreneurs from titular nationalities seeking to retain or establish monopolies over political office and salable resources; their counterparts from nontitular minorities demanding autonomy, independence, or at least access to power; Russians defending their previously protected positions, often with the backing of Moscow's current power holders.

Those processes generate high levels of violence. In Chechnya and North Ossetia (both technically remaining within the Russian Federation at the Soviet Union's breakup in 1991), civil war and ethnic cleansing have bloodied the landscape, with leaders of self-identified Ingush, Ossetian, and Chechen populations at each other's throats. In the Kyrgyz Republic, lethal battles broke out between Kyrgyz and Uzbek clusters as independence approached in 1990 (Tishkov 1997, chaps. 7–10).

As the evidence reviewed in Chapter 3 substantiates, a remarkable change occurred within the broad category of coordinated destruction during the half-century following World War II. Where interstate wars among well-identified national armies had predominated for a century or more, shifts toward a much wider variety of coercive forces and toward campaigns of annihilation elevated civil war (broadly defined) to the chief setting of coordinated destruction. Decolonization, expansion of world trade in arms and drugs, reappearance of mercenary forces, and the weakening of central state capacity in many world regions all contributed to that change. As war shifted from interstate competition to internal struggle, paradoxically, external parties – both other states and international organizations – became more heavily involved as suppliers of military means, allies, aid givers, profiteers, and mediators.

These postwar shifts magnified the importance of two interlocked political phenomena that had receded in importance worldwide after the eighteenth century as Western states centralized at home and divided much of the non-Western world into colonies. The first practice was *subvention* by one state's rulers of rebellion and resistance to central rule in an adjacent state as a way of extending the intervening state's power. That practice did not entirely disappear during the nineteenth century, as recurrent intervention of the United States in Mexico (including the U.S. annexation of Texas) illustrates. But it became less common once internationally recognized boundaries, national and colonial, stood in place.

The second practice was outside *promotion* of political autonomy in resource-rich regions as a way of gaining privileged access to the resources in question. Again, massive Western interventions in China during the nineteenth century as well as twentieth-century U.S. interventions in Central America on behalf of American capital establish that the practice continued well past 1800. But it, too, became less prevalent where great powers agreed on the boundaries. Both practices revived in the decolonizing world after World War II. Despite the decline of Cold War competition for political allegiances, they actually accelerated with the Soviet Union's collapse.

The Lord's Resistance Army – based on the Uganda–Sudan border; led by Joseph Kony; and given bases, weapons, and food by Sudan's military ruler, Omar el-Bashir – offers a lurid instance of the first practice. The LRA organized in the mid-1980s. After mutating from a more conventional guerrilla force, Kony's troops abducted an estimated 15,000 boys and girls from northern Uganda for military or sexual services in their rebellion; UNICEF estimates that 3,000–5,000 have escaped, but many more remain captive and many have died. Perhaps 80 percent of Kony's forces now consist of children between 7 and 17 (Rubin 1998: 57–8; *Economist* 2002). Kony makes defections costly by forcing young recruits to choose between executing those who run away and being killed themselves.

Susan Akello, abducted at age 11 and escaped at age 14, described herself as a seasoned killer:

Once during a raid in Acholiland, Susan's commander ordered her to execute a village woman whom he had accused of being an informant. When she hesitated, she felt the cold, hard thwack of a machete's flat side on her back. "So I shot her dead," she told me. "I gave her two bullets. One here and one here." She touched her chest and the right side of her collarbone. Susan said she didn't know what she would have done if the woman had been her mother; she'd seen L.R.A. commanders order people to kill their own mothers. As it was, she felt confused afterward, especially when the woman's three little children went shouting and crying and running into the hut, where they tried to stay quiet. "But I recovered fast," she said. "You can't show to your boss you felt something bad after killing." (Rubin 1998: 62)

Kony, an Acholi himself, has kidnapped most of his forces from Acholi settlements and turned them to war against their own people. By his tactics of killing civilians, mutilating captives, and raping widely, he has completely discredited himself as the liberator of the North he claims to be (Berkeley 2001: 233).

By now, northern Uganda has become a wasteland with few resources of value to international traders. The Democratic Republic of Congo – the former Zaïre, and successor to the Belgian Congo – differs dramatically. The DRC's territory teems with diamonds, copper, cobalt, zinc, manganese, uranium, niobium, and tantalum (aka coltan), all valuable minerals on the world market. International traders in these minerals, rebel military forces, and the expeditionary armies of adjacent countries have revived the second ancient practice: blocking rule from the DRC's nominal capital, Kinshasa, as they divide up the proceeds of exports from the regions they control.

The illegal mining has been a huge windfall for Rwanda and Uganda. The two countries have very few mineral reserves of their own. But since they began extracting the DRC's resources, their mineral exports have increased dramatically. For example, between 1996 and 1997, the volume of Rwanda's coltan production doubled, bringing the Rwandans and their rebel allies up to $20 million a month in revenue. Also, the volume of Rwanda's diamond exports rose from about 166 carats in 1998 to some 30,500 in 2000 – a 184-fold increase! From 1997 to 1998, the annual volume of Uganda's diamond exports jumped from approximately 1,500 carats to about 11,300, or nearly eightfold; since 1996, Ugandan gold exports have increased tenfold. The final destination for many of these minerals is the United States. (Montague & Berrigan 2001: 17–18)

In the Congo we see convergence of two violence-generating practices: subsidy of rebellion by adjacent states and promotion of internal autonomy to facilitate seizure of resources. Resurgence of the two practices in parts of the world from which drugs, minerals, and cheap labor originate has promoted the rise of civil war to the world's major form of coordinated destruction.

Let us guard against several easy misinterpretations of coordinated destruction. Although young, single males do figure disproportionately as inflictors of its damage (as David Courtwright's stories of American violence suggest they would), sheer concentrations of uninhibited testosterone do not in themselves explain its complexities. Akbar's place in Hyderabad's Hindu–Muslim combats has already alerted us to the importance of political entrepreneurs (many of them no longer young men, some of them even women) in triggering the entry of young enforcers into street fighting. Rwandan genocide, furthermore, underlines the part that more general populations play in coordinated destruction when effectively linked or driven by political entrepreneurs and violent specialists. More generally, the upper right-hand corner of our coordination–salience space does not contain a distinct class of people who remain preternaturally violent throughout their lives. Indeed, as we shall soon see, the same people shift among types of collective violence as well as between nonviolence and violence – depending on well-defined organizational processes.

Nor should we imagine that, in the zone of coordinated destruction, social controls and commitments simply dissolve. Distinct forms of social organization certainly set off coordinated destruction from other forms of collective violence (not to mention from nonviolent contention), but the case of interstate war should remind us how much advance planning, prior training, logistical preparation, and strategic coordination go into efforts at mutual destruction. That participants should then improvise furiously, feel rage, fear, shame, or satisfaction in the face of danger, or manufacture implausible stories about what they are doing does not distinguish them remarkably from those participating in any number of other high-risk activities: police patrols, unsafe sex, fire fighting, brain surgery, team sports, childbirth, drug running, corporate takeovers, and many more. In all these cases, established social ties, shared understandings, and interaction repertoires channel the actors' behavior. Definable social processes – not impulse-ridden anarchy – determine who does damage to whom, and how. Our job as analysts is to trace the more visible and robust of those social processes.

What social processes? – Consider first the features of coordinated destruction that are true by definition. Coordinated destruction, remember, refers to those varieties of collective violence in which persons or organizations specialized in the deployment of coercive means undertake a program of actions that damage persons and/or objects. By definition, then, coordinated destruction results from the political engagement of at least one body of violent specialists. That tautological statement sets the first part of an explanatory agenda: accounting for the creation or activation of forces specializing in coercion. In Rwanda, President Habyarimana's reluctant sponsorship of a Hutu Power militia left a deadly retaliatory force in readiness after his sudden death.

Programs of destruction, likewise present by definition, offer trickier problems of interpretation than does the presence or absence of violent specialists; people tell different stories about their programs before, during, and after violent episodes, and they often modify these programs in the course of interaction. Nevertheless, the prior existence of a destructive program is usually detectable and an important facilitator of coordinated destruction. Such programs can take the form of concrete blueprints for annihilation, conspiratorial plans, or more general stigmatization of a social category – heretics, Jews, communists, Roma, gays, and so on – as falling outside of conventional legal protections.

Beyond tautology, coordinated destruction regularly results from the creation of coalitions among previously segmented wielders of violent means. Political entrepreneurs therefore exercise great influence over the waxing and waning of coordinated destruction, for example by knitting scattered opponents of government exactions into common (if temporary) resistance fronts. In such circumstances, we find entrepreneurs carrying on their usual work of activating, connecting, coordinating, and representing – but now with violent interaction as the object of their efforts. Within governments, precisely parallel processes occur as advocates and opponents of destructive programs negotiate deployment of a government's own violent specialists. In general, coordinated destruction occurs when beneficiaries (governmental or nongovernmental) of exploitation and opportunity hoarding encounter connected resistance to those systems or to their control over those systems. If brokerage fails or multiple boundaries activate, it follows, coordinated destruction mutates into opportunism and/or scattered attack.

Ulster as a Hard Case

Instead of concentrating on armed combats in which these points are obvious, why not examine a sort of lethal contest in which observers do often suppose that violence-prone individuals combine with dissolved social control to produce destruction? We might easily turn to ostensibly ethnic conflicts in Southeastern Europe, Africa, South Asia, or Southeast Asia, but they would still leave open the suspicion that different cultures tolerate or promote violence in ways that the ostensibly mature cultures of Northwestern Europe do not. Of course, we would not have to reach very far back into Italian, Spanish, French, Dutch, or even Swiss history to discover violent events resembling those of today's Liberia or former Yugoslavia (see e.g. te Brake 1998; Dekker 1982; Guenniffey 2000; Head 1995; Henshall 1992; Mayer 2000; Powers 1988; Tilly 1986, 1989; Zwaan 2001). But why not track down the really hard case of Northern Ireland? – clearly within the generally peaceable British Isles, still (if just barely) part of the United Kingdom, but for over two centuries the recurrent site of coordinated destruction.

Easy cases concentrate in low-capacity undemocratic regimes, where petty tyrants acting to maintain or extend their advantages often face either sustained popular resistance from members of distinctive social categories or open competition from other petty tyrants, aspiring or actual. Cases in high-capacity undemocratic regimes are almost as easy, since they bifurcate between external war and government-initiated action against presumed or declared domestic opponents of governmental programs. Ulster presents a serious puzzle because, since its formation in 1801, the United Kingdom, compared to most other regimes, has dwelt in the upper right-hand corner of our capacity–democracy space; with the momentous exception of external war, high-capacity democracies do not host much coordinated destruction.

Ulster and Ireland therefore present an important challenge. Anglo-Norman warriors conquered bits of Ireland during the eleventh-century Norman takeover of England, and a century later England's Henry II launched a serious invasion of the island. Over the thirteenth to fifteenth centuries, English kings tried repeatedly to subordinate the Irish, but outside of the Dublin region – "beyond the Pale" – they did not succeed for long. Serious English colonization and administration did not begin until the 1550s. Most of the earliest settlers were not English, but Scottish. At the succession in 1603 of Scottish King James VI to the English crown as James I, royally sponsored settlements of Scots and Englishmen greatly expanded. They concentrated in Ulster, the nine northernmost counties of Ireland. There and elsewhere in Ireland, English rulers regularly dispossessed Catholic landlords; that displacement of Catholics from land ownership and political power accelerated during the seventeenth century.

During the English civil wars of 1640–1690, Irish leaders tried repeatedly to wrest their territories free of English rule. From opposite sides, Irish activists still celebrate or execrate the Battle of the Boyne (1690), when Protestant King William defeated his rival Catholic King James, who fled to France. From that point until the nineteenth century, English regimes excluded Catholics from almost every form of political power in Ireland, including Ulster. With minor exceptions, Protestants alone enjoyed the right to bear arms. During the late 1770s, indeed, Anglican landlords emulated American revolutionaries by organizing militias – the Volunteers – 80,000 strong. Urban equivalents also formed. In 1778, for example, Belfast formed its own volunteer corps, nominally to protect the coast against a threatened French landing. By 1782, perhaps 90,000 men had joined these militias (Mac Suibhne 2000: 45). In 1782, "delegates from a number of Ulster Volunteer corps gathered at Dungannon in the parish church and pledged their support to resolutions in favour of [Irish] legislative independence" (McDowell 2001: 191). Although a few landlords recruited Catholics to their companies, the militias became overwhelmingly a Protestant force. Political opportunity hoarding pivoted on the Protestant–Catholic boundary.

In Ulster, a triangular relationship emerged: Anglican landlords dominated politics and economic life; leaseholders, skilled workers, and professionals came mainly from the Protestant population; and Catholics concentrated disproportionately in landless labor. From the late seventeenth to the early nineteenth century, however, a prospering linen industry promoted rapid population growth, raised land values, and formed an assertive Protestant commercial class that was prepared to make alliances with Catholics against landlord hegemony. It also introduced further splits between tenants and landlords on one side, between industrial masters and proletarianized workers on the other.

Meanwhile, Catholics were moving into tenant farming, industrial work, and military service; all three sorts of mobility shook previous Protestant monopolies. By the 1790s, Ulster's bourgeois Presbyterian radicals were trying to forge a coalition against the Anglican ruling class by preaching agrarian reform to Protestant tenants and political equality to Catholics. By doing so, they challenged both the exploitation that benefited landlords and the opportunity hoarding that benefited Protestants.

Such a coalition faced two huge obstacles. First, working-class Protestants were actually competing with Catholics for local economic and political priority, proud of their position as Loyalists vis-à-vis the Catholics who had generally opposed English rule a century earlier, and fiercely protective of their exclusive right to bear arms. If the bearing of arms seems a trivial matter, consider the Swiss citizens – exclusively male and a small minority of the total Swiss population – who well into the nineteenth century regularly wore swords, daggers, or bayonets in public to symbolize their membership in the municipal and cantonal militias that constituted the Confederation's armed force. Grouped into opposing armies, mainly Catholic and mainly Protestant Swiss militias fought a crucial civil war, the Sonderbund, in 1847. Through those parts of Europe in which elite civic militias existed, the right to bear arms generally marked social superiority. Ulster's Protestants, in any case, had their own justification to offer for the monopoly of arms: elsewhere in Ireland, through the 1780s armed Catholic bands had attacked landlords, tithe-taking clergy, and their agents, killing half a dozen persons and destroying extensive rural property. Armed Protestants posed as authorized protectors of public order.

Second, Ulster Catholics maintained extensive relations with Catholics elsewhere in Ireland. The United Irishmen first organized in 1791 as a militantly anti-British Protestant organization. They began publication of the influential newspaper *Northern Star* from Belfast on 4 January 1792. But as the organization gained strength outside of Ulster, it attracted Catholics in large numbers. Despite its Protestant initiation and leadership, it eventually became a largely Catholic organization. The United Irishmen began with demands for reform but, during the French Revolution, moved increasingly toward a program of French-backed revolution in Ireland. In fact, French forces tried to invade Ireland in support of the United Irishmen during 1796 and actually succeeded during 1798. The British beat back both French efforts handily and carried out ferocious repression of the United Irishmen on both occasions.

The struggle of British authorities with the United Irishmen undercut radical coalition building as it widened the gap between Protestants and Catholics. In reaction, the British government deeply altered its relation to Ireland. In 1801 it dissolved the Irish parliament, absorbing 100 Irish Protestant members into the parliament at Westminster and establishing a new United Kingdom of England, Wales, Scotland, and Ireland. Although the Protestant MPs of the long-established Dublin parliament had not defended Catholic causes ardently, the move increased distance between lawmakers and Catholic Ireland while validating the claim of Protestants to be the true loyalists.

The two sides solidified their differences by means of political–religious organizations, notably the Orange Order for Protestants and Ribbonmen for Catholics. Those organizations became vehicles for public challenges and shows of strength that have continued from the early nineteenth century to the present day and that have often turned into violent affrays. During the nineteenth century, however, a crucial new element entered the scene. With Great Britain's Catholic Emancipation of 1829, propertied Catholics acquired the right to hold most public offices. As the franchise expanded and party politics began to flourish, election campaigns became new sites of Protestant–Catholic rivalry and also new occasions for collective violence. Mass mobilization of anti-British movements across Ireland as a whole during the later nineteenth century drew in many Ulster Catholics, thus spurring Unionists (as the pro-British Protestant forces began to call themselves) to self-defense. On both sides, arming, drilling, and threatening accelerated into World War I, when Irish nationalists took up arms and declared a republic – only to suffer another round of deep repression.

At first Irish people collaborated with the war effort. To be sure, Ulster's Protestants collaborated much more enthusiastically than the rest of the Irish population. The prewar Ulster Volunteer Force, a Protestant paramilitary unit organized in 1913 to oppose Irish home rule, joined the British army *en masse*. Meanwhile, the British maintained 20,000 troops and police in the rest of the island to contain popular militias of Irish Catholics that started forming in 1914. By that time, Ireland contained five distinct armed forces: not only the British army and the Ulster Volunteers, but also their opponents the Irish Volunteers, the Citizen Army, and the Irish Republican Brotherhood. Still, serious opposition to the British cause did not crystallize until World War I had been going on for almost two years. The abortive Easter Rebellion of 1916 – organized in part from New York, supported by German agents, backed by German bombardment of the English coast, and suppressed brutally by British troops – slowed the cause of Irish independence temporarily. Nevertheless, Irish nationalists began regrouping in 1917.

The parliamentary election of 1918 brought a victory for Sinn Féin, a party popularly identified with the Easter Rebellion and the republican cause. When the U.K. government decreed military conscription for Ireland in April 1918, all Irish MPs except the Protestant representatives of the North withdrew from the U.K. parliament. Returned MPs led organization of opposition back home. In December 1918, Irish nationalists handily won Southern Ireland's votes in a parliamentary election, with 34 of the 69 successful candidates elected while in prison. The newly elected MPs decided to form their own Irish parliament instead of joining the U.K. assembly. On meeting in January 1919, they chose New York–born Eamon De Valera, then still in prison, as their parliamentary president. De Valera soon escaped from prison, but after four months of activity in Ireland he left for the United States.

Soon the British government was actively suppressing Irish nationalist organizations. Nationalists themselves mobilized for resistance and attacked representatives of British authority. By the end of 1919, Ireland reached a state of civil war. As Peter Hart sums up for County Cork:

> Sinn Fein won and guarded its new political turf with the obligatory minimum of street-fighting and gunplay. However, in the course of the revolution the familiar exuberance of party competition turned into killing on an unprecedented, unimagined scale. The political arena was transformed into a nightmare world of anonymous killers and victims, of disappearances, massacres, midnight executions, bullets in the back of the head, bodies dumped in fields or ditches. Over 700 people died in Cork in revolutionary or counter-revolutionary shootings or bombings between 1917 and 1923, 400 of them at the hands of the Irish Volunteers – soon rechristened the Irish Republican Army. (Hart 1998: 50)

The British painfully established military control but also began negotiating with Irish representatives. Within two years, the negotiations led to an agreement: partition of Northern Ireland (Ulster less counties Cavan, Donegal, and Monaghan) from the rest; and dominion status similar to that of Canada and South Africa for a newly created Irish Free State outside of the North. Although hard-line Irish republicans refused to accept the settlement and raised an insurrection in 1922, the arrangement lasted in roughly the same form until the 1930s.

Within Northern Ireland, anti-British forces never gave up. Although the Catholic third of the region's population remained somewhat more rural, more segregated, and more concentrated toward the South than the Protestant population, it still constituted a formidable force. A whole new round of conflicts began with Catholic civil rights marches in 1968, violent confrontations with police, struggles with Protestant counterdemonstrators, and more scattered attacks of each side on the other's persons and property. In 1972, British paratroopers trying to break up an unarmed but illegal march through Derry by the Northern Ireland Civil Rights Association fired on the demonstrators, killing thirteen of them. The uproar following that "Bloody Sunday" induced a worried British government to take back direct rule of the province.

After a bilateral cease-fire declared in 1994, raids and confrontations (including some quite outside Ireland) actually accelerated. A further treaty in 1998 (the so-called Good Friday agreement) initiated serious talks among the major parties and terminated most public standoffs between the sides, but it did not end guerrilla action by all paramilitary units or produce full disarmament of those units. Despite rough agreement between the governments of Ireland and the United Kingdom, while negotiations proceeded paramilitary factions on both sides repeatedly broke the peace. Support of Catholic militants by the well-armed Irish Republican Army, based in independent Ireland and extensively supported by Irish overseas migrants, certainly sustained the conflict. But militant Catholics native to Ulster repeatedly challenged equally militant Ulster Protestants. One of Europe's longest runs of large-scale intergroup violence continues.

The toll is serious. Between 1969 and 1982, Northern Ireland's collective violence laid down the following records:

2,268 persons killed – including 491 military, 187 police, and 1,590 civilians;
25,120 persons injured;
29,035 shooting incidents;
7,533 explosions;
4,250 malicious fires;
9,871 armed robberies;
153 tar-and-featherings; and
1,006 kneecappings (Palmer 1988: 2; see also White 1993).

The numbers bespeak political actors at each other's throats. Although the intensity of violence waxed and waned with the more general rhythms of intergroup struggle in Northern Ireland, mutual attacks continued into the 1990s. Even the tentative settlement of 1998 did not end them:

In the year of the Good Friday Agreement – 1998 – fifty-five people died in violence in Northern Ireland. Three Catholic brothers, aged between eight and ten, died on 12 July when loyalists petrol-bombed their home in a predominantly Protestant area of Ballymoney. On 15 August – a traditional Catholic holiday – twenty-eight people were killed in a car-bomb blast in Omagh. The attack also claimed another victim, who died a few days later. A republican splinter group, the Real IRA, had placed a 500-pound bomb in a parked car in a crowded shopping street on a sunny summer Saturday. It was one of the worst outrages of the Troubles. (Keogh 2001: 332–3)

Repeatedly, groups on the flanks of the two militant movements broke away when peace agreements were crystallizing, using scattered attacks in defiance of national leaders on both sides.

The Stakes of Explanation

Remember what we are trying to explain. The point is *not* to provide a complete account of all Protestant–Catholic struggles in Ulster since the 1790s, much less to explain all violent events in their entirety. As always, we are pursuing an explanatory program of the following kind:

- specify what is distinctive about collective violence in Ulster over the last two centuries;
- specify what is distinctive about the *type* of collective violence – in this case, especially the coordinated destruction – under examination;
- identify causal mechanisms and processes producing those distinctive features;
- reassemble initial conditions, mechanisms, and processes in the correct combinations and sequences to provide a coherent (if skeletal) causal account of those distinctive features.

If the final stage yields no fresh insight into Ulster's peculiarities, to be sure, this exercise will raise doubts about the value of the whole effort to explain variation in collective violence. Why not just study cases closely on their own terms? Only if the analogies suggested by earlier chapters' treatments of regimes, actors, and modes of contentious politics identify genuine causal similarities among apparently disparate episodes will the effort be worthwhile.

What have we to explain? What distinguishes Ulster's collective violence from other instances of coordinated destruction, and from other forms of collective violence in similar social settings? Four features stand out:

1. violence organized around a persistent boundary for two centuries despite enormous shifts in people, organizations, programs, political rights, and external relations on either side of the boundary;
2. the equally persistent and striking conjunction of large-scale public displays of force, only intermittently violent, with small-scale clandestine attacks on persons and property;
3. recurrence of violent encounters despite the absence (except for the British military) of the sorts of competing professional full-time military forces that operate in Colombia, Angola, and Sri Lanka; and
4. repeated fragmentation of the organized forces on both sides such that, when Protestant and Catholic groups reach a settlement, renegade groups of militants form on one or both flanks.

Some sort of Catholic–Protestant division persisted as the basis of cross-boundary violence, but who performed the violence and how fluctuated incessantly. Although coordinated destruction did occur, furthermore, it alternated and interwove with forms of collective violence we could more accurately call broken negotiations, scattered attack, brawls, opportunism, or violent ritual. Disciplined, armed militias rose and fell, but only British military forces figured as participants in Ulster's collective violence more or less continuously over the two centuries. Finally, up to the present, neither side's political entrepreneurs have been able to restrain segments of their coalitions from defecting – and returning to attacks on the other side – as the entrepreneurs approached peace settlements.

Do age-old hatreds explain these four perplexing features of Ulster's conflicts? Certainly Northern Ireland's Protestants and Catholics have fought intermittently for a long time, and Irish Catholics have certainly long suffered political disabilities. As of the nineteenth century, English rulers certainly had stigmatizing stereotypes of the Irish population at hand. The staid *Economist* declared in April 1848:

Thank God we are Saxons! Flanked by the savage Celt on one side and the flighty Gaul on the other – the one a slave to his passions, the other a victim to the theories of the hour – we feel deeply grateful from our inmost hearts that we belong to a race, which if it cannot boast the flowing fancy of one of its neighbors, nor the brilliant *esprit* of the other, has an ample compensation in social, slow, reflective phlegmatic temperament. (Kearney 1989: 160)

The *Economist* did not distinguish between Protestants and Catholics, but nineteenth-century mythology made Protestants somewhat more British than their Catholic countrymen. To some extent, furthermore, Protestants and Catholics shared the idea that they were separate peoples.

Yet, like Bosnia's mixed populations, most of the time most Catholics and most Protestants found ways of getting along. During his long reconnaissance of an Ulster village, American ethnographer and folklorist Henry Glassie found that religious categories organized significant parts of public life – for example, the holidays on which different groups got together and the historical stories Protestants and Catholics told to explain present-day politics. Yet those categories did not bar everyday sociability across religious lines. Glassie muses:

I do not know Belfast, but I know Ballymenone. People there are not religious fanatics. They have not the terrified ersatz faith of zealots who, protesting too much, praise their own sanctity while cluttering their speech with unnecessary references to God. The District's people hold a faith so deep, so sure and serene, that it rarely comes to their lips. They do not quote scripture in vain or discuss doctrine. All are, after all, Catholics, some Roman Catholics, others Church of Ireland. Religious difference, they believe, is a matter more of birth than persuasion, and all forms of religion are valid. (Glassie 1982: 300)

Participation in religious services and some forms of sociability (e.g., musical bands) segment the community along religious lines. Yet others (e.g., the local football team) bring the two sides together. Despite surmounting religious differences in daily social relations, however, villagers line up on occasion along the Protestant–Catholic boundary. That typically happens, as I read Glassie's narratives, under two circumstances: when a local conflict begun on nonreligious grounds happens to oppose factions of different religions; and when outside connections (e.g., solicitations of the Irish Republican Army) draw local people into regional or national politics.

Why should that happen? Think back to the earlier discussion of political identities – with their boundaries, shared stories about the boundaries, social relations across the boundaries, and social relations within the boundaries. Three complementary bundles of mechanisms select certain identities for collective action.

1. When networks of mutual aid segregate on either side of a boundary, a dispute that pits people on the two sides against each other (for whatever reason) – and then leads them to seek support from their fellows – redefines the dispute as categorical. For example, two neighbors get into a fight over a badly dug ditch without any particular categorical definition of their disagreement; however, when they start calling in kin and friends to back them, the contrast in social networks favors a categorical redefinition of the participants and issues. This first process usually reaches a limit as third parties mediate or cooler heads within a category prevail, but it occasionally escalates small-scale disputes into large episodes of coordinated destruction. Call this process *network-based escalation*.

2. Rather than being all-encompassing, political identities connect people with certain social settings and not with others; drawing them into those settings activates the identities. Holidays, weddings, funerals, enrollment in schools, election campaigns, calls to military service, and trips to fairs all place people in settings where identities that play little part in organizing daily life become salient, visible, and compelling. This second process promotes coordinated destruction to the extent that (a) the settings in question bring together members of paired categories that already have a history of conflict and (b) shows of group strength already belong to the repertoires attached to those settings. By itself, however, the process is likely to produce no more than intermittent and scattered violent incidents as a function of schedules attached to the relevant social settings. Call this process *setting-based activation*.

3. Political entrepreneurs (whatever their other talents and appeals) become skilled at evoking certain political identities and suppressing others. As they activate, connect, coordinate, and represent, they draw selectively on networks that will line up on their side of the appropriate boundary. The third process can operate quite independently of the first two, with leaders calling up members of a category who would rather evade service but cannot refuse (Tilly 2001d).

Alone or in conjunction with the first two processes, it can produce coordinated destruction on a large scale. If violent specialists are among those called, the chances of extensive damage increase. Call this process *brokerage*.

All three processes have operated in Ulster intermittently over the last two centuries, in various combinations and sequences. Their triggering and damping help account for the distinctive features of collective violence in that beleaguered land. Network-based escalation accounts for the uneven but persistent hum of low-level conflict returning repeatedly to the same divisions. Setting-based activation accounts for the marked geographical and temporal patterning of medium to large conflicts. Brokerage accounts for the occasional convergence of local efforts into province-wide collective violence.

That very fact, however, helps explain the tendency of extremist groups to break off as peace settlements approach. Most of the time the political entrepreneurs who connect those fragments to the main coalition actually gain power and effectiveness from their relations with more moderate elements. But at a settlement they run the risk both of losing political leverage at large and of losing control over their own militant constituencies. The more those constituencies have become violent specialists, the less they themselves have to gain from peace.

Parades and Confrontations in Ulster

As confirmation, let us close in on the one kind of occasion that has most frequently generated large-scale violence in Ulster over the last two centuries: the party procession. In a wide variety of politics, public displays of disciplined force signal challenges to competitors and authorities, constituting a demand to be taken seriously. In democratic regimes, street demonstrations do just that sort of signaling, which is one reason that organizers, reporters, police, and officials often dispute the number of participants. (Chapter 9 deals with demonstrations in greater detail.) Violence often results from public displays of disciplined force because authorities attempt to squelch them, because rivals try to disrupt them, because participants respond to controls or heckling by fighting back, or because disciplined display gives way to opportunism. The Irish party procession illustrates all these violent outcomes.

During the eighteenth century, ordinary people of Britain and Ireland had no right to gather on their own initiative in substantial numbers. Any group that did so ran the risk of a magistrate's declaring them a riot – a gathering likely to commit a felony – and having them dispersed by shows or applications of force.

But British and Irish authorities tolerated some large gatherings when properly authorized and policed: vestry meetings, assemblies of freeholders, public ceremonies, executions, markets, fairs, funerals, elections, public holidays, religious services, and religious processions. Craftsmen's guilds often paraded in full regalia on their saints' days. Following the craftsmen's model, from at least the 1720s Irish freemasons regularly assembled on St. John's Day (24 June or 27 December) to dine together in some hostelry before marching to church services with music and a display of Masonic emblems (Mirala 2000).

On such occasions, people sometimes took advantage of license and anonymity to voice views on issues and personalities of the day. Within those tolerated forms, furthermore, resourceful political entrepreneurs pushed the limits by such devices as converting the (legal) presentation of petitions into a sort of (questionably legal) street demonstration (Brewer 1976; Brewer & Styles 1980; Palmer 1988; Tilly 1983). On the election of a Captain Wilson to the Irish parliament in 1777, supporters of his stand on behalf of Presbyterians (against the Anglican establishment in Ballymena, Ulster) mounted a procession with

ten thousand men with blue cockades ... next to these 400 freemasons, attired in their jewels, armed with carbines for the purpose of saluting, and preceded by a large band of music, and colours made for the occasion, descriptive of their different lodges, and embroidered with various emblematical figures; to these succeeded 500 young women, habited in white, ornamented with blue ribbons .... The masons lined the street from the entrance into the town, to the tavern, where dinner was served. (Mirala 2000: 125)

About the same time, political activists in Ulster were fusing the militia march and the religious procession into a show of force by followers of the same faith.

The innovation first occurred in Ulster's County Armagh and in Belfast during the 1770s and 1780s. It sprang from co-optation of Protestant guerrilla forces that had formed to disarm Catholics in nocturnal raids after gentry leaders had opened the ranks of the Volunteers to selected Catholics. Those Peep O'Day Boys, as the Protestant gangs were called, agreed to cease their raids in return for expulsion of Catholics from the Volunteers and their own integration into those prestigious military forces. The tamed guerrillas then began marching to and from church armed and in uniform. The Belfast Volunteer Company, to take a major instance, formed in 1778 and soon began parading to church on politically significant holidays (Jarman 1997: 40). When they crossed predominantly Catholic areas, or when crowds of Catholics assembled deliberately to block their passage, scuffles and shootings often followed.

Meanwhile, Catholics created their own guerrilla bands, known generically as the Defenders. They, too, began public shows of strength. In Armagh, an analysis of about 100 violent incidents from 1784 to 1791 identifies a shift from attacks on isolated victims and directly initiated combat between armed bands to public displays of force, which only sometimes led to armed clashes (Miller 1983: 172). After Protestant Peep O'Day Boys had attacked a number of Catholic homes during 1794 and 1795, an armed Defender force from several different parts of Ulster gathered near Loughgall, Armagh, in September 1795. Protestants assembled with arms on an adjacent hill, and members of the two parties began firing shots in each other's direction. Despite a truce organized by a magistrate and a priest, a newly arrived detachment of Defenders attacked the Protestant gathering, whose members retreated to a nearby inn and began firing back. The day ended with about 30 Catholics dead but no Protestant fatalities. That clash entered history as the Battle of the Diamond (Farrell 2000: 25).

The Battle of the Diamond led immediately to the formation of a local Protestant defensive association. Expanded and eventually taken up by city dwellers, the association became the Loyal Orange Order, an organizational base for a large share of Protestant collective action from then to the present. The government's decision to form a volunteer yeomanry in Ulster for self-defense in a time of war with France (1796) permitted local notables to incorporate militant Protestants into military units. In essence, the government recognized military segments of the Orange Order as the provincial army.

The new units retained considerable political spirit and independence. In 1796, the Viscount Gosford, county governor of Armagh, reported that a force of 1,500 men had paraded through his domain,

marching in regular files by two and two with orange cockades, unarmed and by companies which were distinguished by numbers upon their flags. The party had one drum and each company had a fife and two or three men in front with painted wands in their hands who acted as commanders. They posted two men at each side of my gate with drawn swords to prevent any persons coming in but their own body. The devices on the flags were chiefly portraits of King William with mottoes alluding to his establishment of the Protestant religion, and on the reverse side ... a portrait of his present majesty .... They were perfectly quiet and sober. After parading through part of my demesne they took their leave. I was at my gate; each company saluted me by lowering their flags. (Blackstock 2000: 105)

Although the yeomanry boasted a national organization, its Ulster units far outnumbered those elsewhere in Ireland (Farrell 2000: 72). National authorities hesitated to deploy the force widely, precisely because of its identification with Orange politics (Broeker 1970: 36). The rival (and increasingly Catholic) Society of United Irishmen enjoyed nothing like that official standing.

Orange Order members specifically committed themselves to public displays of strength on 12 July, notional anniversary of 1690's fateful Battle of the Boyne. (In fact, the Battle of the Boyne raged on 1 July, and 12 July dates the Battle of Aughrim [1691], when James II had long since fled to France, but that is how historical memory packages events.) In 1798, bylaw article 9 of Orange Lodge 670 in Ballymagerney read:

That We are to mete the 12 Day of July in Every year and go to Whatsoever plase of Worship Shall bee aggred upon and our reason for so meeting and Assembling on that Day is in Memory of King William the prince of ororrnge Who bravly Suported And freed us from Popish Slavery Which ought to be kept By all true prodestants throughout his Mayestys Dominion. (Farrell 2000: 39)

As a matter of practice, lodge members customarily paraded to Protestant services armed and in uniform. In short, they engaged in more or less authorized displays of military strength.

From that point on, Ulster's Orange lodges frequently paraded in regalia with fifes, drums, and banners, and they often fought Catholic hecklers on the way. The annual high point generally came on 12 July. On 12 July 1813, for example, several lodges assembled in Belfast for their annual march to Lisburn, where lodges from elsewhere joined them for a day-long celebration. On returning to Belfast, a detachment marched toward a favorite pub, encountered a hostile crowd, exchanged insults and missiles with members of the crowd, ran into the pub, and endured an attack on the pub's windows. Stepping into the street, some members of the Orange lodge shot at the crowd, killing two young men and wounding four others, only to be stopped by the royal military (Farrell 2000: 32–3).

On 12 July, on other holidays, and at fairs, the performance recurred in Ulster for decades. Catholics fashioned their own shows of strength, mostly in the form of Protestant–Catholic faction fights and attempts to block 12 July processions. (St. Patrick's Day, 17 March, became the favored occasion for Catholic-initiated processions.) Because Protestants owned firearms and Catholics relied mainly on staves and farm implements, fatalities between the 1790s and the 1820s ran heavily against Catholics. After the expansion of Catholic political rights in 1829, Catholics more frequently came armed to their confrontations with Protestants. Hundreds of such affrays unfolded in Ulster during the nineteenth century. They stand out for their combination of apparently incompatible features: stylized interaction scripts, unpredictable outcomes, a more or less constant Protestant–Catholic boundary, and constantly shifting organization on either side of the boundary.

At first, organizational instability ran greater on the Catholic side, as Catholic Freemasons, Ribbonmen, Thrashers, Defenders, and many another organizational form rose and fell. Over time, Catholic urbanization, prosperity, and enfranchisement gave advantages to Catholic political organizers, who helped produce more centralized and durable coordinating structures. From the mid-1820s, for example, Daniel O'Connell's Catholic Association coordinated mass mobilization for Catholic political rights in Great Britain and Ireland alike (Tilly 1998c).

On the Protestant side, in any case, the Orange Order looked more uniform at the top than at the bottom; many differences separated village strongmen from their formally organized urban cousins. By the later 1820s, even the top-down organization was disintegrating. Organizers created new Brunswick Clubs (originating in England but widely supported in Ulster) to oppose Catholic Emancipation, but the clubs faded away after parliament's endorsement of limited Catholic rights in 1829. In 1835, the government banned the Orange Order, which did not keep local chapters from surviving under other auspices.

In rural areas, struggles throughout the nineteenth century over property rights continued to double with partisan alignments. After the abortive anti-British Fenian rising of 1867, any Catholic political action took on an additional taint of subversion. In County Cavan:

When a group of Catholics shouting for tenant rights paraded through the Protestant village of Drumaloor on November 1, 1869, shots were fired from a house along the road. One of the marchers was killed and two others were wounded. The Protestant *Cavan Weekly News* explained that the Protestants had fired when the Catholics refused to lower the green flag. Noting that Drumaloor was an exclusively Protestant neighborhood, the newspaper praised the Protestants as patriots and argued that "Orangeism which is no more than Protestantism in an organized and creative form" was a force for good. (Conley 1999a: 167)

The Catholics had been unarmed, but they carried a banner emblazoned with a harp and crown. (Historical irony smiles on that symbolism, since Protestant Henry VIII imposed harp and crown as Irish symbols when he had himself crowned King of Ireland in 1541.) The courts tried nine Protestants. Their attorneys successfully argued that they had acted in self-defense; they won an acquittal. Nevertheless, police, courts, and public authorities generally acted to channel parades into nonviolence when they could.

On the defensive against Catholic gains, Ulster's local Protestant units engaged in more and more frequent public challenges to their rivals. Across the nineteenth century – as migration swelled Belfast's population, increased the

Catholic share, and produced large, adjacent Catholic and Protestant enclaves – processions and the attendant fighting urbanized as well. Belfast experienced major violent incidents of this kind in 1813, 1843, 1857, 1864, 1872, and 1886 (Farrell 2000: 137–9, 180). With extension of the franchise, shows of strength took on the additional meaning of electoral power, with current political leaders eulogized and portrayed along with ancient heroes.

Still, the prevailing iconography drew on distilled history. From the 1880s onward, for example, Catholics and (especially) Protestants increased their use of stationary triumphal arches to frame parades. Belfast's York Street arch of 1884 was

> formed of iron rods, over which is carefully stretched wire netting and its form is an embattled bridge with six arches between, separated by five Martinello towers each being surmounted by a handsome flag. The design ... is surmounted by the Bible and Crown ... [and] a large well executed oil painting of King William ... each of the towers bears a heraldic shield on each side ... [it] is surmounted by a line of bannerets, the Royal Standard and the Irish ensign being most prominent. (Jarman 1997: 66)

Repeated efforts of parliament and Irish officials to outlaw party emblems and processions – for example, the Party Processions Act of 1832, finally repealed in 1872 – raised the stakes of competitive displays without by any means eliminating them.

The 1921 separation of a truncated Ulster from Ireland as the United Kingdom's Northern Ireland did nothing to terminate such shows of force. In 1926, 100,000 Orangemen are supposed to have paraded through Belfast on 12 July (Jarman 1997: 72). Over the following four decades, Protestant parades in Belfast and Derry worked mainly as triumphal displays and only intermittently produced significant collective violence. But when Catholic activists, emulating American civil rights marchers, began organizing marches of their own in 1968, Ulster's Protestant counterdemonstrators regularly resisted. In fact, Protestant forces adopted the tactic of responding to Catholic announcements of rights marches by initiating an "annual parade" of their own over the same route at the same time. By 1969, competing shows of strength were spiraling into street fighting, barricades, tear gas, and military intervention as Northern Irish governments fell and rose over officials' inability to contain collective violence.

In recent times, the once-religious character of Protestant marches has dissipated. Although small detachments of the Orange Order still parade to church on certain Sundays, if the 12th of July falls on a Sunday then organizers of great Loyalist displays postpone their public showing to the following day (Jarman

1997: 100). It would be hard to state more clearly the distinction between religious fervor and political strength. The sheer number of marches on both sides of Ulster's Protestant–Catholic divide boggles the mind. From 1985 to 1995, the Royal Ulster Constabulary reported an average of 2,430 parades per year, with 237 (just under 10 percent) of them Republican as compared with over 90 percent of them Loyalist (computed from Jarman 1997: 119).

Parades provide entertainment in the form of colorful costumes and loud bands. But they also affirm political identities. Contained by authorities and local negotiations, most occur without open confrontations between Loyalist and Republican forces. Still, since the partially successful Northern Irish ceasefire of 1994, the right to parade has become a major political issue. After two centuries, parades continue to confirm political boundaries, to test the strength of forces on either side of those boundaries, and hence to generate collective violence.

At the same time, the contested parade provides a model and an opportunity for activists at the outer flanks of either side. Instead of simply lining up to block each other's parades by sheer force of numbers, more extreme factions use bombs and other weapons to attack the other side's participants in such shows of strength or to keep the other side's people from reaching public facilities. In June 2001, for example, Protestant militants started blocking North Belfast's Ardoyne Road to keep Catholic schoolgirls from walking to the Holy Cross School, close to the current Protestant–Catholic boundary in that part of the city.

Middle-class Protestants have been fleeing the embattled zone for the Belfast suburbs, leaving behind about 1,000 relatively poor and old Protestants to share the neighborhood with 7,000 Catholics. Some of the Protestant pickets offered an obvious justification: if British authorities keep our boys from marching through Catholic neighborhoods elsewhere, these school children should not be able to walk through Protestant neighborhoods here. Protestant crowds forced early closing of the Catholic school for the summer.

When school resumed in September 2001, Catholic pupils walked up the Ardoyne Road behind a squad of police officers in body armor, military vehicles lined the streets, and a British Army detachment with machine guns at the ready stood by. On the morning of 5 September, one of the Protestant activists threw a homemade bomb at the schoolgirl procession, injuring four police officers seriously. A paramilitary front calling itself the Red Hand Defenders claimed responsibility for the attack. During the first three days of school, Protestant militants threw more than 250 bombs, injuring two soldiers and at least 45 police officers while leaving the streets littered with burned-out automobiles (Lavery 2001a).

Interviewed as the standoffs continued six weeks later, Protestant leader Stuart McCartney made the stakes clear: "We'll call off our protest when they call off their protest" (Lavery 2001b). In case any doubt remained as to the controlled nature of the confrontation, on 9 November local Protestants suspended their picketing temporarily – so, they said, that the schoolgirls could take secondary-school admissions examinations in peace (Lavery 2001c). Soon thereafter, the (Protestant) first minister and (Catholic) deputy first minister of the Northern Ireland Assembly asked local leaders to make the suspension permanent. At a meeting on 23 November, neighborhood Protestants, perhaps sensing the reluctance of their stalwarts to line the streets again, agreed to call off the action. Brendan Mailey of the Catholic parents' Right to Education group offered a suspicious comment: "We welcome this, but we will believe it when we are walking up the road and there's nobody there shouting abuse" (Hoge 2001: A8). Thus Mailey himself indirectly described the standoff as an episode of display and counterdisplay. As it happened, he was right to be suspicious: Protestant attacks on parents at Holy Cross Primary started a new round of violence in January 2002, once again closing the school. Yet another time Catholic and Protestant youths began smashing, attacking, and fighting each other in the streets of Belfast. This time, both Catholic and Protestant leaders decried the new attacks. As leaders approach a settlement, dissident factions on both sides continue to battle for control of public spaces. They do so by means of violent variants on a 200-year-old set of claim-making performances.

Coordination and Salience

Northern Ireland's long experience of collective violence illustrates the interdependence of different sorts of violent politics. Coordinated destruction has occurred repeatedly in the North since the 1780s, but moments of truly extensive coordination and salience have come rarely and passed quickly. They have always arrived in the midst of violence through broken negotiations, violent rituals, opportunism, and scattered attack. We can look at the North's violence in either of two roughly equivalent ways: as collective bargaining by damage and threat of damage; or as a by-product of nonviolent contention. Seen as collective bargaining, the mutual destruction resembles war. Seen as a by-product, it resembles strike violence.

Coordination and salience – and thus the resemblance to war – rise as local struggles connect increasingly to divisions and changes at the national or international scale. Of our three crucial processes (network-based escalation, setting-based activation, and brokerage), brokerage makes the largest difference in this regard. If the major actors finally manage a durable peace settlement in Northern Ireland, it will not be by calming anger, changing beliefs, policing hot spots, interning individual troublemakers, or revamping small-scale interpersonal relations. It will occur through intervention in coalitions among political entrepreneurs, including the segregation or co-optation of violent specialists.

Let me restate my claim and its limits. However rich and relevant, a single case cannot clinch the sort of argument this book is advancing. At most it can show that the argument provides a reasonable fit to significant features of the case at hand and offers interesting, plausible explanations of those features. My larger claim remains untested: that all cases of coordinated destruction bear family resemblances to Ulster's experience and differ systematically from cases of brawls or scattered attack.

The similarities and differences do not result from general laws but rather from the relative prominence of certain mechanisms and processes in different varieties of collective violence. I have singled out the interplay of network-based escalation, setting-based activation, and brokerage as crucial to the emergence of coordinated destruction. A skeptic could therefore refute my claim either by producing a well-documented instance of coordinated destruction in which none of the three processes operated or by showing that similar interplays of the three processes in other settings instead produce broken negotiations, scattered attack, brawls, opportunism, or ritual violence.

The analysis so far carries a further implication that I have not yet emphasized. Variation from one regime type to another shapes some kinds of collective violence more than others. Low-capacity regimes exert less control over coordination among contentious actors than do high-capacity regimes, and they also tolerate a wider range of nonstate specialists in violence. As a consequence, low- and high-capacity regimes differ greatly in their experience with high-coordination, high-salience forms of collective violence: violent rituals and coordinated destruction. Because governments exert their control especially from the top down and at the large scale, lower-coordination forms of collective violence tend to escape that control. Scattered attacks mark a partial exception simply because government action itself so regularly incites resistance. But opportunism and brawls tend to occur below the net of governmental surveillance and thus tend to resemble each other more greatly across regimes than do other types of collective violence.

What should we expect to find happening in the zone of opportunism? Actually, we have already reconnoitered that zone quite extensively as we wandered away from Northern Ireland's ritualized parades. In opportunism we should expect to see less of political entrepreneurs but even more of violent specialists; we should also find more transitions to and from scattered attacks or brawls than in the case of violent rituals. But because of opportunism's lesser scripting and less extensive control by political entrepreneurs, we should also find more volatility in forms, participants, and intensity. Let us look more closely.

6

Opportunism

Opportunists at Work

Chechen guerrillas have created a grisly business on the side: hostage taking for revenge and (especially) profit. They grab journalists when they can, because the journalists usually work for companies that want their employees back and that can afford to pay big money. Former hostage journalist Dmitrii Balburov told ethnographer Valery Tishkov that he suffered bodily pains, hallucinations, and urges to self-destruction for months after his release. He had, he reported, come close to being killed by his Chechen captors:

When they were told a Russian journalist was to be brought to them as hostage, they were all bloody-minded because, after the attack on Dagestan, bombing had begun in Chechnya, with casualties. "Now we'll press him after full program," they said meaning torture or even murder. "But when they pulled you out of the car and took off the hood and the ropes and we saw your mug, we lost all such thoughts – look he's not Russian! Are you a Kalmyk?" Yes, I said, I'm a Kalmyk. "But you, Kalmyks, were also deported, why don't you fight the Russians, why don't you rise against them?"

Later that guard told me that they would have killed me if I were Russian: they had twice decided to cut off my head and lay it out as a threat, as with the Englishmen, when the bombing got worse and when one of them had lost his home and family. My life, he said, hung on a thread, but each time they changed their mind. (Tishkov 2001: 348)

Balburov's Asian features placed him on the rebels' side of the us–them boundary that Chechen soldier bandits had adopted for predation and retaliation; he should have been on the side of the oppressed, against the Russians and Westerners who were oppressing non-Christians across a broad front. But his employment by Russian media pushed Balburov back across the boundary, suspending him half-way. In violent conflicts, that is rarely a comfortable position.

During the late 1990s, the practice of hostage taking accelerated, especially in the North Caucasus. Across the Russian Federation as a whole, 1,140 abductions occurred in 1997, 1,415 in 1998, and more than 1,500 in 1999 (Tishkov 2001: 341). As backing for their demands, hostage takers often mutilated or executed their prisoners, videotaped the violence, and sent the videos to reluctant payers. They meant business.

The high end of the hostage-taking business operated under the sponsorship of guerrilla commanders. At that end a significant share (but not all) of the proceeds went to support the guerrilla movement and not merely to fatten the purses of individual hostage takers. When a major military figure got involved in abductions, he rarely had his own forces perform them. Instead, like a mafia boss, he provided protection, backup, and a reputation for brutality in return for a cut of the take. Away from the most highly coordinated part of the hostage-taking business, however, many an independent entrepreneur took advantage of civil war conditions to seize captives for ransom, rape, or revenge. Chechen hostage taking involved large elements of opportunism.

Opportunism occupies the center right section of our coordination–salience space: medium to low on coordination, but relatively high on salience. The mechanisms generating opportunism concentrate on activating previously available boundaries, stories, and social relations more than on incorporating multiple social sites into coordinated actions. Most opportunistic collective violence occurs when, as a consequence of shielding from routine surveillance and repression, individuals or clusters of individuals use immediately damaging means to pursue ends that would be unavailable or forbidden to them under other circumstances. Opportunism therefore includes most instances of kidnapping and hostage taking, piracy, enslavement, and gang rapes. It likewise includes a series of violent interactions that often take place during or in the immediate aftermath of major conflicts: hijacking, carjacking, looting, rape, and small-scale vengeance.

More so than in the cases of violent rituals and coordinated destruction, placing violent incidents in the category of opportunism requires judgments about the motives and social locations of individuals. Such judgments are always risky business in political analysis – and especially risky when the crucial actors are confused, frightened, enraged, drugged, or drunk. Speaking of the Liberian civil war, Stephen Ellis reports:

By April 1996 many fighters seemed to have no idea why they were fighting at all, other than to acquire loot. When asked why they were killing their own people, they would often mumble something about being "freedom fighters," but could not explain any further. One young man shot his friend in front of a UN official who asked him why he had done it. "He pissed me off," was the reply. (Ellis 1999: 127)

Vicious violence on the small scale: Why do people do it? If this book's task were to provide complete, plausible accounts of motivation and consciousness, now would be the time to confess defeat. No one has come close to identifying the necessary (much less the sufficient) motivational and phenomenological conditions for individual performance of self-serving damage. Luckily, we are trying instead to identify the social processes that make opportunism more or less possible – as well as more or less destructive. We are trying to learn why collective violence, when it occurs, takes the form of brawls, scattered attack, broken negotiations, violent ritual, coordinated destruction, or opportunism. Shifting distributions of motivations and consciousness will not in themselves provide the explanations we require.

We escape that blind alley, however, only to stumble into another barrier. What about governmental agents (and even rulers) who use government-controlled coercive means to seize other people's assets, settle scores with old enemies, extract sexual services, collect protection fees, purvey government resources, or sell confiscated property? At what point should we shrug off these practices as nothing but normal governmental behavior? Here we gain from resisting the temptation to distinguish (legitimate) force from (illegitimate) violence. To the extent that governmental agents do, indeed, use immediately damaging means to pursue ends that would be unavailable or forbidden to them under other circumstances, they are indeed engaging in collective violence. Whether that violence qualifies as opportunism depends on (a) how salient the damage is in all interactions between perpetrators and recipients of violence and (b) how much coordination links the performers of violence. To repeat: opportunism combines high salience with low to medium levels of coordination.

Mechanisms of Opportunism

Over a wide range of opportunistic violence, we see familiar mechanisms of:

- activation of available us–them boundaries;
- response to weakened, distracted, or failed repression;
- signaling spirals that communicate the current feasibility and effectiveness of generally risky practices and thereby alter the readiness of participants to face the risks in question; and
- selective retaliation for previously experienced wrongs.

Taken one by one, all of these mechanisms occur widely through the entire array of collective violence. We have already, for example, seen boundary activation at work in violent rituals and coordinated destruction. But this particular combination of mechanisms appears with special frequency in the zone of high salience and low to medium coordination – the zone of opportunism. Neutralization or absence of the coordinating mechanisms activated by political entrepreneurs or centralized organizations (e.g., brokerage and certification) promotes opportunistic violence. As a consequence, boundaries, stories, and social relations favored by political entrepreneurs commonly give way to those already built into routine social life.

With high levels of coordination and similar levels of salience, collective violence qualifies not as opportunism but as coordinated destruction. State-run protection rackets often permit petty opportunism along their edges, but they generate collective violence chiefly in the forms of broken negotiations and coordinated destruction (Bayart, Ellis, & Hibou 1999; Stanley 1996). The purest cases of opportunistic collective violence initiated by government agents occur when the agents engage in predation that would bring them punishment from their own superiors if the superiors detected it – or if someone more powerful saw the superiors detecting it. By that standard, at least some of Chechen hostage taking and of Liberian shooting qualifies as pure opportunism.

Even more obviously than in the cases of violent rituals and coordinated destruction, opportunism coincides with the generation of inequality by means of exploitation and opportunity hoarding. Existing exploitation allows those who already benefit from inequality to use their power over subordinated populations in the acquisition of new resources, hence new means of exploitation. We have seen a brutal form of that process in Ugandan Joseph Kony's use of child soldiers to abduct more children for use as sexual slaves and child soldiers.

On their own, however, violent specialists often use their armed force and pugnacious prowess to establish new forms of exploitation, for example in the form of local protection rackets. Russian sportsmen and Indian *pehlwans* illustrate such capturing of new advantages by means of force. Similarly, beneficiaries within existing systems of opportunity hoarding – notably hoarding of weapons, drugs, and access to markets – frequently employ those advantages in extending their control over new resources as they come along. Inequality in means of coercion facilitates the extension of inequality to other resources. People who monopolize guns can also monopolize food, drugs, housing, and sexual services.

Regimes differ significantly in their hospitability to different kinds of opportunistic violence. High-capacity regimes, whether democratic or undemocratic, generally leave few high-value resources unclaimed; they exercise wide control over resources within their jurisdictions, guarantee property rights to their dominant classes, and back up those property rights with governmental coercion. Their array of prescribed and tolerated claim-making performances provides little opportunity for large-scale opportunism. As a consequence, within high-capacity regimes genuinely remunerative opportunism takes place chiefly when governmental agents themselves become opportunists, when governmental agents adopt policies of ghettoizing pariah populations instead of controlling them directly, when outlawed actors find ways of circumventing normal surveillance, and when that surveillance itself collapses in war, disaster, or revolution. Otherwise, the opportunistic violence of high-capacity regimes occurs at a small scale, and in the shadows.

Low-capacity regimes offer a wider range of possibilities for opportunism. Whether democratic or undemocratic, they remain susceptible to unauthorized sequestering of resources by violent specialists as well as to seizure or damage of persons and property along the edges of authorized political claim making. As the findings of Collier and Hoeffler (2001) indicate, especially vulnerable are low-capacity undemocratic regimes that combine portable resources of significant value on world markets with large diasporas. (The diasporas probably play a dual role, supporting dissident movements within their home countries and facilitating transit of illicitly acquired resources from those countries.) But low-capacity democratic regimes also invite both small-scale racketeering and forms of political struggle that facilitate private vengeance, pleasure seeking, and profit taking.

A nicely paradoxical example comes from European experience with mercenary soldiers. Between roughly 1400 and 1700, many European rulers who were drawing cash revenues from capitalist expansion built up their military power by hiring mercenaries (Contamine 1984; Corvisier 1976; Covini 2000; Fontenay 1988; Ingrao 1987; Mallett 1974; Redlich 1964–1965; Ribot Garcia 2000; Tilly 1990). Entrepreneurs in such regions such as Ireland, Hesse, Switzerland, and Croatia made a business of recruiting, training, and renting out mercenaries. The paradox consisted in the fact that low-capacity states augmented their military capacity by using mercenaries to conquer others but, by so doing, made themselves beholden to violent specialists they could not easily control.

The balance was delicate: during the 1370s and early 1380s, when his armies were not fighting in the pay of great lords, the notorious English mercenary Sir John Hawkwood repeatedly pillaged towns around Florence. Yet he supported the Florentine oligarchy in its successful coup of 1382. Hawkwood then exacted a large price from his beneficiaries: exemption from taxes and a life pension. At his death in 1394, grateful oligarchs staged a huge public funeral for Hawkwood and commissioned a warlike mural of him, by Paolo Uccello, that is still visible in Florence's cathedral. While alive, Hawkwood had compensated Florence's city fathers by being available for forced loans and by channeling a significant portion of the booty he acquired elsewhere into the city (Caferro 1998: 174–5).

Booty flowing into Florence notably included wealth that Hawkwood extracted from Siena. Siena suffered more seriously from mercenaries than Florence and eventually gave up its independence to Milan in 1399 for the sake of military protection and relief from crushing debts accumulated for payoffs:

Rarely an employer of mercenary armies, Siena was repeatedly their victim. From 1342 to 1399 the city endured at least thirty-seven raids. Such regularity made the raids the most persistent problem faced by the commune in the second half of the fourteenth century. Siena was betrayed by a number of factors, the most prominent of which were its visual opulence and location. The city was conveniently located on the Via Francigena, the great medieval highway that led from France to Rome and was wedged between Florence and the lands of the pope, the two most frequent employers of mercenaries. Florentine use of mercenaries contributed significantly and directly to Siena's miseries. (Caferro 1998: xvi)

Although disbanded mercenaries often looted, raped, and assaulted on their own, mercenaries that remained under command commonly practiced a more coordinated form of opportunism resembling the work of Indian and Russian violent specialists: they *threatened* to loot, rape, and assault unless city fathers paid them off.

Governmental capacity, then, clearly affects the prevalence and character of opportunism. Does democracy also make a difference? The presence of relatively broad and equal rights, equal protection, and responsive government in democratic regimes diverts a share of disputes from private settlement into legal channels. On balance, these features of democratic politics inhibit opportunistic violence. Kidnapping, hostage taking, piracy, enslavement, hijacking, carjacking, looting, and small-scale or group vengeance by violent means all occur less frequently in democracies despite the greater wealth available in the average democracy. Citizens of low-capacity undemocratic regimes suffer the most from opportunistic violence, as they do from coordinated destruction.

The world's postsocialist division of labor is probably aggravating international differences in vulnerability to opportunistic violence. As disparities in income and wealth sharpen across the world, the attractions of capturing and selling off portable resources to rich people increase. In the same Caucasus region where hostage taking has become so prevalent since the mid-1990s, other opportunists are grabbing oil, heroin, and young women for sale to the highest bidders. In the hapless Democratic Republic of the Congo, paramilitary forces are killing for control of minerals that fetch enticing prices on the world's high-tech and luxury markets. Indonesian teak is enriching neither the Indonesian treasury nor the Indonesian people but rather warlords who have made lucrative deals with timber merchants. Once again the high ends of these businesses operate like governments, engaging directly in violence only to drive away rivals and enforce unpopular measures. But on the lower slopes of all these illicit enterprises, opportunistic violence proliferates.

Opportunism in and around Civil War

Like many other forms of collective violence, civil war concentrates in low-capacity undemocratic regimes. On the whole, in such regimes petty tyrants use coercion freely, governmental officials deploy violent punishments when they can catch their enemies, means of violence are widely distributed across other political actors, and ruling classes draw freely on governmental resources in pursuit of their own advantage. Despite the government's weak capacity, differences in advantage between ins and outs loom large in such regimes. Several consequences follow: currently excluded political actors have both the incentive and the opportunity to bid for control of some or all of the governmental apparatus; currently excluded actors can assemble violent specialists and arms with relative ease; and outside powers have both incentives and opportunities to intervene – especially when the government's current jurisdiction contains valuable, detachable resources. All these circumstances promote outbreaks of civil war.

Civil war is a form of coordinated destruction, but opportunism often occurs in its interstices and sequels. Rwanda's struggles from 1990 to 1994 perfectly illustrate this cruel complementarity. Observers impressed or stunned by the government's involvement in the genocide of 1994 might object that the government actually showed high capacity. But such an objection confuses central control over governmental agencies with those agencies' control over resources, activities, and populations within the government's territories; when it came to effective control over Rwandan resources, the central government of the 1990s had little to show. Close observer and aid administrator Peter Uvin has argued, in fact, that by the 1990s the international development community in Rwanda had essentially substituted itself for the central government with regard to the provision of public services (Uvin 1998; see also Uvin 2001; Jones 1995; de Waal 1997, chap. 9).

During the period from 1990 to 1994, Rwanda endured a revolutionary situation. Two military forces – the predominantly Hutu Rwandan army and the predominantly Tutsi Rwanda Patriotic Front – prevailed in different regions and intermittently warred for control of regions where they did not prevail. Both forces expanded rapidly; the Rwandan national military budget rose by 181 percent between 1990 and 1992 alone (Prunier 1995: 159). As of late 1993, a small United Nations peacekeeping force was trying to keep the two enemies apart while taking significant responsibility for public order in and around the capital, Kigali. Rwanda 1990–1994 qualifies all too well as a low-capacity undemocratic regime.

Civil war, genocide, and opportunistic collective violence had all started in Rwanda before the downing of President Habyarimana's aircraft on 6 April 1994. Table 6.1 offers an abbreviated chronology of events before and after that assassination. It makes clear that massacres of Tutsi by Hutu Power activists began soon after the predominantly Tutsi Rwanda Patriotic Front (RPF) invaded the country's northwest from Uganda in October 1990. It also shows that attacks on Tutsi and on opponents of Hutu Power accelerated each time the RPF made significant advances, the government moved toward including Tutsi in the regime, or the same government tried to exclude Hutu Power activists from the governing coalition.

The Coalition pour la Défense de la République (CDR) most consistently promoted anti-Tutsi action. But Hutu Power factions formed in all the regime's major political parties – including President Habyarimana's Mouvement Révolutionnaire National pour le Développement (MRND) – and eventually joined in the genocide (Mamdani 2001: 203, 209). As early as the Arusha peace talks of 1992, the crucial boundary was shifting from strictly Hutu–Tutsi toward Hutu Power versus everyone else; when Félicien Gatabazi, leader of the opposition Social Democratic party, denounced massacres in the Kibuye area that accelerated in August 1992, CDR leaders denounced him as an *ibyitso* – an accomplice of the enemy (Prunier 1995: 162).

Soon after arriving in late 1993, General Roméo Dallaire, Canadian commander of U.N. forces in Rwanda, saw mass killing on the way. Dallaire made repeated requests for military reinforcements and expanded authority to intervene, but U.N. headquarters in New York rebuffed all his requests (Des Forges et al. 1999: 141–79). Still, genocide itself had not yet begun. If the massacres had ceased at that point, we would cite Rwanda as another case of death squads à la El Salvador, East Timor, or Sri Lanka rather than of full-fledged genocide (Mamdani 2001, chap. 7).

In something like the way that the labels Puerto Rican and Dominican work in New York neighborhoods, the labels Hutu and Tutsi – with ample allowances for mixtures and uncertainties – certainly marked divisions within the Rwandan

Table 6.1. *Selected Chronology of Rwandan Conflicts, 1990–1994*

1 Oct 90	(Predominantly Tutsi) Rwandan Patriotic Front (RPF), first organized in 1987 partly in response to Rwandan exiles' loss of property rights within Uganda, invades northwest from Uganda, suffers extensive losses, but then reorganizes under Paul Kagame, back from military training in the U.S.
90–91	Scattered killings of Tutsi begin (e.g., 300 in Kibilira, October 1990).
92–94	Extensive flight and expulsion of Hutu from regions captured by RPF, for a total of perhaps a million refugees.
Mar–Apr 92	Hutu Power activists organize anti-Tutsi CDR (party) and Interahamwe (militia of governing party MRND).
12 Jul 92	Internationally sponsored peace talks begin in Arusha, Tanzania; killings of Tutsi accelerate thereafter.
15 Oct 92	After demonstrations by Hutu activists, Rwandan government repudiates recently signed peace settlement.
Jan 93–Mar 94	Rwanda imports about 580,000 machetes in addition to substantial small arms from France, the U.S., and elsewhere.
8 Feb 93	In violation of cease-fire, major RPF offensive begins, reaching within 23 km of Rwandan capital Kigali.
4 Aug 93	In Arusha, Rwanda's President Habyarimana signs peace treaty with RPF, establishing parliamentary system in Rwanda and (under pressure from negotiators) excluding Hutu hardliners from power.
8 Aug 93	Hutu Power radio-TV Milles Collines begins broadcasting anti-Tutsi messages.
Oct 93	In neighboring Burundi, newly elected Hutu president and thousands of Hutu massacred, with Tutsi-dominated army heavily involved in killing.
Nov 93	First battalion of U.N. peacekeeping mission arrives in Rwanda; Hutu Power forces begin systematic distribution of weapons to militants and militias; attacks on civilians and peacekeepers (especially Belgian) accelerate.
6 Apr 94	Habyarimana's airplane downed by suface-to-air missile as it approaches Kigali airport, killing him, the army chief-of-staff, and the president of Burundi; Hutu-dominated military forces seize government, assassinating prime minister and opposition leaders; almost instantly, roadblocks appear around Kigali and attacks on Tutsi begin (20,000 dead, mostly Tutsi, by 11 April).
7 Apr 94	RPF resumes attacks on Rwandan government forces; widespread killing of Tutsis and unaligned Hutus in Kigali and elsewhere, eventually totaling 500,000–800,000 deaths, perhaps 75 percent men and boys; women and girls raped by the thousands.
16–17 Apr 94	Coup leaders replace military chief-of-staff and regional prefects opposed to killings.
May 94	As RPF continues to advance, increased killing of Tutsi women and children, often previously spared; Hutu militias prey increasingly on fellow Hutu.
4 Jul 94	RPF, commanded by Paul Kagame, takes Kigali.
18 Jul 1994	Mass killing ends.

population of the 1990s; after all, Rwandan identification cards of the time carried explicitly ethnic designations (Prunier 2001: 112; Uvin 2002). (Even then, in everyday life the Hutu–Tutsi boundary marked less profound divisions than those separating ordinary Rwandans from the rich, powerful, French-speaking, Catholic, and mostly white *Bazungu*, both Rwandan and foreign; Uvin 1998: 16.) Unquestionably, Hutu Power political entrepreneurs and violent specialists deliberately activated the Hutu–Tutsi boundary in 1994. But the effective division between killers and killed actually separated Hutu Power activists and their collaborators, on one side, from everyone that opposed them, on the other.

As a result, some 50,000 Hutus died along with ten times as many of their Tutsi compatriots in the 1994 massacres. Mahmood Mamdani reports:

Kodjo Ankrah of Church World Action recounted to me what happened when soldiers entered a church in Ruhengeri and asked that Hutu step on one side, and Tutsi on another: "People refused; when they said, Tutsis this way, all moved. When they said Hutus that side, all moved." Eventually, soldiers killed them all, 200 to 300 people in all. Professionals who refused to join in the killing also met the same fate. Take, for example, the parents of François Nsansuwera, deputy attorney general under Habyarimana, later appointed to the same post under the RPF. Nsansuwera's father was a retired army officer. When thirty Hutu and Tutsi gathered to seek shelter at their house, the militia called in the army; all thirty, including his parents and father-in-law, were killed. Of his family of nine, Nsansuwera said only two survived, himself and a younger brother who had gone through Burundi to join the RPF. (Mamdani 2001: 219–20)

Us–them boundary activation rarely corresponds perfectly to the cognitive categories people employ in everyday life, even when those categories are fairly precise. Boundary activation is an organized political process.

Our task here is not to explain the Rwandan genocide, much less to explain all of Rwanda's collective violence from 1990 through 1994. Rather, it is to single out and explain the opportunistic violence that occurred amid civil war and organized genocide. The task brings its own complications, since participants in Rwanda's violence so regularly raped, stole, extorted, or seized their victims' property, and since organizers frequently used promises of booty as incentives for reluctant participants. How then can we distinguish opportunism from coordinated destruction?

We are looking for low-coordination, high-salience violence that occurs when, as a consequence of shielding from routine surveillance and repression, individuals or clusters of individuals use immediately damaging means to pursue ends that would be unavailable or forbidden to them under other circumstances. In the course of civil war, organized attacks on enemies, or genocide, to the extent that individuals and small groups also engaged in rape, plunder, or revenge without central coordination, we can reasonably call their actions opportunistic violence. That happened frequently in Rwanda, especially as the RPF's advance broke up central Hutu Power control over Rwanda's provinces.

In Rwanda, a great deal of opportunistic violence occurred between 1990 and 1994. It took the forms of rape, plunder, revenge, and extortion. Rape figured prominently. Alison Des Forges reports "tens of thousands" of women and girls raped during the genocide:

Many assailants insulted [Tutsi] women for their supposed arrogance while they were raping them. If assailants decided to spare the lives of the women, they regarded them as prizes they had won for themselves or to be distributed to subordinates who had performed well in killing Tutsi. Some kept these women for weeks or months in sexual servitude. In the commune of Taba, women and girls were raped at the communal office, with the knowledge of the burgomaster. At the Kabgayi nursing school, soldiers ordered the directress to give them the young women students as *umusanzu*, a contribution to the war effort. The directress, a Hutu, Dorothée Mukandanga, refused and was killed. (Des Forges et al. 1999: 215)

According to Lisa Sharlach, Rwandan rapists also deliberately transmitted HIV to their victims (Sharlach 2002: 117). Although assailants may have received sexual gratification from raping their captives, Rwandan rapes also involved bravado, sadism, humiliation of enemy women, and spiting of their male relatives; the frequency with which rapes took place with victims' family members as forced witnesses and with other attackers as cheering audiences suggests as much. In the judgment of the U.N.-backed tribunal charged with prosecuting perpetrators of Rwanda's genocide,

[s]exual violence was an integral part of the process of destruction, specifically targeting Tutsi women and specifically contributing to their destruction and to the destruction of the Tutsi group as a whole.... Sexual violence was a step in the process of destruction of the Tutsi group – destruction of the spirit, of the will to live, and of life itself. (Pillay 2001: 173)

In addition to coerced sexual intercourse, Rwandan predators also imposed a variety of other sexually oriented and demeaning punishments: cutting off of breasts; mutilation of genitals; insertion of bottles, gun barrels, sharpened sticks, or other objects into vaginas; and (for men) castration. Such brutal treatment usually preceded killing.

In May 1994, as RPF forces advanced toward victory, militia members turned increasingly to killing off their enslaved concubines (Des Forges et al. 1999: 296). By that time, Hutu Power central authorities were losing control of their militias as rape, booty, and revenge became more central to the activities of militiamen and of armed deserters from the Rwandan army. At the genocide's beginning, gangs of petty criminals had enthusiastically joined the work of killing and dispossessing Tutsis (Uvin 1998: 219), but by its end the process was reversing: a great many participants were behaving more like bandits than like bloodthirsty ideologues. Just as central incorporation moved most of Rwanda's violence temporarily into the zone of coordinated destruction, disintegration of central control increased the prevalence of opportunism.

Nevertheless, pillage accompanied the genocide's earliest phases. American ethnographer Christopher Taylor was living in Kigali with his Tutsi fiancée when Habyarimana's plane went down on 6 April. That night, raiders attacked the house of Liberal Party leader Landouald Ndasingwa, two doors away from Taylor's house. They murdered Ndasingwa, his Canadian wife, their children, and his wife's aging mother. The next morning, Taylor watched looters carrying the Ndasingwa's belongings down the street (Taylor 1999: 13). The pattern continued into July: when death squads either killed all a dwelling's residents or drove them away from home, squad members took valuables as just compensation for their effort.

Fighting often broke out between Hutu who competed to take over fields, crops, and cattle of refugees and assassination victims (Des Forges et al. 1999: 299). At Rwanda's innumerable roadblocks, armed men who checked identification often demanded valuables or money as their tolls. Opportunism entered the very act of murder, as victims paid their captors to be shot quickly rather than impaled, hacked, bludgeoned, or bled to death. Only those with a good deal of money could buy off their executioners, and even they often died in a second round of suffering. Some Hutu married to Tutsi paid all they had in order to avoid being compelled to kill their own spouses (Prunier 1995: 257).

Clearly the standard package of opportunism-promoting mechanisms was at work in Rwanda between 1990 and 1994. *Activation of available us–them boundaries* obviously facilitated opportunism; political entrepreneurs, furthermore, played visible parts in defining and activating the relevant boundaries, building on widely available cultural divisions between Hutu and Tutsi but recasting them so that reluctant Hutu fell on the dangerous side of the us–them line. Having activated those boundaries, national leaders lost control of their employment in opportunistic rape, plunder, and revenge – so much so that many Hutu regional leaders died accused of sympathizing with the enemy or of being disguised Tutsis.

As such cases indicate, *response to weakened, distracted, or failed repression* likewise promoted opportunism in the course of Rwanda's civil war and genocide. Especially in war zones and in later phases of the genocide, central coordination collapsed, and various forms of banditry became increasingly prevalent. Like demobilized mercenaries in other wars, squads of Interahamwe became free-booting predators.

Rwanda's bloody history also shows us *signaling spirals* that communicated the current feasibility and effectiveness of generally risky practices, and thereby altered the readiness of participants to face the risks in question. Here the process began with the coercion of many Rwandans into killing their neighbors or even their own family members. But it then spiraled into a general recognition of killing justified by defense of Hutu Power as a means of acquiring previously forbidden goods and services.

Finally, *selective retaliation for previously experienced wrongs* occurred repeatedly throughout the period from 1990 to 1994, both at the national level of revenge for Tutsi preeminence under colonial rule and at the local level of vengeance stemming from previous disputes among individuals or households. Indeed, selective retaliation continued after the RPF pushed the major Hutu Power military forces out of Rwanda in mid-1994; the forces that retreated into eastern Zaïre continued anti-Tutsi actions both inside Zaïre and in raids across the Rwandan frontier (de Waal 1997, chap. 10). The four mechanisms – boundary activation, response to failed repression, signaling spirals, and selective retaliation – figure so prominently in Rwanda that they seem like little more than a general description of what occurred. But that is the point: together these mechanisms promote the low-coordination, high-salience forms of collective violence we call opportunism.

Opportunism under Other Sorts of Regimes

Variation among different types of regime strongly affects the coordination of violent action, the involvement of political entrepreneurs, and the political standing of violent specialists. It also affects the range of opportunities for individual and small-group aggrandizement by means of violence at the edges of major political struggles. But within these limits, opportunistic violence varies less in substance from regime to regime than do violent rituals, coordinated destruction, and broken negotiations. Everywhere it occurs chiefly at the margins of existing political controls, either within perimeters that authorities leave unpoliced or at points of breakdown in current systems of surveillance and control. Everywhere it draws in existing bands of nongovernmental specialists in violence. And everywhere its principal components are profiteering and revenge.

Instead of going round the full cycle – from Rwanda's low-capacity undemocratic regime to low-capacity democratic, high-capacity democratic, and high-capacity undemocratic regimes – we may as well move directly to the polar case from low-capacity undemocratic Rwanda: the high-capacity democratic United States. Let us turn to the looting and burning that often occurs at the temporal and geographic edges of those urban uprisings authorities usually call "riots."

American ghetto rebellions of the 1960s provide graphic examples. President Lyndon Johnson's National Commission on the Causes and Prevention of Violence (chaired by Milton Eisenhower, brother of former U.S. President Dwight Eisenhower and former president of Kansas State, Penn State, and Johns Hopkins universities) placed those rebellions in quantitative perspective:

from mid-1963 to mid-1968, protests or counter-protests and ghetto riots involved more than two million persons. Civil rights demonstrations mobilized 1.1 million, anti-war demonstrations 680,000, and ghetto riots an estimated 200,000. Nine thousand casualties resulted, including some 200 deaths. Ghetto riots were responsible for most of these casualties, including 191 deaths. Almost all other deaths, an estimated 23, resulted from white terrorism against blacks and civil rights workers. These casualty figures are for a five-year period, and apart from the ghetto riots, they are comparatively infinitesimal. While they are not to be condoned, in a country with 250,000 aggravated assaults and 12,000 homicides per year, group protests cannot be considered as accounting for a major part of the deliberate violence we experience. (National Commission 1969: 59)

As measured by casualties, ghetto rebellions of the 1960s gave the United States its most extensive concentrated domestic collective violence of the twentieth century.

The events in question commonly began as confrontations between police and local residents in the course of a routine police action that went awry. The vast Los Angeles conflagration of August 1965 began, for example, with the Highway Patrol arrest of Marquette Fry, who was speeding in his mother's Buick after having a few drinks with friends, a block from his home in Watts (Conot 1967). A large street confrontation ensued, with multiple arrests and plenty of additional police. As the police drove away from that first incident, one of the spectators (who had experienced rough treatment from police on earlier occasions) threw a soda bottle at a police car. Then people began tossing rocks, bottles, wood, and metal at whatever vehicles passed through the intersection of Avalon and Imperial. All this happened toward 8 P.M. on a warm summer evening. For the next hour, local people gathered on the street, discussed the incident, and occasionally lobbed objects at passing vehicles.

After 9 P.M., radio, television, and newspaper reporters started arriving, as police sent in plainclothes observers and began setting up a staging area nearby. About an hour later, two squads of ten police each began pushing people away from the intersection of Avalon and Imperial, but further down the street crowds of youngsters continued to taunt the police and throw an occasional rock. After another hour, staff members of the Los Angeles County Human Relations Commission arrived at the scene and persuaded the police to withdraw their forces in the hope that people on the street would give up and go home. The tactic did not work. With the police gone, young people accelerated their attacks on vehicles and began to beat up news reporters as well. More and more people joined the destruction inside Watts, calls for help accelerated, and police returned.

As the conflict spread, open confrontations between police (later, National Guard) and Los Angeles citizens occurred through much of the Watts area. In between those street battles occurred widespread smashing, burning, and looting of neighborhood stores. Many people attacked or looted stores in which they had been doing business. "It dawned on me," one churchgoing woman told her pastor after the violence had ended, "as I was passing a certain store, that I have been paying on my present television set for more than five years. And [therefore] that store owed me five televisions. So I got three and I still believe that they owe me two" (Fogelson 1971: 86). Although parts of the Watts conflict qualify as scattered attacks, broken negotiations, and coordinated destruction, these activities in the interstices qualify as opportunism. They resulted from the characteristic combination of boundary activation, response to failed repression, signaling spirals, and selective retaliation.

A few years after Watts, Swedish ethnographer Ulf Hannerz spent two years (August 1966 to July 1968) in a predominantly black neighborhood of Washington, D.C., learning about ghetto life. When the news of Martin Luther King's assassination reached that neighborhood, crowds gathered, and local people attacked police who arrived to establish control over the streets. For two days, looting and burning occurred. On the second day (Friday):

Some groups went downtown but looting there was rather limited – as we have noted once before, it was particularly men's fashion stores that were hit – and there was hardly any burning outside the ghetto, where most of it continued to be concentrated on the main shopping streets. Some groups seemed to concentrate on going around "opening up" stores which had closed early – that is, they broke doors and windows to leave the way in open to looters. This made it possible for a great many to join in who had qualms about taking the first step themselves. One young mother said afterwards: "Well, you could see all the stuff lying there and all those people going in and out, and somebody was gonna take it, so I thought I could as well get some for myself." (Hannerz 1969: 173)

Fire bombers aimed chiefly at white-owned businesses, but in a high-density area where many black tenants lived in apartments above such businesses, fire wiped out many black businesses and residences as well.

Opportunism of this sort often incites observers, analysts, and critics to concentrate on motives, hence on morality, thence on rights and obligations: If people smash, burn, and steal, can they speak seriously about demanding their rights? In the perspective of contentious politics, however, it is striking how many causal processes opportunism shares with scattered attack, broken negotiations, and coordinated destruction. To say so is not to say that all participants in opportunistic collective violence share the resentment of black people in Los Angeles and Washington during the 1960s. On the contrary, it is to say that the cognitive mechanisms generating resentment in Los Angeles and Washington interact with relational and environmental mechanisms that couple with quite different cognitive mechanisms in other forms of contentious politics.

Detroit, 1967

For sheer destructiveness, Detroit's uprising of July 1967 surpassed all other American urban conflicts of the 1960s and perhaps all other similar U.S. events of the twentieth century. According to the American Insurance Association, the toll included 2,509 stores looted, burned, or destroyed (as compared with fewer than a thousand in the Watts conflict). The damaged businesses included:

611 supermarkets, food, and grocery stores;
537 cleaners and laundries;
326 clothing, department, and fur stores;
285 liquor stores, bars, and lounges;
240 drug stores;
198 furniture stores (Fine 1989: 291).

By the end, 7,231 people had been arrested (almost two thirds for looting) and 43 people had died. Of the dead, law enforcement personnel killed 30, against four deaths of their own. The remaining nine met their deaths through store owners, a private guard, other assailants, asphyxiation in a torched store, or accident.

Like the majority of large 1960s ghetto rebellions, Detroit's massive struggle began with misfire of a police action in the context of many previous police–civilian conflicts. In the face of 1965's emergencies elsewhere, Detroit's police force had adopted a "riot plan" that included a strong initial show of force at the site of police–civilian confrontation combined with containment of the affected area, dispersal of threatening crowds, and intervention to keep them from regrouping. In August 1966, the tactic worked when a crowd gathered as police started to arrest three young black men for blocking traffic.

Soon after bottle-throwing and window-breaking began in the 1966 incident, police headquarters sent in 150 to 175 officers to back up the three squad cars on the scene, outnumbering the roughly 100 people in the gathering. Along a one-mile strip of Kercheval Avenue, black youths threw rocks, broke windows, attempted a fire bombing, and attacked two white men, but did no looting. Police cleared the streets and arrested some black militants who were carrying weapons in their cars. When rock throwing and fire bombing started again the following night, police acted even more quickly to disperse the crowd, making 43 arrests. Heavy rain helped them (Fine 1989: 137–41).

Quick-response police tactics did not prevent a huge conflagration – both figuratively and literally – the following summer. Late on the evening of Saturday 22 July 1967, Detroit police began raids on five "blind pigs": unlicensed after-hours drinking and gambling spots. As their fifth target, police chose the United Community and Civic League on Twelfth Street, a major thoroughfare of black Detroit. After a foiled attempt by a plainclothes officer to enter the League around 10 P.M., toward 4 A.M. on Sunday the 23rd a vice squad finally succeeded in breaking into the bar. When police tried to remove the 85 arrested partygoers from the building, some 200 people gathered and began throwing missiles at the officers. After they had loaded their paddy wagons and suffered one broken cruiser window, the police withdrew from Twelfth Street. When the officer in charge of the precinct drove into the area, he found several hundred people milling on the spot, and someone heaved a chunk of concrete against his head. As his driver raced the car away, people on the street started breaking windows. Looting and burning began soon afterwards.

After about three hours, a police commando unit tried to sweep Twelfth Street, but the two squads of twelve officers each simply moved through a crowd that re-formed behind them. An attempt to cordon off the area fared no better. Nor did a peace patrol of black leaders calm things down. By 1 P.M., thousands of looters filled the streets as at least four big fires roared. At first, black property owners were able to defend their stakes:

State Representative James Del Rio, a Negro, was camping out in front of a building he owned when two small boys, neither more than 10 years old, approached. One prepared to throw a brick through a window. Del Rio stopped him: "That building belongs to me," he said.

"I'm glad you told me, baby, because I was just about to bust you in!" the youngster replied. (National Advisory Commission 1968: 91)

A self-identified looter interviewed by Nathan Caplan in November 1967 called the event "a race riot because the negroes was trying to get the goods from the white folks because the white folks own everything and they [blacks] were just trying to get something so they can own it" (Fine 1989: 352). Racial boundaries did separate the overwhelmingly black looters and fire bombers from the overwhelmingly white fire and police departments. But opportunism crossed racial lines.

The National Advisory Commission on Civil Disorders (the "Kerner Commission," for its chair, Governor Otto Kerner of Illinois) reported that looters soon stopped sparing establishments displaying Soul Brother signs, and arsonists sometimes started fires only to see them consume their own properties; perhaps two thirds of all burned buildings caught fire from adjacent structures rather than being torched deliberately (National Advisory Commission 1968: 92). Though a number of black people on the street shouted anti-white slogans, though some complained to black leaders and law enforcement officers that they were supporting the wrong side, and though (at the start) opportunists concentrated on white-owned properties, the color line soon dissolved.

Following departmental policy (although apparently not on explicit orders from the center), police did not use their guns until late that night. Without intervening, police actually stood behind barricades in sight of attacks on property. During that period, they acted mainly to stop attacks on persons, including fire fighters. Not until the arrival of state police (from late afternoon of the 23rd onward), National Guard detachments (starting around 5 P.M. on the 23rd but mostly arriving on the 24th), and U.S. Army units (toward midnight on the 24th) on the streets did authorities start containing looters, snipers, and fire bombers. Even then, sniper fire reached its peak on the 25th, shooting on both sides continued into the 26th, and troops were patrolling Detroit streets until the 1st of August.

A total of about 17,000 police, National Guardsmen, and U.S. Army troops eventually took part in quelling Detroit's insurrection. Frightened or trigger-happy police and National Guardsmen killed a majority of the 43 people who died in the uprising. (The 2,700 regular army troops, in contrast, fired only 201 rounds of ammunition through their entire stay in Detroit, killing one person: National Advisory Commission 1968: 100, 107.) After that, authorities had to negotiate a delicate balance among warning against renewed violence, processing thousands of arrestees, and maintaining a semblance of justice (Balbus 1973; Bergesen 1980).

Most people who took part in Detroit's 1967 rising were not insurgents in any strong sense of the word. The word might apply to people on the street who challenged the police early Sunday morning, to a small number of snipers, and to some fire bombers. Most participants entered stores and took away merchandise;

they looted. They looted when they saw that law enforcement had disappeared and that store owners had lost control over their premises. In fact, even with police officers on hand, people looted when they saw that the police were outnumbered, under orders not to shoot, and preoccupied with other duties.

Interviewed by the reporters of "Meet the Press" on 30 July, Detroit's mayor Jerome Cavanagh answered a question by recalling his own interviews of Detroit police officers as looting subsided:

One, a patrolman, very interestingly told me just the other day – he said he was one of a squad guarding a fire company that was fighting a fire early on 12th Street, early that Sunday morning, and the mob was all around them, looting down the street. The sergeant in command of that squad ordered them not to fire at those looters, many of the looters being mothers and fathers with seven- and eight-year-old children, walking along in ... sort of a carnival-like spirit, garnering up groceries and shoes and things like that. (Holli 1976: 226)

Not all looters, to be sure, were families on outings. Some professional criminals took advantage of the occasion to grab high-priced portable goods, but the bulk of the looters were local people who responded to an unprecedented opportunity. Interviewed later, a black woman who had a decent factory job reported that

[s]he had come to the riot area where she observed people looting a supermarket and packing their cars with food. "Wow! Free food!" She thought, "I'm going to get some too." She realized as she began helping herself to groceries, "I'm not shopping; I'm stealing!" "I knew I was wrong, but I wasn't thinking about Christianity at the time. I just wanted some free food .... I didn't have to steal. But I figured, 'What the hell? If I didn't take it, somebody else will.'... But I still didn't want my children to think it was alright to steal." (Fine 1989: 345)

At the time, many well-meaning interpreters (myself included) mapped American ghetto rebellions into something vaguely called "protest." We combined the (correct) case that American blacks had plenty to complain about with the (incorrect) case that just grievances explained the whole course of events (see Button 1978; Thompson 2000).

In fact, many black property owners and militants (the two did not much overlap) found Detroiters' opportunism appalling and tried to dampen it. Wayne State University student Earthel Green had participated in civil rights demonstrations in his native Atlanta. He went to Twelfth Street looking for a "true revolt" but found the looters deeply disappointing. "I wanted to see the people really rise up in revolt," he told Kerner Commission staff members.

Opportunism

"When I saw the first person coming out of the store with things in his arms, I really got sick to my stomach and wanted to go home. Rebellion against the white suppressors is one thing, but one measly pair of shoes or some food completely ruins the whole concept." (National Advisory Commission 1968: 93; see also Fine 1989: 347)

Green later volunteered to help fire fighters; he received a citation from Detroit's Fire Department for his aid.

Opportunism's Mechanisms

Once we distinguish clearly between the initial incidents and later interactions of American ghetto rebellions, we can see the importance of the four major opportunism-promoting mechanisms: us–them boundary activation, response to diminished repression, signaling spirals, and selective retaliation. In Detroit's uprising, the selectivity of retaliation raises the greatest doubts. As compared with Rwanda's opportunistic violence, Detroit's looting and burning lacked clear targeting. At least in the conflict's early stages, however, aggrieved blacks focused their attacks on the persons and properties of whites within predominantly black neighborhoods.

The comparison between Rwanda and Detroit brings out the significance of coordination as a background to opportunism. In Rwanda, the initiation of killing and the connection of different sites by anti-Tutsi militias produced a degree of national coordination never faintly approached by American ghetto revolts of the 1960s. As a consequence, ironically and tragically, the Rwandan government's central control over repression diminished rapidly. Free-wheeling militia units, local residents, and bandits all joined in the use of violence to damage and seize persons and property for their own advantage or satisfaction. The advance of RPF forces toward Kigali aggravated that disintegration of central control. In their own retreat, Hutu Power leaders deliberately promoted the exodus of Hutu populations from RPF-controlled areas to disrupt subsequent RPF rule (de Waal 1997, chap. 9). Although we will never know exactly what proportion of Rwanda's assaults, murders, and seizures of property one could reasonably assign to opportunism, the destruction wrought by opportunism in Rwanda surely outweighed Detroit's 2,509 damaged stores and 43 deaths from all causes.

Just as clearly, however, these lethal instances of opportunism differed in character from brawls – occasions on which, within a previously nonviolent gathering, two or more persons begin attacking each other or each other's property.

149

Some analysts of violence take the brawl as the prototype and fundamental building block of all collective violence, the case in which individual propensities to aggression achieve their most direct expression. Although individual-level variation does show up clearly in brawls, we have already learned enough about the social processes shaping violence to doubt that brawls represent collective violence as a whole. Let us look at brawling as a social process.

7

Brawls

Road Rage as Brawling

In his testimony before the U.S. House Subcommittee on Transportation and Infrastructure (17 July 1997), psychologist Leon James from the University of Hawaii vividly reconstructed the steps in an actual episode of road rage that took place near Cincinnati, Ohio, on 27 November 1996.

1. Woman, 24-year-old mother of two in Cincinnati, driving alone in a GrandAm, is following a 29-year-old woman driver in a VW. In front of them are several cars behind a truck going 35 mph. The GrandAm pulls into the left lane in order to pass and speeds up to 55 mph.
2. The VW suddenly pulls out into the left lane, in front of the GrandAm, going 20 mph slower and forcing the GrandAm driver to apply the brakes suddenly.
3. The VW gradually overtakes the slow truck, passes it, and pulls back into the right lane.
4. The GrandAm, still in the left lane, now overtakes the VW, honks several times, makes obscene gestures, and flashes her lights as signs of outrage ("to let her know that she almost caused an accident just then").
5. The VW driver responds by displaying her second finger (meaning "fuck you" or "up yours") and shaking her head.
6. The GrandAm now tries to pull ahead in the left lane in order to reenter the right lane, but the VW accelerates, blocking the way.
7. The GrandAm slows down and pulls in behind the VW, keeping up the pressure by tailgating dangerously.

8. The GrandAm suddenly pulls out into the left lane again, overtakes and cuts off the VW, then gives her a "brake job," slamming on the brakes to punish the VW driver behind her.

9. The VW driver applies her brakes suddenly and they lock, causing her to veer sideways to the right where her car hits a truck parked on the shoulder. She is thrown from the car, taken to the hospital where she recovers from surgery, but she is pregnant and her unborn child dies.

10. The GrandAm driver continues her trip to the office where she tells her supervisor that she has been in an accident, that "the other driver had it coming" and that "she wasn't going to take **** from no one." Later, she is arrested and charged with vehicular homicide for causing the death of an unborn child. She receives an eighteen-month prison term. (Adapted from James 1997: 15–18.)

Evidence presented at the 1997 trial included a photograph of the dead six-month fetus; the GrandAm driver received Ohio's first conviction under a new fetal protection law. The story did not end there. The convicted driver (an administrative assistant and website designer in a wireless communication company) received a release from prison after five months to take care of her 20-month-old daughter, who had suffered brain damage from a tumor. The victim and her husband later sued the convicted woman for being underinsured, claiming that her automobile liability coverage of $25,000 met only a tenth of their $228,000 in medical expenses. Road rage produces plenty of damage.

The term "road rage" only became current during the 1990s, but the phenomenon of brawling by automobile has been with us ever since horses, streetcars, bicycles, automobiles, and pedestrians began disputing public rights of way. As Table 7.1 (which includes the Cincinnati incident) shows, it is by no means a peculiarly American phenomenon. All over the world, drivers who somehow offend one another frequently either use their vehicles to damage each other or stop and attack each other directly. Where reports give sufficient details, they almost always reveal an escalation from small violations to larger ones, with both sides taking increasingly dangerous actions. The fetus-killing Cincinnati crash resulted from a clear escalation beginning with no more than insulting gestures.

Despite the implications of some language in Table 7.1, lethal road rage incidents seldom involve a single angry aggressor and an innocent victim; both sides typically contribute to the violent outcome. For small advantages – for example, one car length in a traffic jam – people take large risks. Short of direct damage, they offer demeaning gestures, shout insults, and engage in maneuvers that threaten each other's safety. They brawl.

Table 7.1. *Some Road Rage Incidents, 1996–2000*

Atlanta, Georgia: A 2-year-old toddler was shot through the neck by an irate motorist engaged in an argument over a road incident with the toddler's father.

Denver, Colorado: A 51-year-old man used a .25-caliber semi-automatic pistol to kill a 32-year-old bicyclist who cut him off on the road.

Detroit, Michigan: A 34-year-old man said he was attacked with a club by another motorist after the two drivers stopped on the road to confront each other.

Cincinnati, Ohio: A 24-year-old woman cut in front of a 29-year-old pregnant woman and slammed on her brakes in an irate gesture following an increasingly angry and risky interaction between the two drivers. The mother-to-be lost control of her car, resulting in a collision with a parked truck that killed her unborn child.

Florida: A 41-year-old man who pulled into an exact change lane at a toll both was shot and killed as he exited his truck to confront an irate driver behind him who was annoyed at the first man's delay in paying the toll.

Mississauga, Canada: A driver of a van was run over by a pickup truck during the truck driver's fit of road rage.

London, England: Two drivers came to blows over who was going to use the car wash first at a service station.

Jerusalem: The stabbing death of a 36-year-old driver occurred after he asked another driver not to scratch his car, and the knifing of a 50-year-old man by a 19-year-old ensued when the elder driver honked his car horn at the younger driver. A 28-year-old man was charged in the beating death of a 46-year-old man who he claimed cut him off on the road; the younger man killed the older one as the elder sat behind the steering wheel of his car.

Ireland: A car driver became angry after a bus overtook him on the road; the car driver pulled in front of the bus, forced it to stop, and attacked it.

New Zealand: A 35-year-old driver became irate when he felt he was being followed too closely by another vehicle; he assaulted the other driver through his open car window.

Malaysia: A 30-year-old man who stabbed another man to death over an incident of road rage was sentenced to ten years in prison.

China: A 44-year-old police officer who killed a 28-year-old man in a fit of road rage was sentenced to death.

India: A popular skating instructor used his vehicle to run over, crush, and kill another man with whom he argued over an incident on the road. Another angry motorist killed a young girl and dumped her body in a drain. A young man on a scooter "thrashed" a couple on another scooter because he was enraged that they stopped at a yellow caution light instead of proceeding through it.

Source: Adapted from K. M. Scott (2000: 2–3).

In a remarkable chapter titled "Pissed Off in L.A.," Jack Katz analyzes about 150 interviews during which drivers reported their own experiences with road rage. He puzzles over testimony of the following kind.

Jan, who lives with her husband and two children in Orange County and works as an athletic coach at a major university, is late to a practice as she drives her red Corvette convertible with a stick shift along a curvy road in Palos Verdes. At a stop sign, a fellow in front of her who is slow to depart irritates her. As she drives behind him, she finds that he slows up. She waits for an opportunity to pass and as they approach a long curve she downshifts forcefully to second, accelerates, and pulls out into the lane of oncoming traffic, only to find that he speeds up, preventing her from passing until they have driven in parallel around a long curve. A few moments later, she stops her car, "dead in the road," forcing him to stop behind her. She walks briskly to his car, puts her head through his window and yells, " 'You ASSHOLE! You could have killed me!!!' " He responds with " 'Shut up, you stupid CUNT!' " Jan immediately "smacked him across the face." After speeding off, she "could not believe she hit the guy." " 'That guy could have chased me and pulled a gun on me and shot me.' " (Katz 1999: 20)

Clearly, not all brawling pits drunken young men against each other. Collective violence qualifies as brawling when, within a previously nonviolent gathering, two or more persons begin attacking each other or each other's property. Although road rage stretches the meaning of "gathering," it certainly qualifies as small-scale, low-coordination, and high-salience collective violence.

Most angry interchanges among drivers stop short of physical damage and seizure of persons or property. But many of them include threats (however serious) of violence, and participants cannot always control whether they give or receive direct damage. To simplify a supremely sophisticated analysis, Katz portrays participants in road rage as engaging in awkward interaction, seeking to gain attention and respect for their personal projects, even to restore what they regard as the proper order of relations between themselves (as expressed by the vehicles they drive) and adjacent drivers. When a first signal does not accomplish what they want, they grow angry and escalate. They grimace, shout, flash lights, honk horns, make ostentatious gestures, or maneuver their cars to signal indignation. Frightened passengers in their vehicles often try to stop them.

Baffled communication generates danger. Katz tells the story of Ralph, an employee of a Beverly Hills architectural firm, who is driving his girl friend and his brother to Las Vegas. At 70 mph on a steep mountain road, the driver of a van behind him flashes high beams and tries to pass. Ralph slows down deliberately. When they reach a wider part of the road and the van succeeds in passing, its driver gives Ralph the finger and cuts in close. Ralph flashes his car's high beams at the van, speeds up, passes, and again slows down dramatically. He resists his passengers' pleas to stop:

I didn't respond to their comments. I looked at my girlfriend to the right and noticed that she was holding on to the handle on the passenger door. I didn't care though. I didn't care if I was scaring her and my brother. I felt my face really flushed as I kept trying to catch up to the van. As I was driving, I was cussing the guy out at the top of my lungs. I said things like, "You fucking asshole! Who do you think you are? You don't own the fucking road! I'll show you who owns the fucking road!" Immediately after the incident, I looked at my girlfriend. She was shaking her head in disapproval and told me that my temper is exactly like my father's temper. (Katz 1999: 32)

After the fact, drivers themselves often express amazement, confusion, and embarrassment at their own behavior. Caught up in the logic of baffled competition, they transgress limits they would ordinarily respect and enforce. After the fact, they regularly explain their risky behavior as an effect of uncontrollable anger; hence the label "road rage." But the process generating the anger consists of social interaction that commonly begins with no more than the usual anxieties of driving on crowded roads.

Road rage provides a valuable limiting case for the study of brawls as collective violence. It transmutes the highly routine and generally nonviolent interactions of highway traffic into infliction of damage. It rarely lasts more than a few minutes. Most participants flee the scene as soon as they can. Although drivers certainly differ in their overall levels of aggression, drivers involved in road-rage incidents do most of their driving without direct damage to others. Yet they draw on a shared store of signals, understandings, and stories – frequently declaring and acting out their versions of proper behavior to passengers or witnesses.

In all these regards, episodes of road rage caricature common features of brawls: rapid mutation from routine nonviolent interaction, quick termination and dispersal, operation through conventional understandings and signals, and generation of anger. They move from phase to phase through signaling spirals during which even infuriated participants usually remain aware of how the contest is going and react accordingly. The spread of automobiles has certainly introduced new understandings, practices, technologies, dangers, and anxieties, but long before the automobile the intersection of different transportation modes produced other sorts of brawls (see e.g. Schneider 1980; Stowell 1999). As in the case of opportunism, the effective way to reduce highway brawling significantly would not be to alter the moods of drivers, much less to instill ideas of proper driving in them, but to intervene in their social interactions.

Brawling parallels violent ritual and sometimes emerges from violent ritual, but nonetheless it has some distinct properties. The differences stem from significantly lower levels of coordination in brawls than in violent rituals. Violent rituals stand out for their following of known scripts, fixing of competition's stakes, drawing of sharp perimeters around their central conflicts, distinguishing sharply between proper and improper participants, objects, and means, establishing clear distinctions among spectators, monitors, and participants, and generally reducing the uncertainty that promotes cross-boundary violence. Brawls, in contrast, commonly feature weak scripts, shifting stakes, blurred boundaries, no monitors, and great uncertainty. All these features result from lower levels of coordination.

Despite appearances, these features do not mean that brawls only occur randomly, accidentally, or as a consequence of sudden impulses. Some settings – like crowded highways – lend themselves to brawling precisely because they cluster weak scripts, shifting stakes, blurred boundaries, no monitors, and great uncertainty. Settings with these characteristics distribute systematically through inhabited space – for example in unpoliced ghettos, flea markets, red-light districts, and abandoned buildings (Bayat 1997; Harison 2000; Polletta 1999; Tilly 2000). In a brilliant passage, Argentine-born political analyst Guillermo O'Donnell compares driving into major thoroughfares from side streets during rush hour in major U.S. cities, Rio de Janeiro, and Buenos Aires. In the Argentine capital, he reports,

we are apparently equals: the rule is that if there is no police officer in sight (and if it is unlikely that one is hiding out nearby) each driver should go first. Therefore, the crux of the matter is to impede the passage of others. The way to do this, illegal but universally practiced, is *meter la trompa,* that is, to edge one's car in front of another's, to "sneak it in," or "slide it in." As a result, the cars at the intersection advance to the point where they almost hit one another. One line of cars is crossing bumper-to-bumper (so that those who are coming from the other direction cannot get through), and the cars in the other line are millimeters away from the doors and fenders of the crossing cars, ready to take advantage of the tiniest hesitation in order to "sneak it in" and victoriously inaugurate the flow that now begins from the cross street, until someone else *achique* or *arrugue* ("gives in" or "chickens out") and therefore opens the way once again for cars coming from the other direction. The consequence of all this, of course, is monumental inefficiency, insults, fights, and often that gesture of a thumb and index finger closed in an evocative circle which celebrates one's "sticking it" to the other who is left *frenado y con rabia* (stranded and humiliated) (this sounds like the title of a tango) a few millimeters away from the car now sliding forth in victory. (O'Donnell 1999: 84–5)

Given the prevailing interaction routines, the setting begs for brawls. In fact, as we will see later, participants can deliberately precipitate brawls in such settings – taking advantage of signaling spirals to inflict vengeance, seize property, demonstrate superior fighting skills, or otherwise pursue agendas that ordinarily would face serious obstacles to their realization.

Remember the major mechanisms we encountered in violent rituals: boundary activation and deactivation, polarization, competitive display, monitoring, containment, and certification–decertification. The first three – activation, polarization, and competitive display – all occur in brawls and help explain their violence. But in brawls they operate on a smaller scale and more intermittently than in violent rituals. The other three – monitoring, containment, and certification–decertification – depend on and constitute high levels of coordination. The weakness or absence of monitoring, containment, and certification helps explain the development of brawls. So does an additional mechanism that plays a lesser part in violent ritual: the signaling spiral by which (in the presence of uncertainty about the other side's next move) defensive action and retaliation escalate. When activation, polarization, competitive display, and signaling spirals begin in the absence of monitoring, containment, and certification, brawls emerge.

Nevertheless, brawls resemble violent rituals in making damage (of one kind or another) central. Their high salience, low coordination, and small scale combine to provide exceptional scope for violent specialists, including violent specialists who are exiting from well-coordinated violent rituals. As a result, per-capita damage in brawls exceeds per-capita damage in violent rituals. Consider an example from medieval Arboga, Sweden. On 11 July 1468,

a courtier (*bovman*) named Silvast and his servants behaved provocatively towards a miner in the street. Silvast shoved the miner so that his sword fell to the street. The miner objected that it was not a deed worthy of a man to throw *his* sword in the dirt. One of the courtier's servants then called the miner a whoreson and hit him on the head with the sword. Then out rushed Jöns Djäkn from his yard, evidently sympathizing with the miner and outraged by the injustice of the situation. Jöns told the courtiers that they did wrong to strike a poor man who had done them no harm. The conflict then spiraled and ended in manslaughter. (Österberg & Lindström 1988: 49–50)

With higher levels of coordination, this brawl could easily have mutated into another form of collective violence, especially some form of coordinated destruction pitting miners against nobles and their servants. Medieval Europe overflowed with brawls as well as with parallel episodes on a larger scale, involving greater coordination. Event for event, brawls are no doubt the most frequent episodes of collective violence in low-capacity regimes.

Despite their abundance in many settings, brawls present two related problems of evidence that set them off from other types of collective violence:

problems of documentation and problems of distinction. As for documentation, most brawls leave few traces: cuts, bruises, broken glass, blurred memories, not much more. The incidents of road rage in Table 7.1 attracted attention from media and police, but thousands more disappeared from the public record. As Chapter 4 showed us in the case of half-brawl, half-ritual soccer violence, it takes sturdy ethnographers and hardy reporters to assemble documentation on most people's day-to-day involvement in brawling. Every other form of collective violence has a greater chance of leaving visible traces, even when regimes try to hush up the damage. As a consequence, available knowledge on brawling slants toward its larger-scale and more destructive forms.

Distinction of brawls from higher-coordination or lower-salience forms of collective violence also presents subtle difficulties. Remember the flagellants' fracases and gang battles in Chapter 4? Precisely because violent rituals sometimes devolve into brawls as coordination collapses, it takes considerable information about what was happening *before* and *after* the relatively indiscriminate fighting to know whether an episode qualifies as an occasion on which routine nonviolent interaction turned into small-scale attacks on persons and property. Similarly, in nineteenth-century America, many a free-for-all started with an official's attempt to seize property, make an arrest, or shut down an illegal but peaceful assembly; such events teeter on the boundary between scattered attack and brawls.

Let us be clear about what these cautions mean and what they don't mean. They make it difficult to test propositions about brawls as distinctive forms of violence by collecting uniform, representative samples of events. In most circumstances, cataloging is easier for other sorts of violent episodes because (a) authorities, observers, and participants record them and (b) whether a violent episode actually included coordinated destruction or scattered attack poses fewer problems of definition. These practical and logical problems, however, need not hinder our main enterprise: to explain how and why collective violence takes different forms and often shifts from one form to another. In the case of brawls, their distinctive properties matter less than what causes collective violence to occur with salient damaging interactions and low coordination among damage doers. Even an incomplete, selective, and truncated collection of brawling episodes will help decide that question.

Brawls in Eighteenth-Century France

Among relatively high-capacity undemocratic regimes, the experience with violence of eighteenth-century France has drawn exceptional attention from generations of scholars. Because a major revolution closed the century, scholars have scrutinized conflicts during earlier decades to see whether they could identify antecedents, rehearsals, or even causes of 1789's great explosion. In addition to scattered resistance and large-scale rebellion, brawls have received more attention than elsewhere because of the supposition that they provide evidence of the popular temper before the Revolution. This book's arguments and evidence cast doubt on anyone's ability to read back popular consciousness from overall levels of any particular kind of violence. But we can take advantage of talented historians' contributions to look more closely than usual at the character of brawls in eighteenth-century France both before and during the Revolution of 1789–1799.

Authorities and chroniclers of the time applied many terms to small-scale violence involving ordinary people, notably *émeute, émotion, sédition, pillage, rébellion,* and *attroupement.* Although events called by these names sometimes began with attacks on pariahs or dishonored persons, the terms all implied some sort of confrontation with officials, property holders, or other important people. Looked at closely, episodes receiving these labels usually turn out not to have been brawls in this book's sense of the term but to qualify instead as scattered attack, broken negotiations, or coordinated destruction. However, the disparaging word *rixe* typically designated occasions on which, within a previously nonviolent gathering, two or more persons begin attacking each other or each other's property; *rixe* meant brawl. A *rixe* became a *sédition* or *émotion* if participants began coordinating their action more extensively in resistance to authorities or in attacks on common enemies. But most *rixes* remained within the limits of the brawl.

Who participated in France's eighteenth-century brawls? France had no American-style cowboys in the eighteenth century, but it had plenty of other youthful groups that frequently brawled – especially students, soldiers, artisans, village youths, and retainers of magnates' households. Each of them brawled in triple mode: sometimes engaging in fights that began with a hostile pair and spiraled from there, sometimes activating an established boundary between two units within the same broad category, and sometimes pitting members of the category against outsiders. Sometimes they switched modes rapidly, as when battling groups of students from rival schools banded together against the police who arrived to calm them down. The widespread organization of work, study, and social life in guilds, confraternities, and similar parallel, competitive structures promoted the outbreak of cross-boundary brawls in response to insults and challenges.

Parisian lawyer and chronicler Edmond-Jean-François Barbier noted a fine example in his journal for March 1721:

At the start of the Saint-Germain fair last month, the pages of royal houses and great families had a great quarrel with the pages of foreign ambassadors and lords. The former did not want the latter to enter the show of tightrope dancers. There was a big fight; [the foreigners] disarmed the watch and for three days paraded through the fair armed with walking sticks. That battle settled down, but yesterday the royal lackeys made up their minds. They gathered at the fair, broke into the tightrope dancers' space, raised a hullabaloo, and kept the show from going on. The authorities called not only the fair guards but also troops stationed in the faubourg Saint-Germain, who arrived with fixed bayonets on their rifles. The lackeys disarmed a few soldiers, but finally gave up. Almost all of them were carrying clubs inside their clothes; the authorities made them leave one by one, took their clubs, and arrested six from different households. (Barbier 1847–1856: I, 41)

As Barbier's account suggests, many people routinely carried weapons in eighteenth-century France. Nobles, guild members, and officials routinely wore swords; important people traveled with armed guards; and clubs, staves, or walking sticks served for those who lacked the right to carry lethal arms. Over the century, royal police worked hard at disarming urban populations, restricting duels, and disciplining their own violent specialists. Yet at the time of the Revolution, plenty of Frenchmen continued to pack weapons. When they used those weapons in small-scale conflicts, brawls often resulted.

Ménétra the Brawler

An extraordinary autobiography places French eighteenth-century brawls within local lives. Jacques-Louis Ménétra, son of a Parisian master glazier, was born in 1738 and died in his 60s, a few years after 1800. He began writing his autobiographical *Journal de ma vie* in 1764, shortly after his 26th birthday and about eleven months before he married Marie-Élisabeth Henin. Between 1757 (when he was 19) and his marriage, Ménétra spent much of his time traveling from town to town and working for local contractors as part of his Tour de France, a standard routine for journeymen of the time. On his tour, he passed through a remarkable series of jobs, adventures, love affairs, and brawls. He seems to have remembered them well. At least his journal recorded them in detail.

During the sixteenth century, French journeymen (*compagnons*) in a wide variety of construction trades had started to join the secret societies known collectively as Compagnonnage. They fell into three main divisions – Enfants de maître Jacques (Compagnons du Devoir, or Dévorants), Enfants de maître Soubise (chiefly carpenters), and Enfants de maître Salomon (Loups or Gavots) – all three of them claiming descent from master builders of Solomon's temple. In all important cities, each division of the Compagnonnage designated an inn as its headquarters; the workers who lodged in those inns called the innkeepers their Mother and Father. When Ménétra arrived in Tours during the spring of 1758, established journeymen there inducted him as a Compagnon du Devoir. That ceremony set him on the side of his fellows against the Enfants de Soubise and, especially, the Enfants de Salomon. Many of Ménétra's subsequent brawls pitted Dévorants against Gavots.

The first violent episode that Ménétra narrates in detail led from a small brawl to an event resembling American gang rumbles of the 1960s. It took place in Angers, just north of the Loire in Western France, during the summer of 1758. A journeyman locksmith from the Devoir went to a tailor's to fetch the outfit he was planning to wear at the local festival on the following day. A group of Gavots attacked him and took his new clothes. The Dévorant locksmith returned to his inn and complained to the Mother. A number of journeymen from the inn went to the Gavots' inn, demanded return of the suit, but received only insults. At that, the Dévorants challenged their enemies to a pitched battle. The two forces lined up with about 750 on the Gavot side and 500 on the Dévorant side. The city's militia surrounded the space. After much maneuvering and some defections, a battle royal with clubs and stones began. Ménétra reported seven dead and forty wounded. Pursued by police, Ménétra and sixty of his colleagues fled Angers that night (Ménétra 1982: 57–8). A brawl had spawned a violent ritual.

Ménétra fled to Poitou, worked intermittently, spent a month in jail with other workers on a trumped-up accusation of vandalism, then trekked to Saint-Malo to sign up on a privateer engaged in raiding the English during what would eventually be known as the Seven Years War. After five months of seafaring, he deserted in a small Breton port and tramped back to Poitou. On his way to Nantes (in Brittany, near the Loire's mouth) after spells of work in Poitou and southern Anjou, he met two Gavots who tried to take his backpack; as he was defending himself, two journeymen hatters came along, joined his side of the fight, and beat up the Gavots.

During his eleven-month stay in Nantes, Ménétra brawled some more. But he also negotiated settlement of a long dispute that had divided masters and journeymen there, as well as setting up housekeeping with a master glazier's widow. He had to leave the city suddenly after an adventure that began when he and two friends were strolling through the city. The friends

dared me to kiss a lemonade vendor. Since I was well dressed, I introduced myself and politely asked her permission, which she gave. To my surprise, a little fart objected (for there are people like that in Nantes just as in Paris). He pushed me away roughly. I pushed back. He drew his sword and I disarmed him. Other guys of the same type drew their swords, but I attacked so fast that all three of them were wounded. As I ran away, I heard them calling the cops, who grabbed me. Luckily for me sergeant Gaborie [of the watch] was a master glazier who let me get away. I went to my good widow, who hid me in her sheets. The next day a bailiff came to call, and she said I hadn't come back. After that visit I realized I wasn't safe any more, so I sent a message to the Mother. More than sixty journeymen arrived and accompanied me across Pirmil Bridge. (Ménétra 1982: 65)

The bridge took him across the Loire – out of the city and therefore out of its police jurisdiction.

Brawls continued as Ménétra explored other regions of France, including the Midi. In 1760, on his way from Narbonne to Béziers with a journeyman cabinet-maker named Saint-Germain, Ménétra had an unpleasant surprise:

Eight husky Gavots were waiting to ambush us. I saw them and told Saint-Germain to hold steady. I cocked my pistol, which I carried when traveling in a holster hidden in the folds of my jacket. When they saw that I was armed they said that they weren't after me but wanted to get my companion. I told him to stand fast and they didn't dare to advance. (Ménétra 1982: 83)

It turned out that Saint-Germain had previously been a leading Gavot but had defected to the Devoir. When the pair arrived in Béziers, Saint-Germain asked Ménétra to go to the local Mother and ask her to send journeymen to protect him from the local Gavots. Ménétra then made a serious mistake: he asked directions to the mother house of cabinetmakers without specifying which *order* of cabinetmakers. He found himself at the wrong inn, surrounded by Gavots rather than Dévorants. The Gavots demanded that he drink to their health; he refused, and only the arrival of the Gavots' Father kept him from a beating. He returned to the glaziers' mother house to find journeymen gathering for an effort to rescue him from the Gavots. He led them instead to Saint-Germain's hiding place, from which they led him in triumph through the streets to the Dévorant cabinetmakers' mother house.

The young Ménétra was a brawler, but mainly on behalf of his workers' order. Once married and settled as a master of his own shop in Paris, he left his fighting days behind except for an occasional street quarrel. When the Revolution arrived, 51-year-old master glazier Ménétra served as a National Guard officer, thus moving to the side of the repressive forces he had once battled. As a National Guard he engaged in a number of military actions, but none of them quite qualified as a brawl. A loyal Jacobin despite the disapproval he recorded of many executions under the Terror, he became president of his local assembly and held a number of other Revolutionary offices. By that time, Ménétra's own son was serving in the French army on the front. The father's days as a brawler had ended.

Table 7.2. *Selected Parisian Brawls Noted in Siméon-Prosper Hardy's Journal for 1753 to 1789*

Apr 1767	Musketeers, wagoner, and city watchmen battle after a wagon splashes a musketeer and he attacks the wagoner.
Feb 1775	After drawing lots for militia service, young men from two villages in Paris suburbs gather in a café, argue about the drawing, then fight each other with clubs.
Feb 1776	Porters, fruit sellers, and egg merchants of Paris' central market (les Halles) engage in free-for-all.
Aug 1776	Rival groups of clerks at Palace of Justice battle each other on an outing.
Jun 1778	In St. Cloud, members of a dissolved brotherhood fight with church's canons, who have excluded them from carrying the banner in a religious procession.
Oct 1781	At the Royal School of Surgery, students battle with a school security officer (Suisse).
May 1785	Stonecutters break up bar and then attack the watch, who arrest two of them; battle ensues.
Oct 1785	A violent struggle breaks out among soldiers, Suisses, and civilians at the Palais Royal, then a major center for drinking, gambling, free speech, and illegal activity.
Sep 1788	Some 200 youngsters rush through Right Bank streets celebrating political reforms; they encounter four squads of French Guards, who push them back with bayonets and fire on them, with a final count of many wounded and at least one dead.

Source: Hardy (1753–1789, vols. 1–8).

Brawls Blend into Revolution

Table 7.2 lists the major brawls that meticulous Parisian bookseller and chronicler Siméon-Prosper Hardy described in his entries for 1767 through 1788. Hardy did not record events in his eight-volume diary unless they piqued his curiosity. Ordinary barroom brawls and fights among workmen, of which plenty occurred in Paris during that period, did not make it into his pages. He noted events that produced more damage than usual, attracted exceptional public attention, involved significant categories of actors, or simply followed intriguing scenarios.

The first brawl listed (April 1767) spiraled from an eighteenth-century version of road rage. As four musketeers left a restaurant, a passing wagoner accidentally splashed mud on one of them. The offended musketeer struck the wagoner with his walking stick; the wagoner kicked him back. All the musketeers began to attack him. Just then, an officer of the watch in civilian clothes came by on his horse and admonished the musketeers, only to be attacked by them. When two squads of watch arrived, a battle ensued, with several people wounded and nearby shops shot up (Hardy 1753–1789: I).

The 1781 incident pitted medical students against the school guard. The Swiss (as uniformed guards of public institutions were by then commonly called, regardless of their actual nationalities) followed the rules by stopping a student from entering a lecture hall with his walking stick, grabbed the stick, and received a blow in the belly from the student. The Swiss grabbed his assailant by the collar, whereupon many other students "seized the Swiss by the hair, which started a sort of battle between them and him." An Inspector stopped the fight and suspended the Swiss, but a facultywide council later reinstated the guard as having behaved properly (Hardy 1753–1789: V).

May 1785 brought an even more classic instance of a Parisian brawl. Stonecutters smashed up a bar where they were drinking and then started to leave without paying. The bar's owner called the watch, who arrested two stonecutters – only to have sixty more attack their squad in an attempt to rescue the two prisoners. The watch fixed bayonets on their rifles, and the stonecutters began to pelt them with rocks until military reinforcements arrived (Farge 1979: 155–6). As in most eighteenth-century *rixes*, members of an established corps acted together against members of another established corps.

Hardy did not call the final episode in the set (September 1788) a brawl. I have included it to point out the difference that coordination can make. In this case, young people were celebrating the return of the popularly supported sovereign courts with which the king had been struggling. The celebration took place in the context of extensive old-regime style demonstrations against major figures in the king's government as well as regular baiting of royal troops by students, law clerks, and other civilians (Egret 1962; Monin 1889; Tilly 1986, chap. 7). In this case, two bands of about a hundred young people each formed in the Left Bank student quarter and then crossed the Ile de la Cité to the Right Bank, "carrying torches and laurel branches, singing and seeming to have no other purpose than to rejoice." Several detachments of French Guards – a total of 54 men, according to Hardy – blocked their way near the rue des Mathurins, pushing them back with sabers, bayonets, and finally gunfire. A shoemaker's son died of his wounds (Hardy 1753–1789: VIII).

The confrontation with French Guards resembled a brawl, except that the context immediately broadened the event's scope on both sides. Coordination arose from the extensive availability of shared stories, boundaries, and relations among potential participants. From the middle of 1788 to the invasion of the Bastille in July 1789, brawl-like confrontations between troops and crowds became increasingly frequent.

Those violent episodes divided roughly into two types: occasions on which people gathered to jeer or pelt royal troops in the course of the troops' regular duties, and other occasions on which troops (including the city watch) tried to break up popular displays of opposition to the regime. Clerks of the Palace of Justice, who vociferously supported the courts whose autonomy the king had been attacking, formed a major nucleus of such displays. They often took place in and around the Place Dauphine, between the Palace of Justice and the Pont Neuf. On Friday the 29th of August 1788, following several days of what Hardy called "open war" between the watch and local crowds,

[t]oward 9 P.M., the populace of the faubourg St. Antoine and the faubourg St. Marcel having augmented the number of mischief-makers in the neighborhood, disorder only grew progressively. Instead of limiting themselves to setting off firecrackers, which already bothered nearby residents, they set a large fire in the middle of the Place Dauphine, feeding it with everything they could carry in from the surrounding area, such as a sentry box from the Pont Neuf, the stalls of orange- and lemon-sellers from the same place, and the trellises of poultry merchants on the Quai de la Vallée.

Members of the crowd burned an effigy of Attorney General Lamoignon (major agent of royal actions against the courts) and then went out to attack city watchmen and destroy their guardhouses. In the fighting that ensued, three people died and forty were wounded (Hardy 1753–1789: VIII). This time a semi-brawl spiraled into coordinated destruction pitting the military against civilians.

As the Revolution proceeded, France polarized: first between enemies and defenders of the royal regime; then between rival factions in struggles for control of the revolutionary regime. At the same time, the disarmament of civilians that had been proceeding for a century reversed to some extent: militias broadened their social bases, became more durable, and turned into National Guard units. In a parallel process, governmental patrolling and surveillance of public spaces intensified. As a result, such brawls as occurred more frequently involved armed men, more regularly drew intervention from armed forces, more often activated existing boundaries between competing factions, more easily mutated into scattered attack or coordinated destruction, and therefore became more lethal. As a result, relatively inconsequential brawls grew rarer – at least as a share of total violent interaction.

Switches to and from Brawls

When activation, polarization, competitive display, and signaling spirals begin in the absence of monitoring, containment, and certification, brawls emerge. French eighteenth-century experience shows us, however, the ease with which brawls change form: fragmenting into individual aggression; receding into scattered attack; following increased coordination into opportunism or even coordinated destruction. These other forms of violence also convert into brawls as a function of shifts in coordination and salience. Switches to and from brawls occur with particular ease and frequency when some of the participants are themselves violent specialists (police, soldiers, guards, thugs, and the like). We have already seen switches occurring in Ménétra's reports of individual aggression that turned into brawls and of brawls into coordinated destruction when activation of boundaries between categories of journeymen brought more fighters into the fray and polarized them across boundaries. Hardy's catalog of brawls likewise shows us shifts among individual aggression, brawls, and coordinated destruction as a result of signaling spirals, boundary activation, and the intervention of violent specialists.

Let us ransack a source that provides more than the usual detail concerning switches between individual aggression and brawls. Between 1973 and 1979, Raphael Samuel repeatedly interviewed former London thug Arthur Harding, who was 87 years old when the interviews began. Harding engaged in individual fighting, brawling, and petty crime from boyhood into his 40s. Here was his own recitation of his early indictments.

10 April 1901	Suspected person; 100 yards from my home; this case was dismissed. Age 14 years.
4 March 1902	Larceny simple; 12 months hard labour; attempt to steal bag of rags from a van. Age 15.
10 March 1903	Larceny to the person; discharged. Age 16.
21 April 1903	Larceny to the person; 20 months and hard labour; taking a metal watch from another lad I knew. Age 16.
17 January 1905	Larceny to the person; discharged. Age 18.
28 May 1905	Larceny to the person; discharged. Age 18.
6 April 1906	Shooting with intent; acquitted. Age 19.
13 April 1906	Assault; £5 or 1 month. Age 19.
24 July 1906	Robbery; discharged. Age 19.
26 Sept 1906	Assault; discharged. (Samuel 1981: 187)

After marrying in 1924, Harding set himself up as a cabinetmaker and stayed out of the law's way. For years before then, however, most of Harding's income came from illegal activities. He spent ten years (1911–1916 and 1917–1922) in prison for committing major crimes. Over his criminal career, he went to court as a defendant 32 times and won discharge or acquittal 27 times. He was a rough youngster.

Harding's prime as a brawler occurred between 1905 (when he reached 19) and 1920 (when he reached 34). "One time," Harding recalled,

about 1908 we had a quarrel with the Titanics. We got involved with them because of a man named Pencil. He used to go with some of the brides [prostitutes] down Brick Lane. Me and some others set about him one night at the coffee stall in Shoreditch High Street, top of Bethnal Green Road. They were taking liberties with the chap who had the stall and I knew him so we belted him and that led to a bit of gang warfare between us and them. Stevie Cooper was in it. The next night they come down from Hoxton. But what they done was crafty. They set a trap for us. They was well in with the police and directly the fight started the police were there. They got hold of us – including Cooper, who had a loaded gun on him. It wasn't an offence to carry a gun, but we got a week's remand for causing an affray. (Samuel 1981: 147–8)

First Harding and his friends "belted" Titanics member Pencil, then the whole Titanics gang fought Harding's gang, only to call in the police as their allies. The process moved from individual aggression through brawling to coordinated destruction.

Signaling spirals alone could expand a brawl without producing higher levels of coordination. At one stage in his criminal career, Harding made much of his income from fixed games of "crown and anchor," the local equivalent of three-card monte. During one game, a lookout came to report that a plain-clothes policeman was on his way:

He must have pushed against a couple of chaps in the crowd, and a fight started. Well all along Sygnet Street there were stalls dealing with auxiliaries for bikes and motor bikes. Some of the barrows had bottles of petrol and when the fighting spread they got knocked over. "Bang! Bang! Bang!" people thought they were guns. The cry went up, "They're shooting," and that started a stampede. It was 1911, the time of Sydney Street, and everyone thought it was the anarchists and the police.

There was a terrific rush to get away. Nearby in Club Row was the great bird market and thousands of birds were trampled underfoot. The stampede spread out like a wheel, with people running in all directions to get away. A couple of people got killed. A policeman is said to have put a stop to it. He was on point duty at the top of the Wheeler Street Arch, just where Club Row starts, and when the panic reached him it is said to have stopped. He got a reputation for it, the great big London policeman who put a stop to the stampede. Everyone wanted to give him a pint on the strength of it. But he no more stopped it than he could fly. It just weakened at the edges. I knew that policeman well. He was absolutely bloody useless as a policeman – he would never trouble to arrest anybody for fear of endangering himself. (Samuel 1981: 177)

Shop owners and other victims sued the police for failing to protect them. The police came to Harding and asked him to find witnesses who would testify that the officers present had done their duty. Harding obliged; he found friends who would tell an inquest that an everyday quarrel had simply spiraled out of control, that "the police had acted very bravely, and come out of it with flying colours" (Samuel 1981: 178). Harding's recollections overflow with stories of how regularly he and his fellow criminals conspired with, paid off, and provided information to their local police.

One more insight about switching comes from Arthur Harding's reminiscences. On some occasions, deliberately initiated brawls become occasions for revenge or covers for individual aggression. In 1911 a pimp Harding knew asked for his help in "straightening out" another pimp with whom he was competing for control of neighborhood whores. Harding recruited six or seven of his friends for a Saturday night visit to the pub where the targeted pimp and his "mob" hung out. When the targeted man handed Harding a drink, Harding took it and emptied the glass on him. Then Harding and his companions broke glasses and began fighting, cutting up the opposition very badly. When the police arrived with an ambulance, Harding and friends decamped. Two days later, Harding led his gang to police court, where Saturday night's chief victims were swearing out complaints against them. Unfortunately for the gang, some of Harding's sidekicks carried weapons into the court – a felony and a direct threat to the police. Eight members of his gang, including Harding, went to prison for the affair. Police–criminal cooperation had its limits.

Looked at closely, brawls have much more structure than their chaotic reputation suggests. That structure results from two different bundles of causes. First: social settings with weak monitoring, containment, and certification favor brawls, and they distribute systematically in time and space; brawlers cluster in these settings or move to them for brawling. Second: activation, polarization, competitive display, and signaling spirals generate brawls, and each of them draws on previously established culture.

As eighteenth-century French brawls and twentieth-century English brawls demonstrate, all the crucial mechanisms commonly align combatants along boundaries well marked by previous social interaction. Whether Dévorants versus Gavots, students versus police, or East End gang versus East End gang, available divisions channel the collective violence despite relatively low levels of overall coordination. But these same characteristics also give brawls porous boundaries; more so than other types of collective violence, they easily emerge from or convert into adjacent types of violence. All it takes is activation of mechanisms that alter the salience of violent interaction or coordination among damage doers.

So far we have concentrated on high-salience forms of collective violence: violent rituals, coordinated destruction, opportunism, and brawls. It is now time to examine lower-salience forms: scattered attacks and broken negotiations. They will show us similar violence-producing mechanisms but in different combinations, sequences, and initial conditions. Even more so than the high-salience forms, they will show us collective violence as a by-product of mainly nonviolent social processes.

8

Scattered Attacks

Resistance to Revolution

When Muslim clerics won out in Iran's 1979 revolution, they inherited massive national unemployment but generated still more unemployment on their own. Many capitalists had fled the country or shut down their enterprises while revolutionary turmoil spread from October 1978 on; their departure left many employees out of work. As the clerics gained control, they began shutting down enterprises they deemed immoral – not only brothels and liquor stores, but also restaurants, theaters, gambling parlors, and other purveyors of what they regarded as un-Islamic goods or services. After checking the large movements of unemployed that challenged the government in 1979, officials began dealing with the street vendors who had multiplied in Tehran and elsewhere. Street vendors actually included many laid-off workers who had taken to retailing food and sundries. But they also included numerous sellers of politically dubious books, tracts, and other materials. Many political vendors were former students who had earlier joined the rising against the Shah but now opposed his clerical successors.

As the regime began major repression of its secular opposition in 1981, it also began a campaign to clear city streets of vendors – especially vendors of subversive publications. Its violent vigilantes, the official Pasdaran monitors and their fellow-traveling *hizbullahi* street toughs, began tearing down stalls and seizing petty merchants' goods. "Groups of thugs," reports Asef Bayat, "often escorted by the Pasdaran, went around kicking down stalls and *basaats* [stands] and confiscating merchandise and other belongings. Subsequent scuffles and fistfights resulted in many injuries and deaths" (Bayat 1997: 147).

By April 1984 the government reported that it had eliminated more than 90 percent of the 120,000 unlicensed vendors and kiosk holders from Tehran

(Bayat 1997: 148). The remainder, however, continued to resist. Sometimes they actually marched and sat in on public authorities. Mostly they practiced sell-and-run tactics. But now and then they fought off the raiders:

On December 15, 1985, CCMAOT [Committee for Continuing Mobilization Against the Obstruction of Thoroughfares] squads, along with groups of Pasdaran, raided a fruit market located in the Falake-ye Dovvom-I Khazaneh, a poor neighborhood in South Tehran. They began to collect handcarts, scales, and similar belongings, throwing fruits into the sewage ditches running through the market. The vendors responded with their fists, inciting the Pasdaran to shoot into the air. One cart owner reacted by throwing a heavy scale weight at the agents, knocking one down. They beat him up and dragged him to the Security *Komiteh*. Reportedly, the women present defended the vendors, screaming at the agents and blaming the troubles on them. (Bayat 1997: 150)

Little by little, the streets emptied of vendors. But as they went, the vendors engaged in scattered attacks. Bayat makes the surprising claim that they mobilized through what he calls passive networks – "instantaneous communication among atomized individuals, which is established by the tacit recognition of their common identity and is mediated through space" (Bayat 1997: 16). His own evidence of extensive connections and sometime coordination among vendors belies that claim. Nevertheless he establishes firmly that their collective action consisted chiefly of localized and short-term resistance.

Most revolutionary regimes (and many nonrevolutionary conquerors as well) generate scattered attacks as they first consolidate their control. They lay down rules and forms of organization that threaten previously established routines; parties that have depended on those routines for their welfare often fight back. As Chapter 3 showed, although some collective violence under the French Revolution consisted of revolutionary attacks on old authorities and struggles among revolutionary factions, the most intense domestic violence pitted revolutionaries and their military forces against reluctant citizens. The new Iranian regime of 1979 likewise generated that sort of reaction. Scattered attacks combine weak coordination and low salience of violent interactions. We have already seen scattered attacks at work around the edges of coordinated, provocative, or repressive but nonviolent campaigns such as Ulster's party processions and scattered attacks on patrolling police.

Collective violence qualifies as scattered attack if, in the course of widespread small-scale and generally nonviolent interaction, a number of participants respond to obstacles, challenges, or restraints by means of damaging acts; examples include sabotage, scattered clandestine attacks on symbolic objects or places, assaults of governmental agents, and arson. As compared with the forms of collective violence we have already reviewed, scattered attack stands out for the relatively low salience of violent interactions; damaging acts occur in the midst of mostly nondamaging interactions. As in the cases of violent rituals and coordinated destruction, we can usefully make rough distinctions among three different configurations of scattered attack.

1. Where two or more participating parties are more or less evenly matched, and nonviolent interaction generates occasional violence; *skirmishes* have this character.
2. Where one party enjoys the preponderance of force and uses violence uni-laterally to advertise or support that preponderance; *shows of force* have this character.
3. Where again one party enjoys the preponderance of force but now the other side responds to its demands or interventions with intermittent, dis-persed damage; *resistance* has this character.

As compared with other forms of collective violence, all these varieties of scat-tered attack occur more frequently when violent specialists do *not* initiate the doing of damage, when relations among the parties are relatively stable, when stakes of the outcome for the parties are fairly low, and when third parties are present.

Here is another way of saying the same thing: under these conditions, even when collective violence occurs, a high proportion of the interaction among con-tending parties tends to be nonviolent. In the purest forms of scattered attack, violent interactions occur at the edges of nonviolent confrontations – often out-side of or after asymmetrical confrontations during which subordinates simulate compliance with authorities. Under some circumstances, however, scattered at-tack shifts into coordinated destruction as coordination increases and damage becomes more salient (Gamson, Fireman, & Rytina 1982).

Without using this book's terminology, I once mistakenly argued that, outside of interstate war and small-scale aggression, most politically significant collec-tive violence took the forms of scattered attacks or broken negotiations (see e.g. Tilly 1975). I thought that when violence occurred at all, low-salience collective violence predominated over a wide range of political life. I made that mistake for three related reasons.

1. I joined with other populists in thinking of violence as an expression of popular grievances that the historical record usually concealed; I concentrated on the view from below, asking chiefly how and why relatively powerless people engaged in interactions that produced collective violence – a question that draws attention away from violence initiated by governments and political leaders.

2. I was studying the relationship between political change and collective violence over the last few centuries in Western Europe, where resistance to the expansion of state power and the growing power of capitalists figured importantly in political violence and where workers, peasants, landless laborers, and other relatively powerless people did often find that their nonviolent claims met with violent repression.

3. I failed to recognize how often political entrepreneurs and violent specialists pursued their own agendas by means of damage and threats of damage, thus promoting the high-salience forms of collective violence this book calls brawls, opportunism, coordinated destruction, and violent ritual.

Those widely shared mistakes provided some benefits: they promoted criticism of readings of collective violence as straightforward expression of impulses, and they spurred detailed investigations of such conflicts as grain seizures, shaming ceremonies, and peasant rebellions (for reviews, compilations, and syntheses, see e.g. te Brake 1998; Hanagan, Moch, & te Brake 1998; Hanagan & Stephenson 1986; Moss 1993; Randall & Charlesworth 2000). But they fortified the interpretation of violence as the solo voice of the people. I learned better as I assembled systematic catalogs of violent events and compared my own enumerations with other people's catalogs of violence. All well-prepared catalogs reveal the large share of interpersonal damage that occurs in the course of coordinated destruction and opportunism.

Coming from that direction, however, makes it easier to avoid the opposite mistake: assuming that participants in collective violence uniformly intend and desire to do damage. On the low-salience side of our coordination–salience space, violence often emerges from initially nonviolent (even if rancorous) interactions greatly resembling other interactions in which no damage occurs. Examples include seditious meetings broken up by authorities, roughing up of insistent tax collectors, and demonstrations in which police clash with marchers. Scattered attacks occur especially when power holders attempt to impose novel, onerous, or threatening forms of organization that some subjects of their demands refuse to accept.

Scattered attack offers two rather different conundrums to analysts of contentious politics. First, governmental repression generally dampens collective claim making, but heightening of governmental repression nevertheless often generates waves of resistance (at least in the short run); what resolves this apparent contradiction? Second, if we suppose that ostensibly altruistic acts (in which actors sustain losses while others gain as a result) actually spring from egoism (because the actors gain self-satisfaction or otherwise benefit invisibly), how can we explain the self-destruction and mutual destruction that sometimes occur in the course of scattered attacks?

Much governmental repression does dampen collective claim making by raising the costs of claim making across the board or for particular actors: seizing the media, restricting public assembly, and intensifying surveillance generally reduce overall levels of claim making. Under some circumstances, however, increased repression has the opposite effect, actually generating increased collective action (Khawaja 1993; Lichbach 1987; Mason 1989; Mason & Krane 1989; Moore 1979; O'Brien 1996; Olivier 1991; Schneider 1995). Three processes seem to favor resistance: (1) hesitation, faltering, or visible division on the part of repressive authorities; (2) defensive intervention of powerful allies; and (3) direct attacks by repressive forces on persons, objects, and activities that sustain a population's collective survival. These processes increase the scope and intensity of scattered attacks.

The same processes – especially attacks on persons, objects, and activities that are crucial to collective survival – help produce self-sacrifice on the part of persons who under other circumstances act more egoistically. People become more willing to engage in risky and costly actions, including violent actions, when valued others will clearly benefit from the sacrifice; when not to sacrifice would betray weakness, fear, or disloyalty; when visible suffering has a chance of attracting third-party intervention; and when inconspicuous exit is difficult (Tilly 2001d).

Scattered attacks concentrate in undemocratic regimes. They do so because oppressed parties have fewer alternatives and potential allies than in democratic regimes. They also occur more frequently when regime capacity is changing rapidly, either increasing or decreasing. Rapid changes in capacity promote scattered attacks by shifting the threats and opportunities that bear on oppressed populations. Rapid increases in capacity often threaten group survival, as governments start intruding on previous areas of protected autonomy; states that mobilize for war often meet just such resistance (Levi 1988, 1997). Rapid *decreases* in capacity signal the vulnerability of authorities to forms of resistance that previously would have been hopeless; defeated states often face that sort of resistance as their wars end (Bearman 1991; Lagrange 1989; Tilly 1992).

The word "terrorism" often elbows its way into political conversation at precisely this point. Beginning with citations from the 1790s, the Oxford English Dictionary gives two definitions for terrorism: "1. government by intimidation as directed and carried out by the party in power in France during the Revolution of 1789–94 .... 2. a policy intended to strike with terror those against whom it is adopted." Both definitions point to the asymmetrical deployment of threats and violence against enemies outside the forms of contention routinely operating within the current regime. By now it should be clear that a wide variety of violent interactions qualify: spectacular exemplary punishment in some regimes, assassination of political leaders in others, attacks on citizens at large in still others.

One of the twentieth century's most effective terrorist forces in this sense was the Apartheid regime's South African Defense Force (SADF), which long deployed intimidation and violence against people – black *and* white – whom it had identified as opposed to the regime; SADF members no doubt shared the racism of their employers but did not otherwise stand out from the South African population by distinctive ideological coherence or extremism. Nor, for that matter, did the French Resistance activists who struck at the regime's railroads, military installations, and leaders during World War II qualify as extremists except from the perspectives of Vichy and Berlin. As a general rule, the attribution of terrorism to extremism, fundamentalism, or delusion makes little sense.

Yet a kernel of truth hides within that common error. On the whole, the political actors most likely to employ extraordinary forms of threat and violence against their enemies come from two categories of the excluded: (i) people aligned with external enemies of the regime and (ii) people within the regime who are barred from the usual forms of claim making. That barring may actually occur in the course of routine contention, as the militant activists of contending parties resist a settlement under negotiation by their leaders; we have already seen both Protestant and Catholic paramilitary forces break away repeatedly in Ireland as settlements approached, only to see their previously justifiable attacks labeled as terrorism. We have also witnessed the opposite evolution in Rwanda, where the scattered attacks of Hutu Power activists on Tutsis and their sympathizers accelerated after the RPF invasion of 1990, then acquired government sponsorship in 1994, mutating temporarily into coordinated destruction before devolving into widespread opportunism.

We have encountered most of the mechanisms and processes that cause scattered attacks in previous chapters, but in different combinations. They include

- *Network-based escalation* – networks of mutual aid segregate on either side of a boundary; a dispute that pits people on the two sides against each other (for whatever reason) and then leads them to seek support from their fellows redefines the dispute as categorical.
- *Setting-based activation* – political identities connect people with certain social settings and not with others; drawing them into those settings activates the identities.

- *Signaling spirals* that communicate the current feasibility and effectiveness of generally risky practices and thereby alter the readiness of participants to face the risks in question.
- *Polyvalent performance* – individual or collective presentation of gestures simultaneously to two or more audiences in ways that code differently within the audiences.
- *Selective retaliation* for previously experienced wrongs.

In scattered attacks, these mechanisms and processes combine into more complex processes that convert routine nonviolent contention into small-scale, segmented collective violence. Sometimes they also initiate shifts from scattered attacks into opportunism and coordinated destruction.

Weapons of the Weak

James Scott's analyses of peasant resistance to landlords and governments in Southeast Asia have made famous the idea of everyday resistance comprising sabotage, mockery, foot dragging, and related hindrances to hegemony (Scott 1985; Scott & Kerkvliet 1986; for critiques, extensions, and applications, see Guttman 1993; Joseph & Nugent 1994). Although Scott develops ideas about the rare conditions under which clandestine opposition becomes concerted and open (Scott 1990, 1998), most of the violence he documents from his own research qualifies as scattered attack. In the Malaysian villages for which Scott first formulated his ideas, resistance usually involved delays, evasions, informal pressure, and theft rather than direct damage.

Scott does report outright violence, however, in two circumstances: reprisals against neighboring farmers' trespassing animals and attempts to stop adoption of harvesting combines. We have already encountered the anti-combine actions in Chapter 1. According to Scott:

Starting in 1976, when combine-harvesting began with a vengeance, peasant acts of vengeance likewise spread throughout the paddy-growing region. Poor villagers in Sedaka can remember several incidents, which they recount with something akin to glee. Tok Mahmud, for example, told me that he knew exactly how to jam a combine's auger – where to put the barbed wire or nails – because he had friends who had done it. He declined to elaborate because, he said, if he talked openly his friends might be arrested. Sukur described a more dramatic incident, two seasons before I arrived, near Tokai, just a few miles south of Sedaka, where a combine was set on fire. A number of poor people, he said, surrounded the Malay night watchmen and asked him who owned the machine. When he replied that it belonged to a Chinese syndicate, they ordered him to climb down and then poured kerosene over the engine and cab and set it alight. (Scott 1985: 148–9)

But such openly damaging acts occurred amid a much wider range of semi-violence and nonviolence: blocking the paths of combines, withholding labor from farmers who adopted them, and grumbling noisily.

Populist historians and social scientists find the analysis of everyday resistance attractive despite its difficulty. It allows them to voice sympathy for underdogs and losers without lambasting the same underdogs and losers for passive acceptance of injustice. It also offers evidence that great top-down transformations such as the expansion of capitalism and the growth of centralized states affected the lives and politics of ordinary people by means other than turning them into desperate, rootless masses. Much of the resistance documented in available historical records takes the form of violent encounters in the course of widespread small-scale and generally nonviolent interaction – when a number of participants respond to obstacles, challenges, or restraints by means of damaging acts. The records feature scattered attacks.

Because capitalism was expanding and states were gaining power most of the time, European history from the sixteenth to nineteenth centuries overflowed with scattered attacks. Across much of the continent, bourgeois landlords were expelling hunters, fishers, gatherers, herders, and householders from their increasingly enclosed properties, merchants were collaborating with officials in freeing food markets from local controls, and employers were liberating themselves from customary forms of hiring and payment; government officials not only supported these efforts but also expanded taxation, conscription, and registration of populations. The growth of state-backed policing resulted largely from these processes but then became another form of intervention in routine social life. All these changes generated scattered attacks: pulling down of enclosures, killing of forbidden game, sniping at forest guards, mobbing of tax collectors, driving off of census takers, roughing up of police, and more. Those were the sorts of clashes I was studying when I wrongly concluded that low-salience collective violence prevailed across the world.

A colorful, well-documented example comes from France's struggles over forests before, during, and after the revolution of 1830. In 1827, France enacted a new forest code that extended the powers of landlords, big contractors, and state authorities while radically diminishing the rights of local people to pasture, gather, clear, and cut wood in private or public forests. Among other things, the code authorized private owners to hire their own armed guards as it reinforced the powers of government-hired guards. On the French slopes of the Pyrenees, scattered attacks against authorized charcoal burners (who used forest lumber to fuel metal-working forges) and forest guards multiplied in 1829. Groups of men disguised as women, with blackened faces, gathered wood in forbidden forests, threatened charcoal burners, destroyed guards' houses, and assaulted the guards themselves.

Masked or face-blackened avengers in women's dress frequently took part in the rural violence of Western Europe from the seventeenth to nineteenth centuries. The Pyrenean avengers ostentatiously took on the name Demoiselles. When the bishop of Pamiers told parish priests to preach against the forest depredations, he received a letter containing these words:

> We insurgents, under the mask of the women called *Demoiselles;* Garchal, curé of Biert, and Séres, of Soulan, have had the imprudence to preach against us. The said parishes have written you several times. You are unrelenting, but we will know how to teach them ... the lesson which was given to the clergy and to the nobility in 1793. Their residences will be torn down and burned, their properties pillaged and burned, their bodies torn to pieces, their limbs will be sent by the parishes of the *arrondissement* to better set an example. (Merriman 1975: 98–9)

Although the threatened new Terror never materialized, the Demoiselles' action continued to broaden without acquiring central direction. With the revolution of July–August 1830, scattered attacks increased and some violence consolidated into coordinated destruction: early August brought the Ariège concerted attacks on castles, forges, forest guards, tax collectors, and the homes of local notables.

At the same time, assemblies of peasants besieged officials and landlords, sometimes successfully bargaining out formal concessions of their forest rights. On the whole, however, the concessions were few and temporary. An amnesty and a governmental commission failed to satisfy local demands but did break the peasants' momentum. Scattered attacks in the Pyrenees' forests continued intermittently at a diminished pace into the 1870s but never again approached the surge of 1830. They were clearly weapons of the weak.

The Swing Rebellion

About the same time that Pyrenean peasants were insisting on their dwindling forest rights by means of scattered attacks, landless agricultural laborers in Southeastern England were employing similar tactics to defend their jobs. The so-called Swing Rebellion of August to December 1830 occurred during vast popular mobilization for parliamentary reform, but it constituted a distinct set of episodes. Across urban Britain, political associations (such as the Birmingham Political Union) and national federations of workers (such as the National Association for the Protection of Labour) were organizing mightily, holding mass

meetings, and peppering power holders with their demands. In London, resistance to Robert Peel's New Police coupled with demands for parliamentary
reform. But these great stirrings intersected very little with the Swing Rebellion.

Following similar but smaller bursts of agrarian conflict in 1816 and 1822, the
huge wave of 1830 eventually covered much of London's agricultural hinterland. In that region, large farmers (who generally leased their properties from
absentee landlords) had been increasing the scale of their operations, enclosing
and putting into cultivation previously unplowed land, cutting workers' wages,
and introducing machines – especially threshing machines – since the close of
the Napoleonic Wars. The day laborers who worked the farmers' land had been
fighting back with various weapons of the weak but, by 1830, were losing ground
badly.

Locality by locality, a split was opening up between large capitalist farmers
and the rest of the agrarian world. Very large farmers profited from economies
of scale in mechanical threshing, which allowed them both to save on labor costs
and to control the timing of their grain's entry into national markets. Smaller
landlords and farmers found themselves mechanizing to compete but failing to
gain from scale economies (Hobsbawm & Rudé 1968: 359–65). This division between large and small producers helps account for the surprisingly sympathetic
local hearings laborers sometimes received from members of the landed classes.

Beginning southeast of London, parish by parish and day by day, bands of agricultural workers gathered to confront farmers and local officials with demands
for redress (for a compact summary, see Charlesworth 1983: 151–5). Their demands varied by locality: higher wages; more secure employment; reduction of
tithes; abandonment of agricultural machines; and occasionally distributions of
money, beer, or food. In some cases, they organized a kind of strike, declaring
that no one would work for local farmers until all the farmers raised their wages.
Sometimes, in contrast, they enlisted tithe-paying farmers in proposals to reduce the tithe and simultaneously raise laborers' wages. In Romsey, Hampshire,
agricultural workers proposed a parishwide program:

Gentlemen Farmers we do insist upon your paying every man in your parish 2 shillings
per day for his labour – every single man between the ages of 16 and 20 eighteen pence
per day – every child above 2 – to receive a loaf and sixpence per week – the aged and in-
firm to receive 4s. per week. Landlords – we do also insist upon your reducing their rents
so as to enable them to meet our demands. Rectors – you must also lower your tithes
down to £100 per year in every parish but we wish to do away with the tithe altogether.
(Hobsbawm & Rudé 1968: 197)

Usually, however, a parish's wage laborers directed threats and demands at farmers or landlords who were cutting wages and employment.

Most such gatherings featured threats but no outright damage to persons or property, but a substantial minority linked with collective violence. I use the term "linked" intentionally: in the course of very few parleys between laborers and farmers or officials did any violence occur. Yet before, after, and outside of public gatherings, laborers sent threatening letters, broke up threshing machines, torched hayricks, and (more rarely) sacked or burned farm buildings. They often sent letters or announced their deeds in the name of a mythical avenger, Captain Swing – whence the name that outsiders eventually attached to the whole series of episodes. Instead of consolidating into a regionwide rebellion, Swing activities typically occurred in clusters of adjacent parishes – a parish or two on any given day – and then moved on. Until the national government started sending out serious numbers of troops late in November, the actions multiplied. Eventually 252 participants received death sentences, and 19 of them hanged.

In 1968, E. J. Hobsbawm and George Rudé published an admirable study of the Swing Rebellion. Within a larger study of contention in Great Britain from 1758 to 1834, my own research group prepared several catalogs of Swing events (Tilly 1995: 315–21, 402–3). Hobsbawm and Rudé listed every threat, fire, machine attack, and gathering they found in an extensive search of published accounts and archival sources – a total of 924 incidents. In its main catalog, my group included only events reported in one of seven national periodicals (*Gentleman's Magazine, Annual Register, Morning Chronicle, Times, Mirror of Parliament, Hansard's Parliamentary Debates, Votes and Proceedings of Parliament*) during which ten or more people gathered in the same place and interacted, for a total of 285 such "contentious gatherings." Hobsbawm and Rudé therefore listed 3.3 times as many Swing incidents as the Tilly group. For well-dated events, nevertheless, the correlation over time between the two series is .95.

Figures 8.1 and 8.2 show the course of events from late August to the end of December 1830. In Figure 8.1, both the Hobsbawm–Rudé and the Tilly series reveal a dramatic increase of events in November and a rapid decline once Home Secretary Melbourne began serious repression the day after taking office on 22 November. The "Tilly" line represents larger-scale gatherings whereas the "Hobsbawm–Rudé" (H & R) line includes not only those gatherings but also threats, machine breaking, and arson. Comparison between the two lines therefore makes it clear that, near the high point of conflict, threats and small-scale attacks on machines accelerated even more greatly than collective confrontations.

Figure 8.2 uses the Hobsbawm–Rudé catalog to make a rather different point: during the peak mobilization from early November to early December, open confrontations and collective assaults on machines constituted a much larger

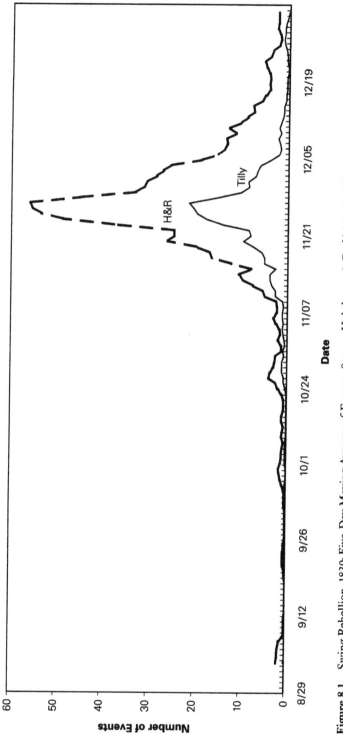

Figure 8.1 Swing Rebellion, 1830: Five–Day Moving Average of Events. *Sources:* Hobsbawm & Rudé (1968); Tilly (1995).

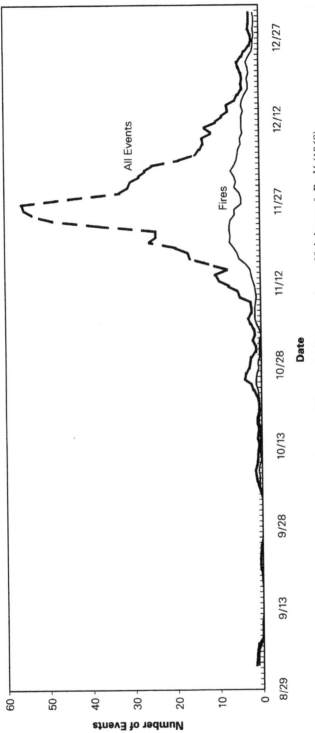

Figure 8.2 Swing Rebellion, 1830: Five–Day Moving Average of Fires and All Events. *Source:* Hobsbawm & Rudé (1968).

share of all Swing events than before or after; the rest of the time, most events consisted of scattered attacks by means of arson. Signaling spirals worked in both directions: first indicating to landless laborers in previously unaffected parishes that pressure on farmers had some chance of working; then (from late November onward) broadcasting the increasing danger and futility of collective attacks. When signaling from other places indicated that rejection and repression were the likely outcomes of public parleys, laborers turned to anonymous threats and arson. The other standard mechanisms – network-based escalation, setting-based activation, polyvalent performance, and selective retaliation – also played their part.

No encompassing organization lay behind the Swing Rebellion. Clusters of events moved along market connections such as canals and highways, often affecting a number of villages in a given town's market region within a few days. As Hobsbawm and Rudé remark:

The path of the rising therefore followed not the main arteries of national or even county circulation, but the complex system of smaller veins and capillaries which linked each parish to its neighbors and to its local centers. Thus in Kent the machine-breaking began in the triangle enclosed by Canterbury, Ashford and Dover, and the tracks which linked such places as Upper and Lower Hardres, Barham and Elham, were of much greater importance to its diffusion than either Watling Street or Stane Street. (Hobsbawm & Rudé 1968: 190)

Undoubtedly peddlers, tinkers, and other itinerants carried the news of gatherings, fires, and machine breaking from place to place along the main lines of communication (Charlesworth 1978). The events themselves frequently reveal conversation and collaboration among laborers in adjacent places. But the movement as a whole arose from a vast, decentralized, incomplete, changing network of connections among agricultural workers in far-flung villages.

British authorities and property owners, to be sure, often connected the Swing events with the recent French and Belgian revolutions as well as with the unprecedented mobilization for parliamentary reform that was accelerating in 1830. An article from the *Brighton Gazette* (reprinted in a broadsheet by radical Henry Hetherington in October) reported that, in Kent:

It appears that the conspirators do not seek for money or plunder of any kind. On the contrary, when offered money not to destroy property, they have uniformly refused it, and they have on no occasion robbed. I understand that the *High Sheriff of the county lately attended one of their meetings in the open air, and addressed them*, pointing out to them the folly and wickedness of their proceedings. They appeared to attend to his observations; but previous to dispersing one of them said *"We will destroy the corn-stacks and thrashing-machines this year. Next year we will have a turn with the Parsons, and the third we will make war upon the Statesmen."* What will such a state of things as this end in? (PRO HO 40/25 [Public Record Office, London, Home Office Papers, series 40, box 25; italics in original])

Hetherington took the opportunity to brandish the Belgian example as a warning to greedy, heedless aristocrats. For the most part, however, laborers themselves stuck to local affairs.

The national government stepped in decisively only after the Whigs took power from Wellington, Peel, and the Tories late in November. Before then, local magistrates did the bulk of the repression. Most of the time they tracked down suspects after fires, attacks on machines, or public confrontations, but now and then they met the laborers on their own ground. A report from Kent on 16 November gave these details:

Sir William Cosway has routed the Mob of Labourers in their progress out of the Marsh thro' Ham Street & into Buckinge where he met them (Mr Deedes Jr was with him) he refused to accede to their Terms, he seized one of the most active Men and held him fast notwithstanding two blows on the head. Mr Deedes' keeper, one of the party ... was severely cut in the face in the affray. They took two or three into Custody and the Mob, then consisting of the forced Men chiefly, many having deserted them, began to parley. (PRO HO 40/27)

Sir William lectured them and kept them from pressing their demands for higher wages in Buckinge, but he could not keep them from moving on to the next parish. Their system was simple and effective: men from one parish walked into the next, recruited or forced a following, then made their demands in the second parish. That work finished, the group moved on to a third parish as most of the men from the first one returned home.

The presence of authorities did not necessarily deter participants in the Swing Rebellion. Wiltshire Member of Parliament John Benett testified in December 1830 that, on 25 November, he had tried unsuccessfully to break up a crowd of about 400 men near the lime kiln of Ponthill Gifford:

This Deponent observed one Charles Jerrard the elder acting at the time as the foremost man or the Leader of the Mob and a young man near him wore a party coloured sash and these with many other violent men who were forward rushed on towards the parish of Ponthill Gifford while this Deponent continued to address others as they came up in succession many of whom gave anxious attention to his observations till they were driven on by the pressure of sticks and pushing of the more violent, who were behind them. This Deponent rode with them and saw them break the Drum of a Threshing Machine which had been taken down at the Farm occupied by Mr Candy at Ponthill Gifford and a whole machine which had been taken down and placed out in a field near the Inn in the same parish by Mr Lampard and the Horse House and a Great part of a Barn from which the last mentioned machine had been taken down at Lawn Farm in the parish of Fishny in the said County the property of Mr Lampard. And this deponent then and there (meaning Lawn Farm) again addressed them at some length entreating them to desist but refusing to comply with their demand then tumultuously made for raising wages and destroying his this Deponent's own Threshing Machines, alleging as a reason that he would not listen to any demands or complaints made by persons riotously assembled and with arms in their hands. (PRO HO 40/27)

The group returned to Benett's own farm. While he watched, helpless, the laborers smashed one of his threshing machines and then rushed off to destroy another. A troop of yeomanry (the farmers' militia) came by unexpectedly. Benett led them to where the machine breakers were just leaving the site of their second attack. Although the attackers disappeared into a nearby wood, when they emerged from the other side half the mounted yeomen were waiting for them. The laborers came on with hatchets, wrenches, pick axes, sticks, and stones, but the yeomen replied with swords, guns, and the sheer force of their horses. It was a losing battle; the 40 or 50 cavalrymen killed one of the estimated 300 attackers still at hand and arrested 29 of them (PRO HO 52/7).

By this time, magistrates all over England were responding to newly installed Home Secretary Melbourne's call for vigilance and repression by swearing in reliable local men as special constables and sending requests for military assistance when crowds gathered. As repression tightened and the frequency of open confrontations declined, however, a previously rare form of scattered attack became more common: the rescue of prisoners taken by the yeomanry or the military. On 1 December, for example, R. Buckland reported from Shaftesbury, Dorset, that when prisoners taken in a nearby machine-breaking episode came through the town,

[a] mob of disorderly persons in considerable force collected, and immediately without the Town completed their rescue from a party of Mounted Constables, after which they proceeded to two farms in the immediate neighborhood and totally demolished the machinery thereon. A Military force arrived this Morning. The principal ring leader in the Rescue has been taken & conveyed to the County Gaol & the Town is at present quiet. (PRO HO 52/7)

Little by little, however, both the scale and the frequency of attacks diminished. Furtive arson again became the laborers' principal form of violence (Archer 1990).

Even in its waning phase, the Swing Rebellion frightened authorities across Great Britain. If ordinarily slow and docile farm workers could produce such widespread havoc, perhaps a French- or Belgian-style revolution could occur in the orderly British Isles as well. A junction of agricultural laborers with the industrial workers, small masters, and merchants who were already mobilizing so

Doncaster, December 4, 1830

At a MEETING of the MAGISTRATES for the West-Riding of the County of York, acting in the Lower Division of Strafforth and Tickhill, the Mayor of Doncastor (sic), and of several Gentlemen from the Neighborhood, PRESENT, THE FOLLOWING MAGISTRATES:

Sir W.B. Cooke, Bart., Sir Joseph Copley, Bart., The Mayor of Doncaster, Edmund Denison, Esq., Godfrey Higgins, Esq., Geo. Broadrick, Esq., Thos C.R. Read, Clerk., John Forster, Clerk., Alexander Cooke, Clerk., Thos. Cator, Clerk,, E.H. Brooksbank, Clerk.

IT WAS RESOLVED That although they do not apprehend any such unlawful and riotous proceedings will take place in the said Lower Division of Strafforth and Tickhill, as have recently occurred in and disgraced some of the Southern Counties, viz. breaking Thrashing Machines, destroying Houses, Corn and Hay Stacks, or other property; nevertheless they feel called upon to put the said Division in such a condition as will, in all probability, effectually prevent, or immediately put down all unlawful attempts.

RESOLVED - That in each Town, Village, or Hamlet, within the said Division, a sufficient number of Householders and Labourers shall immediately be sworn in as Special Constables, and be placed under the direction and control of a Head Constable, to whom further directions and orders shall from time to time be given by the said Magistrates.

INSTRUCTIONS TO ALL SPECIAL CONSTABLES . . .

IN case you have any reason to suspect that any Person or Persons intend to commit any Outrage, such as breaking THRASHING MACHINES, setting FIRE to CORN or HAY STACKS, or BUILDINGS of any description, or riotously assembling for the purpose of *pulling down or destroying the same*, or *disturbing* the Peace, you will immediately give information thereof to the Person who may be appointed your Head Constable, whose instructions you must steadily follow; and provided you unexpectedly hear, that any Person or Persons are *actually breaking any Machine*, or committing any of the above named offences, you will immediately let your Head Constable know, and go as quickly as possible, with as many Special Constables as you can conveniently muster, for the purpose of putting a stop to the Outrage, and taking into custody every Person whom you have reason to suspect of being concerned in the same offence.

Figure 8.3 Excerpt from Anti-Swing Proclamation of Yorkshire Magistrates. *Source:* Public Record Office, London, Home Office Papers, Series 40, Box 26.

vigorously against the establishment could cause serious trouble for the ruling classes. The northern county of Yorkshire, which had only four threshing machines broken over the entire period from 1830 through 1832 (as compared with 97 for Wiltshire; Hobsbawm & Rudé 1968: 199), provides a case in point. Early in December, a group of its magistrates posted the proclamation excerpted in Figure 8.3. It bespeaks the desire to co-opt or cow agricultural workers and organize armed force in advance of any challenge.

Compared to the other types of collective violence reviewed in previous chapters, Britain's Swing crisis nevertheless displays two surprising features: containment and segmentation. Despite occurring simultaneously with an enormous national political mobilization, Swing events almost never involved public references to parliamentary reform, taxes, or rights of labor to organize. Their participants rarely included political activists or unionized workers. Although by definition these scattered attacks included moments when participants were doing damage, whole episodes rarely shifted into opportunism, brawls, or coordinated destruction.

In all these regards, the hundreds of Swing events remained strikingly contained. They also followed an extremely segmented pattern among themselves: almost never touching more than a handful of adjacent places on the same day, with few participants traveling far from their home bases, and the targets of violence commonly persons and places already quite familiar to the perpetrators. Low coordination beyond a very local scale, relatively high shares of talk, threats, and bargaining among all the interactions, and small amounts of damage per participant mark the Swing episodes as exemplary instances of scattered attacks.

Switching to and from Scattered Attacks

Not all scattered attacks, however, remain contained and segmented. In principle, we might expect salience and coordination to increase, and scattered attacks therefore to shift toward opportunism or coordinated destruction, if political entrepreneurs or violent specialists join the action on either side. Even the Swing stories reveal some shifts in that direction at the intervention of militias in the repression of laborers' assemblies. Conversely, we might expect broken negotiations and coordinated destruction to generate or mutate into scattered attacks as political entrepreneurs and/or violent specialists withdraw from the action.

Dingxin Zhao's comprehensive analysis of Beijing's struggles in 1989 offers a close look at the process by which scattered attacks shift toward more coordinated and high-salience collective violence. As we saw in Chapter 3, the peak of the city's mobilization arrived after students began a hunger strike in Tiananmen Square on 13 May. Little violence of any kind occurred in Beijing until the government declared martial law and troops started arriving in the city on 19 May. Troop movements and the declaration of martial law alerted city residents who had already been showing massive support for the student strikers that the situation was changing fast. In many Beijing neighborhoods, encounters with troops led simply to the soldiers' immobilization on the spot, but a number of them generated scattered attacks. In some, police attacked taunting crowds; in others, local people threw bricks at troops.

Most such events remained within their neighborhoods, unconnected with similar events elsewhere in Beijing. But from the top down, student organizers were mapping troop movements and sending coordinators to hot spots. Businessmen had organized a motorbike team called the Flying Tigers, which also spread news of concerted action from one neighborhood to the next. When one of these connecting networks intersected with local activism, a higher level of coordination emerged, sustained resistance became more likely, and collective violence resulted. A young teacher told Zhao how the connecting process worked:

On May 19 we knew that the army would come that night. Many young teachers came to my dormitory. We discussed what we should do when the troops came. Eventually we decided to persuade the soldiers to withdraw. We decided to write a statement, print it on handbills, and record it on a cassette. When we met the troops we could give them the handbills, and turn on our cassette players ....

In the night, we headed toward Liuliqiao .... When we arrived at Liuliqiao, we found that the troops had arrived and that some people were already there trying to stop the troops. We went over and turned on our cassette players. Somehow, we were separated and I was now alone. Then I met two students from our university. We three became a new team. The two students told me that there were more troops in Babaoshan, so we went there. (Zhao 2001: 186)

Note the resemblance to the process Asef Bayat describes as the operation of "passive networks" in Tehran a few years earlier. No centralized organization planned the disposition of Beijing citizens on the streets as troops arrived. Networks of acquaintance nonetheless facilitated low-level coordination and adaptation. When those same networks connected people with top-down organizations, the scale of coordination rose. Tehran's vendors remained at the level of scattered attacks, but a coalition of Beijing's students, workers, and neighborhood residents sustained resistance to the Chinese government for three weeks before massive repression put them down.

A similar consolidation of scattered attacks into concerted resistance occurred during Barcelona's Tragic Week of 1909. Having lost many of its remaining colonies in the Spanish-American War, the Spanish government was struggling to expand its exploitation of African colonies. In 1909, it faced serious guerrilla activity in Morocco and sent in troops to put down the rebels. The Spanish troops took humiliating defeats. At that point, the government called up six battalions of reservists, largely men from low-income Barcelona families. As reservists marched to the harbor for embarkation on 18 July, families gathered at the port, and rich women (many of whom had paid bounties to exempt their sons from military service) distributed religious medals and cigarettes to the troops. Some soldiers threw the medals into the harbor, family members broke into the ranks to hug their departing heroes, and crowds began to shout against the sending of their kin to Morocco. After a few days of widespread demonstrations and police action against demonstrators, a coalition of political activists called a general strike.

Like the Tiananmen crisis, Tragic Week featured intermittent, incomplete connections between scattered attacks and coordinating networks. Women figured importantly as connectors. On Monday 26 July, opening day of the strike:

At the Plaza of Catalunya at 6:00 that morning, a woman named Mercedes Monje Alcázar called on the men to prevent the drafted troops from leaving for Morocco. The Civil Guard intervened and arrested her, despite the large number of people around. By 10:00 other women, joined by young men, were demanding that merchants close their shops. All kinds of women joined the fray. Some had already participated in Radical party politics as the Red or Radical Women (Damas Rojas or Radicales). Others were active in street politics. Among these was "Forty Cents," the nickname given María Llopis Berges, a prostitute: she led a group that strong-armed shopkeepers along the Parallel, forcing them to close in support of the general strike or face destruction of their windows and furniture. Some two hundred men and women attacked the police station on New Street of the Rambla, where they liberated a woman who had just been arrested. (Kaplan 1992: 96)

Later, women led attacks on trolleys, police stations, and military outposts. By the next day, a general insurrection had begun. Although troops began trying to clear the streets almost immediately, insurgents controlled central city streets for most of the week. Scattered attacks had mutated into coordinated destruction.

In another, less heroic, version, scattered attacks occur as local majorities punish or even expel members of pariah minorities. Members of the majority lynch, burn, beat, or otherwise make life unbearable for people who are at least legally entitled to some sort of protection. Such attacks become more likely when they draw on a widespread consensus and extend an established pattern of day-to-day denigration and harassment against the minority. Donald Horowitz cites the case of Romania from 1990 to 1997, which "experienced more than two dozen episodes of arson perpetrated in separate villages against Roma (Gypsies) resident there" (Horowitz 2001: 479). Every instance, according to Horowitz, followed either a fight between Roma and Romanians or a public complaint that Roma had committed a serious offense, including insulting a Romanian. The violence in question focused on the alleged offenders and never spiraled into pogroms, but it generally sufficed to drive Roma villagers from their homes. What is more, authorities rarely prosecuted the perpetrators. Here we can see resemblances to American lynching of blacks as well as to early phases of the Swing Rebellion.

We are, then, actually looking not at twins but at first cousins: two concatenations of similar mechanisms that produce somewhat different outcomes. In the first concatenation, scattered attacks connect intermittently with other sorts of struggle but also continue on their own – with lesser salience and lower levels of coordination. In the second, scattered attacks as such disappear in the creation of new or consolidated forms of contention. The mechanisms are similar, but the second includes further mechanisms that foster increases in salience and/or coordination. Most often, such shifts occur when violent specialists or political entrepreneurs (or both) intervene in previously segmented conflicts.

Romanesque Violence

Yet sometimes the two cousins dance together: scattered attacks, coordinated destruction, and the transformation of one into the other all occur simultaneously. Just such a *danse macabre* took place in France's Piedmont region east of the Rhône during 1579 and 1580. At the time, the compact city of Romans had about 7,500 inhabitants and dominated an important rural hinterland. It lived from rents, administration, river trade, and production of woolen cloth. Civil wars between Catholics (who controlled the state) and Protestants (who prevailed in a number of segregated enclaves) had been racking much of France for almost two decades. Romans' region itself divided between a Catholic majority and a Protestant minority that concentrated in a few small towns. Twenty years earlier, Protestants had temporarily won control of Romans. By 1579 the city's Protestants had lost ground to intimidation, emigration, and conversion; they then constituted less than 10 percent of the city's population and occupied no distinctive place in public life. The city divided much more sharply between artisans, on one side, and rentiers, officials, clergy, and merchants, on the other.

Over the region as a whole, sharp divisions of interest aligned well-defined categories against each other – not just Protestants versus Catholics, city dwellers versus country people, and noble bandits versus peasants, but also tax-exempt segments of the population (clergy, nobles, and urban notables who paid taxes at home but not on the rural properties they were increasingly buying) against the householders who had to pay the rising costs of war. In a classic conjunction of exploitation and opportunity hoarding, the ruling classes and the crown drew taxes from the rest of the population, using those taxes both to support military activities from which the bulk of the population did not benefit and to maintain their control over the populace. They also hoarded an extensive set of privileges, honors, rights, and emoluments for members of the nobility, the clergy, and/or the honored urban classes.

Struggles opened up along these boundaries of exploitation and opportunity hoarding. In January 1579, villagers who had been meeting and arming themselves attacked troops of royal soldiers that passed through the region. The next month, a clothmakers' holiday brought out an armed parade of workers and small masters within Romans. The "king" of that festival was a master draper nicknamed Paumier; born Jean Serve, he had acquired his nickname through prowess in the tennis – the *jeu de paume* – of the time. Paumier continued to lead popular movements in the city until his murder in 1580; he also provided a link with peasant leagues outside of Romans and so became a crucial political entrepreneur.

On the 10th of February, artisans and city-dwelling agricultural workers, led by Paumier, invaded a city council meeting to demand major tax reductions, redistribution of the tax burden, and publication of the city's fiscal accounting. In March 1579 a peasant league formed to battle a noble warrior-bandit assembled in Romans, named Paumier its captain-general, and marched off to storm the bandit's castle. Presented with a *fait accompli*, the city fathers created their own force to join the action and co-opt it for the forces of order. Paumier prudently stayed in Romans while his troops went out, failed in a badly organized siege, and then found themselves shoved aside by a detachment under orders of the king's regional military commander. The royal Lieutenant General (the term means, literally, one who holds a place for a superior) used his artillery to finish the job successfully. That did not keep Paumier's league from taking credit for the victory or from returning to the city under arms.

As various peasant bands attacked other offending nobles in the countryside, struggles continued inside Romans. Workers who were allied with Paumier tried to throw off the bourgeois leaders of the urban militia in favor of their own men. Although the members of the Paumier coalition failed in their attempt to gain a voice in the city council, they organized widespread resistance to the city's augmented taxes and continued to demand publication of accounts. The crisis sharpened after Candlemas (2 February) 1580, the traditional opening of pre-Lenten festivities in Romans. Candlemas came the day before the anniversary of the clothmakers' festival (St. Blaise, 3 February) on which the artisanal party had first paraded in force. On St. Blaise's day, Paumier donned a bear skin, climbed on a horse, rode through the streets to drumbeats as festival king, and ostentatiously took an unauthorized seat in the city hall. Some of the people who danced in the streets that night brandished swords, while others wore funerary robes as they carried rakes, brooms, and flails. The notables read plebeian dancing as a threat against their power and their lives. They read rightly.

During the raucous festivities that stretched from Candlemas to Ash Wednesday, a split appeared within Romans' popular faction; beneath the cover of Carnival, a rival group to Paumier's, backed secretly by members of the city elite, began to challenge Paumier's dominance. Beside the plebeian "kingdom" of the

Rooster-Eagle created for festival purposes, bourgeois leaders created an elite "kingdom" of the Partridge; both aligned against the popular "kingdoms" of the Hare and the Capon. Each kingdom held its own games, parades, tableaux, and feasts. Each also took the occasion to mock the others and sometimes to interfere with the others' celebrations. From that arose ample opportunity for scattered attacks that could turn into sustained combat. Before Mardi Gras (16 February), the rivalry among Hares, Capons, and Partridges produced extensive bloodshed in Romans.

In fact, Fat Monday (Lundi Gras, 15 February) became the critical day. That evening, a herald from the Rooster-Eagle Kingdom entered the banquet of the Partridge Kingdom in full regalia. He delivered a card from his king complaining of a slight earlier that day. In a previously plotted scenario, members of the two kingdoms carried on a ritual joust and then reconciled ceremoniously. Later an armed band left the Partridge ball, divided into three squads, and marched into the artisanal quarter. One of them went straight to Paumier's house, called him into the street, and slaughtered him on the spot. All three troops then went on to take control of the artisans' neighborhoods and the nearby city gates.

Many of Paumier's allies slipped out of the city, but others threw up barricades and fought the invading force. According to the powerful judge who later wrote the elite account of the whole struggle, the squad sent to seize the guard post adjoining the drapers' neighborhood of le Chapelier "encountered resistance and some barricades ... and were therefore forced to bloody their hands with the rebels. Because of that the rebels who feared for their hides gave up the post to the forces of order" (Le Roy Ladurie 1979: 263). Some of the escaping partisans reached villages around Romans, where peasants assembled in arms for an assault on the city. Some 800 to 900 men marched to the walls of Romans. A few broke into the city, found no allies, and left again. City leaders began bargaining with the force outside the gate, promising them no harm if they left in peace. They dispersed, and repression began. A special court convened on 27 February sentenced two of Paumier's surviving lieutenants to be dragged through the streets, tortured, and hanged. Later the courts condemned another three followers to execution. All five died in March 1580. No one prosecuted Paumier's killers.

In Romans, we do not discover class consciousness in a classic *Communist Manifesto* sense of the term. Yet unequal divisions formed and sustained by exploitation and opportunity hoarding clearly underlay the major conflicts of 1579–1580. Boundaries between haves and have-nots took on the names noble–commoner, bourgeois–artisan, rentier–peasant, or soldier–civilian rather than more conventional class names, but they certainly separated people who were aware of their antagonistic interests. Under some conditions, they inflicted damage on those antagonists. The prevailing sorts of damage alternated between scattered attacks and coordinated destruction.

Emmanuel Le Roy Ladurie, whose ornate reconstruction of Romans' struggles I have plundered for my (much more linear) narrative, treats the city's conflicts primarily as an expression of sixteenth-century mentalities shaped by long-term demographic, economic, and political realities. As he puts it with characteristic bravura:

Romans' Carnival makes me think of Colorado's Grand Canyon. An event-filled furrow, it cuts deep into structural stratigraphy. With a saw's incision, it reveals the mental and social levels that constitute a very Old Regime. In Renaissance twilight, it uncovers a whole tinted, tortured geology. (Le Roy Ladurie 1979: 408)

While it does all that, the Romans crisis of 1579–1580 also provides insight into relations among different kinds of collective violence. Founded on wide-ranging, culture-bound, but relatively decentralized interpersonal networks, scattered attacks remained the characteristic response of both workers and peasants to the threats and depredations of more powerful actors. They lashed out at soldiers who not only marauded through the land but also lived on the crown's rising taxes. But on Fat Monday the opposition between urban notables and their enemies turned to coordinated destruction three times: first in the organized massacre of Paumier and his stalwarts; then in the battle for control of the artisans' quarter; and finally in the abortive assault on the city by peasants from surrounding villages. For good measure, the parties acted out their hostility in well-contained violent rituals, drenched in the symbolism of Carnival.

If we look closely enough at Romans and its hinterland in those troubled times, we also detect some collective violence in the form of broken negotiations – more highly coordinated on one side or both than the scattered attacks just reviewed but still leaving direct damage that is less salient than in ritual violence or coordinated destruction. Authorities first and normally used non-violent means to convert Protestants, collect taxes, and billet soldiers. They commanded, threatened, cajoled, bribed, and colluded in preference to inflicting outright short-term damage. In this setting of widespread communication and solidarity among oppressed populations, however, those initially nonviolent interventions generated not only scattered attacks but also widely coordinated campaigns of evasion, subversion, and resistance. Under those conditions, broken negotiations and coordinated destruction became the dominant forms of collective violence.

9

Broken Negotiations

Indian Police versus Villagers

Rice- and sugar-growing Narayanpur village lies in the northeastern reaches of India's Uttar Pradesh, near the border with Nepal. In the region, members of elite castes generally support the Congress Party and sometimes carry their clients with them. But the bulk of the peasant population tends to favor left and agrarian opposition parties. A large divide opens up between rich and poor. On either side of the divide, party politicians provide important links between national centers of power and local politics, including violent politics. Police forces usually line up with the same party politicians for protection and promotion. A road accident in 1980 activated just such alignments in village violence.

On 11 January, a bus operated by a private company ran down and killed a Narayanpur grandmother. The victim had supported two grandchildren by herself. Local people surrounded the offending bus, demanding that the company offer compensation to the family members who would now have to bring up the children. The driver escaped by promising that the bus operator would pay up. Later that day, people in the village stopped a second bus from the same company. The bus's sequestration brought the owner onto the scene; he offered a small amount of money as compensation, only to face rejection from the crowd. (Some observers reported a remark from the owner that if he had to pay full compensation every time one of his buses killed someone, he would go bankrupt.) Police arrived, freed the owner, and helped him get away with a commitment to pay the proper amount.

Having received no further response from the bus operator, three days later villagers stopped yet another bus belonging to the same company. They declared they would not let the bus leave until the owner paid for his company's malfeasance. When police arrived and tried to free the bus, a battle broke out between the officers and local people. In one local version of the story, violence began when a villager accused an officer of having taken a bribe from the bus owner.

Eventually, several police units came to reinforce their colleagues in Narayanpur. After negotiations over which place would be safe for the delegates, a group went to the Hata police station to work out a settlement. "At the Hata police station," reports Paul Brass, who investigated the episode,

an agreement was reached in which the bus owner was to pay Rs. 5,000 – the standard money value attached to a poor person's life in those days – in compensation to the surviving family members for the upbringing of the children. However, the police then detained a number of the male villagers – variously estimated at between eleven and fourteen persons – at the Hata police station, where they were beaten and grossly abused. They were then taken to the Captainanj station for further beatings and humiliation. Finally, they were put in the Kasia jail. (Brass 1997: 136)

That night (14 January), almost a hundred police arrived in the village and attacked residents. Exactly what happened that night became a nationwide matter of dispute. Local leaders complained of beatings, rapes, looting, humiliating punishments, and further arrests, but a parliamentary commission eventually concluded that no rapes or looting had occurred. The commission left unresolved whether – as some locals reported – police had destroyed village property, stripped their victims, stuck police batons into their anuses, or forced them to drink their own urine.

What happened became a national political issue in part because national elections were under way. Uttar Pradesh state remained under control of the Lok Dal Party, local legislators all belonged to Lok Dal or the temporarily allied Janata Party, but some police officials had acquired office under auspices of the nationally powerful Congress Party. Congress supporters had reasons to blame regional administrators, while Lok Dal and Janata activists had reasons to blame the police. Within the next three weeks, national Congress leaders Sanjay Gandhi and his mother Indira Gandhi both visited the village to publicize and deplore the incident as an atrocity – a gratuitous attack on Harijan (untouchable) and Muslim households. The Gandhis' public account conveniently ignored the fact that the victims also included members of several different Hindu castes.

The national debate settled nothing. The anti-Congress newspaper *Statesman* commented on 9 February:

Narayanpur's moment of glory is over. The Prime Minister has come and gone. Other politicians will shortly come and go, perhaps even the Chief Minister will come and then go along with his Government.

For a while longer tears, real and crocodile, will be shed and the dust will continue to rise in the village as cars filled with VIPs tear in. Then, Narayanpur will become another paragraph in history. (Brass 1997: 170)

As Brass points out, it takes a great deal of unpeeling to uncover the core of what happened in Narayanpur from 11 to 14 January 1980. (In fact, I have had to do some reconstructing of Brass's own account, which contains minor inconsistencies.) Clearly, however, the event went beyond road rage, protection racketeers' opportunism, or straightforward retaliation. An accidental death occurred. Negotiations over just compensation ensued – negotiations that, under a wide range of circumstances, would have produced a nonviolent settlement. Instead, at seven different reprises (three seizures of buses, one battle between villagers and police, three attacks of police on villagers), violent interchanges occurred in and near Narayanpur.

Taken together, we can reasonably consider the series of incidents a characteristic case of broken negotiation; they combined medium to high levels of coordination among the parties with relatively low salience of damage across all the relevant interactions. More often than not, the combination of medium-high coordination and low salience results from various forms of collective action that generate resistance or rivalry, to which one or more parties respond by actions that damage persons and/or objects. In the most common episodes of this kind, some of the participants are already engaged in bargaining by relatively peaceful means before substantial collective violence occurs.

Broken negotiations differ from the scattered attacks we have just been reviewing; broken negotiations depend on significantly higher levels of coordination. They also differ from the coordinated destruction we examined earlier; in broken negotiations, nonviolent interactions occupy a significantly higher proportion of the social process. In general, participants in broken negotiations are carrying on a relatively organized nonviolent interchange that produces collective violence as a by-product.

Mechanisms That Break Negotiations

Broken negotiations matter because a significant share of public violence actually occurs in the course of organized social processes that are not in themselves intrinsically violent. That is notably the case in collective political struggle. Political regimes differ dramatically in the scope they allow for nonviolent collective making of claims – for example by petitioning, shaming, marching, voting, boycotting, striking, forming special-interest associations, and issuing public messages. On the whole, democratic regimes tolerate such claim making more readily than do their undemocratic neighbors; that is one way we recognize a regime as democratic. Yet even in democratic regimes, such forms of collective claim making occasionally generate open violence. This occurs for three main reasons.

1. Every regime empowers agents – police, troops, headmen, posses, sheriffs, and others – to monitor, contain, and on occasion repress collective claim making. Some of the agents are violent specialists, and most others have violent specialists under their command. These agents always have some means of collective coercion at their disposal and always enjoy some discretion in the use of those means. In one common sequence, claimants challenge repressive agents, occupy forbidden premises, attack symbolically significant objects, or seize property; then agents reply with force. Because variants on that sequence occur frequently, when repressive agents are at hand they actually perform the great bulk of the killing and wounding that occurs in public violence.

2. Collective claim making often concerns issues that sharply divide claimants from regimes, from powerful groups allied with regimes, or from rival groups; examples are campaigns to stop current wars, outlaw abortion, or expel immigrants. In these circumstances, offended parties often respond with counterclaims backed by governmental or nongovernmental force.

3. In relatively democratic regimes, an important share of collective action centers not on specific programs but on identity claims: the public assertion that a group or a constituency it represents is worthy, united, numerous, and committed (WUNC). Assertions of WUNC include marches, demonstrations, mass meetings, occupations of plants or public buildings, vigils, and hunger strikes. Even when the means they adopt are currently legal, all such assertions entail implicit threats to direct WUNC energy toward disruptive action, implicit claims to recognition as valid political actors, and implicit devaluation of other political actors within the same issue area. These features sometimes stimulate counteraction by rivals, objects of claims, or authorities – with public violence the outcome.

Broken negotiations also include some encounters that do not begin with concerted collective making of claims. Border guards, tax collectors, military recruiters, census takers, and other governmental agents, for example, sometimes generate intense resistance on the part of whole communities as they attempt to impose an unpopular measure. Similarly, audiences at theatrical performances, public ceremonies, or executions occasionally respond collectively to actions of the central figures by attacking those figures, unpopular persons who happen to be present, or symbolically charged objects. By and large, broken negotiations connect with issues over which groups are also currently contending in nonviolent ways.

One subclass of broken negotiation, however, displays a rather different pattern. Some organizations specialize in controlling coercive means, threatening to use those means if necessary but seeking compliance without violence if possible. Examples include not only established agents of repression but also mafiosi, racketeers, extortionists, paramilitary forces, and perpetrators of military coups. When such specialists in coercive means encounter or anticipate resistance, they commonly mount ostentatious but selective displays of violence. Their strategy resembles that of many Old Regime European rulers, who lacked the capacity for continuous surveillance and control of their subject populations but often responded to popular rebellion with exemplary punishment – rounding up a few supposed ringleaders, subjecting them to hideous public executions, and thus warning other potential rebels of what might befall them. The strategy is most successful, ironically, when specialists in coercion never actually have to deploy their violent means.

Broken negotiations, then, cover a diverse and interesting array of collective encounters that vary systematically as a function of regime type. They have in common relatively low salience of damage and relatively high coordination among damage doers. Recurrent mechanisms and processes causing violent breaks in negotiations include the old standbys brokerage, certification–decertification, polarization, and network activation, as well as newcomer object shift.

Object shift means alteration in relations between claimants and objects of claims, as when contending parties and their brokers in Narayanpur moved up the Indian administrative hierarchy looking for allies and thus promoted new definitions of their local conflict. Object shift often occurs in the short run, during the strategic interaction of contention; battling gangs unite against the police, the intervention of an official in a market conflict diverts customers' attacks to him, a besieged tax clerk calls in the mayor. Of course such shifts commonly alter the actors and the paired identities they deploy, but they likewise affect the forms of collective claim making that are available, appropriate, and likely to be effective.

Over the long history of armed forces recruitment, object shift often occurred during impressment: the capture of a man for service in the army or the navy. In a recurrent routine, friends or bystanders tried to prevent the capture but a local official intervened to stop them; what had been a fight between a few sailors and a recruiting gang became a confrontation between lawbreakers and public authorities. When Massachusetts was still a colony, for example, British warships often sent press gangs into the port of Boston to look for new hands. Press gangs worked the port so actively during the 1740s that many American sailors left town for safer havens. At that, the Boston town meeting protested to royal officials. The town's prosperous merchants not only believed in free labor but also depended on the availability of sailors for their own ships.

A crisis began in 1747 when 50 sailors deserted the H.M.S. *Lark*. The ship's captain, Commander Charles Knowles, sent a press gang ashore to recruit replacements for the deserters (Linebaugh & Rediker 2000: 215–16). On 16 November 1747, a crowd of 300 sailors and dockworkers tried to stop the gang by seizing a lieutenant from Knowles's squadron. (The anti-conscription activists reportedly included blacks and, especially, Scotsmen.) When the County Sheriff and his posse tried to rescue the lieutenant and arrest two of his captors, members of the crowd attacked the Sheriff. Meanwhile, the Speaker of the Massachusetts House of Representatives brought two naval officers to the royal governor's house for protection.

Governor William Shirley sent orders to raise the militia, authorizing the use of firearms to quell the rebellion if necessary. Shortly after, as the governor reported in a letter to the Lords of Trade:

they appear'd before my gates, and part of 'em advanc'd directly through my court yard up to my door with the Lieutenant, two other sea officers, that part of the mob which stay'd at the outward gate crying out to the party at my door not to give up any of their prisoners to me. Upon this I immediately went out to 'em and demanded the cause of the tumult, to which one of 'em arm'd with a cutlass answer'd me in an insolent manner it was caus'd by my unjustifiable impress warrant; whereupon I told 'em that the impress was not made by my warrant, nor with my knowledge; but that he was a very impudent rascal for his behaviour; and upon his still growing more insolent, my son in law who happen'd to follow me out, struck his hat off his head, asking him if he knew, who he was talking to. (Hofstadter & Wallace 1970: 61)

The governor took the captive naval officers into his house, locked the door, and readied the people inside for an assault. The assailants "beset the house round" and beat the deputy sheriff on watch in the yard before placing him in the public stocks.

That evening, a larger crowd broke the windows of the city hall, invaded the building, but could not get past the militia force on the ground floor. The governor (now gathered with his council in the city hall) parleyed with leaders of the invaders; the protesters demanded release of the men who had already been impressed for naval service. Reaching an impasse, the governor retreated to his council chambers as the crowd went off to capture more naval officers and burn a barge (wrongly) reputed to come from the British fleet. When Boston's militia resisted his orders to put down the rising, Shirley fled to Castle William in the harbor. Impressment ceased for a while in Boston. Object shift had magnified small-scale struggles between press gangs and their victims into a general division between royal officials and Boston's citizens.

Object shift also occurs over the longer run and outside of contentious interaction. When elected legislatures gain power vis-à-vis kings, warlords, or political patrons, for example, claim making not only moves toward the legislature and its members but also shifts toward electoral campaigns, demonstrations of electoral power, and such devices as lobbying (Tilly 1997). This sort of parliamentarization generally promotes changes in standard forms of claim making. Claim making shifts from locally variable to nationally standardized, from small-scale to large-scale, and from mediated by local notables to either direct or mediated by political entrepreneurs and legislators.

Formation of the Indian National Congress in 1885 and its Gandhi-coordinated adoption of a hierarchical structure corresponding approximately to the British system of top-down administration both promoted and resulted from the increasing orientation of Indian leaders to the British parliament; within their sphere of action, those moves generated standardized, large-scale, relatively unmediated claims on British parties, administration, and parliament (Johnson 1996: 156–62). During its early years, the Congress made its claims in the manner of an orderly British pressure group – by lobbying, petitioning, and drafting addresses (Bose & Jalal 1998: 116–17). They even staged decorous demonstrations; Mahatma Gandhi's nonviolent but still revolutionary repertoire included several adaptations of the demonstration. In 1930, for example, Gandhi led a march from his ashram at Ahmedabad to the sea at Dandi, where he planned to challenge British colonial law by evaporating sea water and making salt. The colonial government sent in troops to break up the demonstration, which ended with injuries and arrests.

The Demonstration

In twentieth-century democracies, demonstrations have recurrently generated violence in the form of broken negotiations. Demonstrations pose interesting puzzles for analysts of violence because of their ambivalence. On one hand, the characteristic actions of demonstrators – marching, assembling, and displaying shared will – are in themselves nonviolent. On the other hand, conventional demonstrations share enough form and genealogy with the military parade and review to convey a threat of force. When and how does that threat become reality? To answer this question, we must look closely at what happens in and around demonstrations.

Although you will not find it inscribed in constitutions, the demonstration is a remarkable political invention. It consists of:

- gathering deliberately in a public place, preferably a place combining visibility with symbolic significance;
- displaying both membership in a politically relevant population and support for some position by means of voice, printed words, or symbolic objects;
- communicating collective determination by acting in a disciplined fashion in one space and/or moving through a series of spaces – for example, by marching from Washington's Vietnam Memorial to the Capitol building.

Demonstrations display WUNC: worthiness, unity, numbers, and commitment. If we thought of the four items as varying from 0 to 1 – from the lowest to the highest values ever seen within the current regime – then we could then compute WUNCness as a multiple of the four: $.8 \times .6 \times .5 \times .9 = .216$ for a demonstration with high worthiness and commitment but lower scores for unity and numbers. (Imagine a demonstration bringing together fasting clergymen visibly representing a wide variety of faiths on behalf of peace.) The frequency with which supporters and opponents of a given demonstration disagree publicly over each of the four items – are they *really* worthy, unified, numerous, and/or committed? – indicates that participants and observers do employ something like that scorecard.

Demonstrations deploy WUNC on behalf of two main kinds of claims. *Existence claims* are that a certain political actor exists and has a right to exist; *program claims* are that a political actor or set of actors supports a program. The two kinds of claims are of course compatible, but demonstrations vary significantly in their relative emphasis on one or the other. Existence claims assert political identities; they announce that a connected set of people have entered the political scene, possess the capacity to act together, and deserve attention as players. Program claims announce that significant categories of people support or oppose some person, organization, proposal, or public action. Sometimes demonstrators actually come from the constituencies they claim to represent – workers, women, neighborhood residents, military veterans, and so on. On other occasions, however, demonstrators assemble on *behalf* of slaves, fetuses, war victims, animals, trees, or other absent constituencies. Despite considerable standardization of form, demonstrations adapt to a startling range of actors and programs.

Across the nineteenth and twentieth centuries, all democracies created legal niches for demonstrations. Those niches never acquired the depth and precision of the niches occupied by the strike, the electoral campaign, and the public meeting, but they certainly distinguished demonstrations from the more heterogeneous episodes authorities called "riot," "insurrection," and "terror." Within limits renegotiated incessantly and varying from regime to regime, such niches guaranteed a wide range of self-organized citizens the rights to assemble, occupy public space, identify themselves as a collective interest, and make demands.

So far as I can determine, no demonstration ever occurred anywhere in the world before the 1760s. (According to the *Oxford English Dictionary*, the term "demonstration" itself did not come into common use in this sense until British Whigs began using it during the 1830s.) Then demonstrations rapidly became common in Western Europe and North America before spreading across much of the world (Tilly 1989). By the 1850s, demonstrations had become recurrent features of public life in most relatively democratic countries; even in a number of undemocratic regimes, leaders of popular mobilizations were trying to organize demonstrations when they dared.

British and North American activists of the 1760s and 1770s pioneered the demonstration. They synthesized two established forms of public display: (1) the procession, in which groups from different corporate social units (organized trades, militias, parishes, religious sodalities, etc.) marched through streets to a common meeting place; and (2) the presentation of collective petitions to authorities. Supporters of the renegade gentleman John Wilkes probably deserve pride of place in the demonstration's history; from 1768 onward, they repeatedly pushed out the boundaries of tolerated processions and petitions by bringing thousands of people into London's streets on behalf of their hero, his defense of multiple freedoms, and (eventually) his opposition to British policy in North America (Tilly 1977).

A few excerpts from the *Annual Register* for 1768 offer a taste of London's street actions at the time of Wilkes's first great mobilization.

A great number of Spital-fields weavers, masters and journeymen, went in grand procession from Spital-fields through the city to St. James', in order to return their thanks to his majesty, for his declaration to shorten, for the future, court mournings. [12 February; long mournings meant fewer sales of the colorful silks produced in London's Spitalfields district]

Being St. David's Day, the stewards of the Society of Ancient Britons went in procession to St. James's, where they were admitted to see his royal highness the prince of Wales, to whom they presented an address; and his royal highness was pleased to present the charity with a purse of 100 guineas. [1 March]

This morning Sir William Beauchamp Proctor and Mr. Wilkes, two of the candidates for the county of Middlesex, set out for Brentford, where the election came on that morning for knights of the shire for the said county. Mr. Cooke, the other candidate, was confined with the gout. Mr. Wilkes went in a coach drawn by six long-tailed horses, and was attended by an amazing number of people to the place of election, which was held in the middle of Brentford Butts, a temporary booth being erected there for that purpose. The majority of hands appeared in favour of Sir William Beauchamp Proctor and Mr. Wilkes, who were accordingly returned ....

The mob behaved in a very outrageous manner at Hyde-park-corner, where they pelted Mr. Cooke, son of the city marshal, and knocked him from his horse, took off the wheels of one of the carriages, cut the harness, and broke the glasses to pieces; several other carriages were greatly damaged. The reason assigned for these proceedings is, that a flag was carried before the procession of Mr. Wilkes's antagonists, on which was painted, "No Blasphemer." There has not been so great a defection of inhabitants from London and Westminster to ten miles distance, in one day, since the lifeguardman's prophecy of the earthquake, which was to destroy both those cities in the year 1750 ....

At night likewise were very tumultuous; some persons, who had voted in favour of Mr. Wilkes, having put out lights, the mob paraded the whole town from east to west, obliging every body to illuminate, and breaking the windows of such as did not do it immediately.... At Charing-cross, at the duke of Northumberland's, the mob also broke a few panes; but his grace had the address to get rid of them, by ordering up lights immediately into his windows, and opening the Ship ale-house, which soon drew them off to that side. [28 March]

All these actions included some elements of the demonstration as we know it, but none of them constituted a full-fledged display of WUNC. Important innovations were occurring, but it would take another half-century before the full complement of demonstration actions appeared regularly in British and American streets. Benjamin Franklin, who lived in London as an agent of Pennsylvania at the time of the 1768 elections, found the actions of Wilkes's supporters dismaying. "Tis really an extraordinary event," he wrote to his son,

to see an outlaw and exile, of bad personal character, not worth a farthing, come over from France, set himself up as a candidate for the capital of the kingdom, miss his election only by being too late in his application, and immediately carrying it for the principal county. The mob (spirited up by numbers of different ballads sung or roared in every street) requiring gentlemen and ladies of all ranks as they passed in their carriages to shout for Wilkes and liberty, marking the same words on all their coaches and chalk, and No. 45 on every door, which extends a vast way along the roads into the country. (Franklin 1972: 98–9) ["No. 45" referred to an infamous 1763 issue of Wilkes's *North Briton* newspaper, which contained Wilkes's lightly veiled attack on the king's speech celebrating the settlement of the Seven Years War and defending his regime's American policy. Wilkes's number 45, in turn, recalled the 45 Scottish members integrated into the Westminster parliament in 1707, when Britain dissolved the independent Scottish parliament; the number therefore symbolized resistance to centralizing tyranny.]

By the 1770s "Wilkes and Liberty" had become a rallying cry for opposition to royal tyranny on both sides of the Atlantic (Brewer 1976; Hoerder 1977; Rudé 1962). Although people also shouted "Wilkes and Liberty" at authorized public meetings and banquets, the slogan linked indissolubly with street demonstrations before they had acquired that name or their full nineteenth-century form.

To be sure, public displays resembling demonstrations in some regards existed long before then; earlier chapters have described Italian penitents' processions and Carnival as occasions for collective assertions of existence, precedence, and support. But in the same sense that popular, contested legislative elections combined established devices such as representative assemblies and voting for candidates into striking new institutions, the emergence of the demonstration as an established political form wove familiar strands into fresh fabric. Its antecedents all involved authorized public assemblies such as festivals, submission of petitions, religious processions, military parades, official ceremonies, and electoral meetings. But the new form synthesized existence and program claims.

As binding, contested elections became more significant and engaged more of the population, participants in election contests (including nonvoting adherents of parties and candidates) increasingly reshaped old forms of assembly and procession into collective expressions of support and opposition. Even with a relatively narrow electorate, the existence of binding, contested, and consequential elections provided occasions, justifications, and legal toeholds for demonstrations reaching outside the range of candidates and parties. Such demonstrations depended on some minimum freedoms of assembly, speech, and association, but when effective they extended the boundaries of assembly, speech, and association.

From this derives the potential of demonstrations for violence: they became a means of drawing forbidden or divisive issues, demands, grievances, and actors into public politics. Demonstrations rose with electoral campaigns, public meetings, lobbying, mass petitioning, and pamphleting as means of placing controversial questions and groups on the political agenda. Rivals, opponents, and authorities therefore frequently sought to block the agenda changes; they sometimes attacked the persons and property of demonstrators as they did so. Over the long run, a large majority of demonstrations passed without collective violence, but a significant minority produced violent clashes; that minority qualified as broken negotiations.

Increasingly, authorities assigned police forces the responsibility of containing demonstrations. In the very process that gave workers and other common people political rights, nineteenth-century Western European countries created new police forces. Before the nineteenth century, private guards, game wardens, local constables, posses, militias, and regular armies had done whatever policing occurred in Western Europe. Bounty hunters and thieftakers also tracked down criminal suspects for posted rewards. During the nineteenth century, however, salaried police forces operating in uniform under civilian control began to take over policing of cities and some rural areas. Fear of crime in fast-growing cities provided one spur to the creation of specialized police forces, but concerns about public order provided another.

Once ordinary people had the right to assemble and organize – that is, once it became difficult or even illegal to send in regular troops simply because people were demonstrating or striking – authorities created specialized police forces. They hired men (before the twentieth century, they were always men) whose job was not only to patrol streets looking for drunkards and criminals but also to contain or disperse crowds that got out of hand. The authorities put police in uniform to mark them off from the general population and to advertise their presence. Just as police facilitated their daily work on the beat by creating networks of informers and collaborators, they dealt with crowd control in part by infiltrating dissident organizations, bargaining out parade routes with leaders of protests, and calling out extra forces to police elections, public ceremonies, mass meetings, and major strikes.

Early stages of the transition to policed demonstrations usually produced extensive violence (Ballbé 1985; Lindenberger 1995; McCarthy & McPhail 1998; McCarthy, McPhail, & Crist 1999; Palmer 1988: 54–6; Price 1982; Storch 1976). They did so because rights of assembly and speech remained in dispute, because people challenged the authority of the new police, because at first all parties were jockeying for advantage in unanticipated ways, and because it took time to work out standard rules of engagement. All these circumstances made scattered attacks fairly frequent accompaniments of demonstrations. They also opened the way to signaling spirals that generated coordinated destruction.

The creation of specialized police forces nevertheless changed the relationship between demonstrations and collective violence. Police generally worked to prevent or contain demonstrations. They threatened, patrolled, spied on, and infiltrated – but also negotiated with – organizers. Several consequences followed.

- Police and organizers took to bargaining out itineraries and forms of action both before and during demonstrations.
- Leaders of demonstrations themselves began to impose limits on itineraries and action.

- Such violence as occurred in the course of demonstrations increasingly flowed from encounters between police and demonstrators rather than from direct confrontations between demonstrators and authorities, enemies, counter-demonstrators, or other repressive forces.
- Demonstration-related violence bifurcated between central struggles of demonstrators with police at major points of assembly and peripheral attacks by dissident factions, opportunists, and dispersing participants.
- More precisely, collective violence emerged from demonstrations most frequently in two circumstances: (a) when police barred the way to symbolically important persons or objects and demonstrators tried to break through; or (b) when – at the edges or ends of demonstrations – subsets of participants attacked symbolically charged persons, objects, or properties.
- Preventive measures such as prohibition of assembly and anticipatory arrests reduced the frequency and scale of demonstrations but increased the likelihood of violent encounters between police and hard-core activists.
- When police themselves took to demonstrating (as they did increasingly when they organized as workers), their voicing of demands in this way posed a serious political threat, often incited authorities to take exceptional measures including the calling in of regular troops, and frequently generated violence between demonstrators and those assigned to contain them.

A dramatic variant on the last sequence occurred in the wake of New York's World Trade Center attacks of 11 September 2001. Shortly after hijacked airliners crashed into the two main WTC towers, the collapse of those towers killed 23 police officers and 343 fire fighters among the thousands of people who died. In the aftermath, members of the fire department took the lead in searching the smoldering debris first for survivors, then for bodies, then for remains of any kind. They established rituals for removing and preserving objects that could be identified with people who died in the disaster. When they did find a body, police, demolition teams, and fire fighters regularly ceased work to form two ranks of solemn guards as their comrades removed the cadaver.

After several weeks, however, the city administration began reducing the number of fire fighters allowed on the site. On 31 October, the city reduced the permitted number of searchers from 64 to 25. On 2 November, called out by their union, several hundred fire officers came to the disaster site for a demonstration. They called for the removal of Mayor Rudy Giuiliani and Fire Commissioner Donald Von Essen, shouting "Bring our brothers home!" One fire fighter told the crowd about the solace his family had felt when searchers found the body of his fire fighter brother in the rubble and the family gave the body a proper burial. A retired fire captain spoke of his fire fighter son, still among the missing.

City police were manning barricades set up to keep unauthorized persons from entering the site. The union president used his bullhorn to ask the police to open a path to the area and allow the demonstrators to walk through it. Then:

The protesters pushed aside a steel fence and began marching south down West Street, closer to the disaster site, while police officers watched, as if taken aback. It was not until the protesters pressed against a second barricade that matters turned ugly.

Punches were thrown, profanities exchanged. People either fell or were pushed to the ground. Police officers grabbed whom they could and, after brief struggles, slapped on handcuffs. Then the scuffling ended almost as quickly as it had begun, and the police officers stepped aside. (Barry & Flynn 2001: B10)

Construction workers formed two ranks of an impromptu honor guard as the fire officers walked off the site and over to City Hall for a (nonviolent) continuation of the demonstration. Meanwhile, police arrested eighteen fire fighters, including five of high rank. On the previous day, the fire union had already announced its intention to stage a demonstration, but somehow fire fighters and police had failed to negotiate plans for a peaceful encounter. Violence resulted from that failure.

Over the demonstration's long history, organizers frequently struck bargains in advance with authorities and police. Negotiation among organizers, demonstrators, authorities, and police took place both before and during demonstrations. Negotiation created limits on all parties and increased the predictability of encounters in the course of demonstrations. As a consequence, most demonstrations unfolded without direct damage to persons or property. Violence that did occur resulted mostly from failed bargaining, unanticipated encounters, breakaways by dissidents, or disruptions of coordination on one side or another. Demonstration violence came to concentrate heavily in the category of broken negotiations: relatively low salience of damage and fairly high levels of coordination as a by-product of largely nonviolent interactions.

Demonstrations in France

French demonstrations lived a more discontinuous history than those of Great Britain (Robert 1990). In retrospect, we might see some assemblies and marches of the 1789 revolution as precursors of demonstrations. During the postrevolutionary decades, public meetings, funerals, and banquets occasionally took on the air of demonstrations. But only with the revolution of 1848 did mass public gathering, marching, displaying membership, and communicating of demands become frequent. Louis Napoleon's coup d'état (1851) and subsequent establishment of a repressive empire again squeezed out demonstrations until the late 1860s.

With the Third Republic (1870–1940), the demonstration became standard practice for a wide range of claimants in French politics. The German Occupation (1940–1944) again marginalized demonstrations. After 1944, however, they acquired a prominence in French popular politics – left, right, and center – that they had never previously enjoyed. French police became specialists in repressing, containing, and managing demonstrations, modifying their tactics in antagonistic collaboration with activists (Bruneteaux 1993; Fillieule 1997b; Fillieule & Jobard 1998).

In the case of Lyon ("Lyons" for English speakers), Vincent Robert argues that, despite a flurry of demonstrations under the Second Republic (1848–1851), demonstrations did not really become readily available ways of pressing collective claims until the great May Day mobilizations of the 1890s put them on the map. Authorities themselves did not publicly recognize demonstrations as valid forms of political action, according to Robert, until just before World War I. At that point, Lyonnais authorities began assigning police to protect and channel demonstrations instead of routinely breaking them up as illegal assemblies.

Nevertheless, Lyon had seen plenty of demonstrations during the nineteenth century. When the Lyonnais workers' militias that formed early in the revolution of 1848 turned over the forts they had seized to the duly constituted National Guard, according to a popular newspaper:

> They went through the rue de la Barre and paraded in perfect order at the Place de Bellecour. There we saw these men who had so frightened the aristocracy for three weeks and that evil tongues had described as brigands.... In the midst of them was the city council of the Croix Rousse; next came a group of armed men carrying a bust of Liberty on a platform. Behind them followed the National Guard of Croix Rousse. They went to the Prefecture, where delegate [of the central government] Arago gave them a moving speech. Then the cortege went off to the City Hall, where it was received with enthusiasm. They installed the bust of Liberty in the museum of the Palace of Fine Arts. (Robert 1996: 84–5)

At least seven more demonstrations followed within the next month (Robert 1996: 94). Soon women's groups, political clubs, veterans of Napoleonic armies, school children, workers from the national workshops set up to combat unemployment, and even strikers who actually had jobs were demonstrating in Lyon. Most of them demonstrated in displays of solidarity with the new regime combined with statements of particular demands. They made both existence and program claims.

All these demonstrations went off without significant violence. However, when the municipality sought to rebuild the customs wall (and thus to resume collection of taxes on goods entering the city from the industrial suburb Croix Rousse) in December 1848, collective violence returned. At first, boys and men 15 to 20 years old simply threw stones at soldiers guarding the construction site. When two or three hundred of the youths pelted the soldiers and began to demolish their guard post, only to be driven away by reinforcements, one group of youngsters marched through the neighborhood carrying a red rag as their banner. The following day, crowds gathered to stop the construction, and authorities called in a military battalion to protect the building project.

Over the next two days, multiple groups of young men and women marched in Lyon, despite the banning of street marches by the repressive decrees that followed the Parisian insurrection of June 1848. Marchers confronted police (with some arrests) on one occasion, and burned an effigy of French head of state General Cavaignac on another. With military protection, authorities still got their wall rebuilt. Nationally and in Lyon, power was already shifting back to conservative elites. The following year, demonstrators gathered in Lyon's Perrache quarter to protect the statue of the Man of the People rumored to be slated for destruction by the authorities. After several days of confrontations between police and demonstrators, on 19 February 1849 a troop of dragoons charged people in the square, killing one and seriously wounding another (Robert 1996: 108).

Soon popular street marches and assemblies ceased under the weight of repression. They did not again assume prominence in Lyon's public life until the late 1880s. Lyon's experience between 1848 and 1914 confirms three important principles: that demonstrations thrive on relatively democratic regimes; that once installed in public politics they generally proceed without much violence; and that the violence that occurs in them most commonly occurs as a by-product of ongoing nonviolent interactions.

Twentieth-century demonstrations have inevitably figured in major catalogs of contentious events for a number of different countries (see e.g. Beissinger 2001; Deneckere 1997; Giugni 1995; Imig & Tarrow 2001; Kriesi et al. 1995; Mueller 1997; Oberschall 1994; della Porta 1995; della Porta & Reiter 1998; Sugimoto 1981; Tarrow 1989; Tilly, Tilly, & Tilly 1975; Titarenko et al. 2001; for reviews, see Hug & Wisler 1998; Olzak 1989; Rucht & Koopmans 1999; Rucht et al. 1998). When it comes to catalogs focusing more specifically on demonstrations, however, the United States and France have predominated (see Duyvendak 1994; Favre 1990; Favre, Fillieule, & Mayer 1997; Fillieule 1997a,b; McCarthy, McPhail, & Smith 1996; Oliver & Maney 2000; Oliver & Myers 1999; Tartakowsky 1997, 1999).

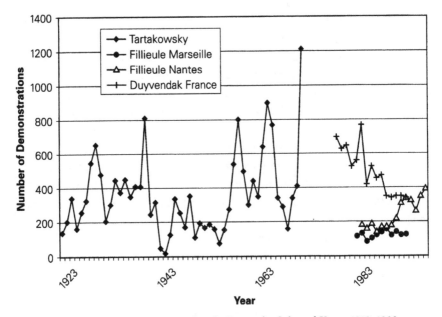

Figure 9.1   Number of Demonstrations in France for Selected Years, 1919–1993.

Specialists in French history have assembled the fullest long series of demonstrations. In addition to the work of Vincent Robert on Lyon, Danielle Tartakowsky has inventoried demonstrations over France as a whole from 1919 to 1968, Olivier Fillieule for Nantes from 1975 to 1990 and Marseille from 1980 to 1993, and Jan-Willem Duyvendak for France as a whole (but drawing events from just one newspaper issue per week) from 1975 to 1990. Figure 9.1 groups their findings together.

Tartakowsky's 15,000 catalogued events and the smaller collections of Fillieule and Duyvendak establish that, after World War I, the demonstration became a major means of advertising political identities and programs in France. Every major political controversy produced its own surge of demonstrators – and often of counterdemonstrators as well. Both right-wing (e.g., Croix de Feu) and left-wing (e.g., Communist) groups initiated disproportionate shares of demonstrations; more often than groups in the center of the right–left continuum, they were the political groupings that recurrently asserted their identities as significant actors and sought to place forbidden issues on local or national agendas. Demonstrations served both purposes in France. World War II and the German occupation, as we might expect, produced the low point of demonstration activity registered by these series. During that exceptional period, women complaining to authorities about food shortages and high prices became the most frequent initiators of the rare demonstrations.

Although differences in method and geographic scope forbid strict comparisons, the data also make clear that demonstrations became far more common after World War II than they had been before. Even the 814 demonstrations Tartakowsky identified during the great Popular Front mobilization of 1936 did not match the 899 of 1961 (massive conflict around the Algerian war) or the 1,213 of 1968 (immense movement activity mostly opposing the de Gaulle regime). As students of new social movements will not be surprised to learn, the all-time peak arrived in 1968. Whether the demonstration has since begun to fade away is less clear; the partial findings of Fillieule and Duyvendak contradict each other on that score. Still, the broad correspondence between periods of relative democratization and periods of frequent demonstrations comes across strongly.

What about collective violence in demonstrations? The long term trend looks paradoxical: the share of demonstrations producing violence declined significantly, but the sheer quantity of killing, wounding, and property damage done in demonstrations increased. Between 1919 and 1938, Tartakowsky estimates 60 deaths in French demonstrations; for 1939 through 1968, the figure soared to well over 200, with anti-Algerian police actions of 1961–1962 the peak (Tartakowsky 1997: 685). Deaths in French demonstrations averaged three per year in 1919–1938 and eight per year in 1939–1968.

When great surges of demonstrations occurred as in 1936, 1961, and 1968, furthermore, total damage rose dramatically but the proportion of all demonstrations producing damage diminished. These apparently contradictory trends occurred because, when demonstrations accelerated, a few (but only a few) of them featured violent confrontations. That happened especially when (1) authorities ordered police to crush an already organized demonstration; (2) activists broke from the announced scenario by assaulting police, attempting to reach police-protected locations, or attacking symbolically charged objects and properties; and/or (3) the central action of the demonstration itself consisted of occupying, blocking, or destroying property.

Table 9.1 illustrates these tendencies by listing some of the best-known violent demonstrations that occurred in Paris between 1919 and 1968. Over this period – and especially after World War II – demonstrations became one of the principal means by which popularly based French organizations made their presence and programs known. The roster omits two common violence-producing sorts of demonstration: first, the cortege of striking workers between workplace and seats of civil authority; second, the deliberate blockage of thoroughfares and/or

Table 9.1. *Examples of Violent Demonstrations in Paris, 1919–1968*

1 May 1919	Organized workers march to the Chamber of Deputies demanding an eight-hour day; police and troops block them, demonstrators build barricades, battles produce at least one death and 600 wounded.
23 Aug 1927	After a long series of demonstrations in Paris and elsewhere, Communists and anarchists call supporters to multiple locations in central Paris for protests against the recent execution in the U.S. of Italian immigrants and anarchists Sacco and Vanzetti; major groups gather on the Grands Boulevards, with a barricade on the boulevard de Sébastopol, stores broken into, and repeated fights between police and demonstrators along the boulevards and the Champs Elysées.
6 Feb 1934	Multiple right-wing groups gather at the boulevard Saint-Germain, the Place de la Concorde, and the City Hall, attempt to reach the Chamber of Deputies, battle police and Communist-led counterdemonstrators, for a total of fourteen dead, 1,700 wounded, 600 arrested; the Daladier government resigns.
16 Mar 1937	When 400–500 members of a right-wing group gather at a cinema in working-class Clichy, 5,000–6,000 demonstrators respond to a call from Communist officials; riot police protect the cinema, demonstrators sack right-wing properties, and in the struggle (possibly started by shots from the crowd) police gunfire kills seven, with 257 police and 107 demonstrators (the latter surely an undercount) wounded.
28 May 1948	After numerous demonstrations on previous days in Paris and elsewhere against the installation of American General Ridgway as NATO chief, columns of demonstrators armed with clubs, projectiles, and a few firearms converge on the city center, attacking and battling police at many locations, leaving one dead and a reported seventeen wounded among demonstrators against 372 police wounded.
13 May 1958	As the Algerian war heats up and as disputes between its proponents and opponents exacerbate within France, demonstrators demanding a stronger French hand in Algeria (including Jean Le Pen) march from the Arc de Triomphe to the Place de la Concorde, then try to reach the Chamber of Deputies; pushed back by riot police, some of them rush to the Tunisian Embassy and break windows.
17 Oct 1961	Perhaps 25,000 Algerians gather unarmed on the Champs Elysées and the major boulevards to protest a curfew imposed on North African Muslims alone, but 8,000 police ordered to clear the streets kill some 200 demonstrators and arrest another 11,500 of them.
3 May 1968	After the Sorbonne's rector has students (assembled to debate reforms) expelled from the university's main buildings, multiple student demonstrations form in the nearby streets, police attempt repeatedly to clear the streets and engage in minor scuffles with demonstrators; the movement expands for another six days, with barricades, burning vehicles, and street fighting the night of the 9th to the 10th.

Sources: Tartakowsky (1997); Tilly (1986).

ostentatious destruction of crops or other goods by aggrieved farmers, truckers, and shopkeepers. Those forms of demonstration occurred mainly outside of Paris. Otherwise, the chronology rightly portrays major processes by which previously nonviolent demonstrations turned violent: the authorized police attack on a march or a gathering; the taunting confrontation between police and demonstrators; the turning back of demonstrators from a symbolically important target. Brokerage, certification–decertification, polarization, network activation, and object shift were all clearly at work within these violence-generating processes.

Note, for example, the enormous place of brokers based in parties and organizations. Over the long run of 1919–1993, the French Communist Party specialized in bringing out not only its own stalwarts but other sympathetic groups on May Day and the sorts of special occasions described in Table 9.1; newly recruited Communist militants soon learned how to organize demonstrations. Right-wing organizations such as the Croix de Feu (which often recruited members from military veterans and disaffected workers) likewise produced cadres specialized in organizing demonstrations, creating counterdemonstrations, and subverting police controls.

Although the sheer exercise of brokerage did not in itself cause violence, the particular groups it connected (and how strongly) affected the likelihood that a demonstration would produce damaging encounters. Despite its appearance and reputation of spontaneity, the student–worker rising of May 1968 depended heavily on coordination by such brokers as Daniel Cohn-Bendit and Georges Séguy (Tartakowsky 1997: 748–82). Those brokers, in turn, promoted certification of the rebels as serious political interlocutors by left-wing intellectuals such as Edgar Morin and Alain Touraine (Morin, Lefort, & Coudray 1968; Touraine 1968). Polarization and object shift produced a new, if temporary, alignment of rebels against the French state, thus facilitating cross-boundary violence. And people continued to join the movement through network activation.

Resistance to Taxation

The violent demonstration offers us a privileged case of broken negotiations because it centers on a form of negotiation between two or more organized bodies. Collective violence of a similar sort also occurs, however, when well-organized authorities attempt to impose unpalatable measures on populations that belong to no single organization but are already connected by common residence, trading networks, kinship, religion, or other shared categorical memberships.

Expanding governments throughout history and across the world have incited violence in the form of broken negotiations by instituting conscription, censuses, cadastres (property lists), religious conformity, government-issued currency, or taxation.

Although over the long run some governments deliver net benefits to their subject populations in the form of security, roads, contract guarantees, and other collective goods, all governments exploit in the short run: they extract money, goods, and services from their subject populations and then deliver the returns from the investment disproportionately to officials and ruling classes. They also impose beliefs, practices, and definitions of identity that often clash with those held by members of the subject population. Governments therefore incite resistance in three overlapping but different ways:

1. imposing burdens that, by local standards, are visibly unfair as compared with what others are providing;
2. seizing resources (land, labor, cattle, money, and more) that are already committed to locally crucial enterprises and social relations;
3. insisting on affiliations, acknowledgments, displays, or supplies of information that conflict with locally salient commitments.

Most resistance consists of nonviolent weapons of the weak: subterfuge, evasion, sabotage, or flight. As Chapter 8 showed for the case of sixteenth-century French conflicts, some of it takes the form of scattered attacks. But on occasion sufficient coordination occurs to qualify resistance as broken negotiations.

The occasions in question are those in which brokerage, certification or decertification, polarization, network activation, and object shift work together, creating well-connected coalitions aligned along the boundary that separates them from agents of the central power. Decertification of the central power as illegitimate by significant third parties (for example, priests or outside authorities) promotes such an effect. So does certification of those who resist as legitimate actors. Indeed, a shift from broken negotiations to coordinated destruction sometimes occurs when brokerage and certification go far enough – notably, when armed elite opponents of the central power ally with different local groups of resisters and incorporate them into an already reputable common cause. In Europe from the fifteenth to eighteenth centuries, major rebellions most often occurred through just such alliances of armed noble opponents of ruling dynasties with multiple local and regional clusters of people resisting demands by the central government (Tilly 1993).

Most resistance of this kind never reached beyond the local or regional level. When it produced collective violence, it more often took the form of broken negotiations than of coordinated destruction. In European experience, resistance to increased or novel taxation occurred in the company of resistance to conscription, to imposition of new religious identities, to freeing of food markets, and to exclusion of ordinary people from previously common properties. But because tax increases and innovations occurred frequently in every expanding or war-making state and also commonly affected numerous adjacent localities simultaneously, tax resistance remained for centuries the most common basis of direct popular participation in Europe's large-scale collective violence.

Europe was not alone. Despite the relative durability of its empires, China long experienced rebellions against demands from the center. Imperial land taxes often generated resistance and sometimes open rebellion. During the late nineteenth century, several struggles over taxes spiraled into major rebellions against the Qing government. Widespread mobilization occurred especially when the government rapidly increased its demands, when local officials added surcharges or illegal taxes, when officials persisted in requiring payment at times of disaster, or when inequities of assessment and collection suddenly became visible (Perry 1981; Wakeman 1966, 1985; Wong 1997).

In 1852, for example, opening of the Shanghai port to Westerners and their textiles threatened household producers in nearby Qingpu county. When the county magistrate ordered payment of grain tribute taxes that had been suspended two years earlier, a local clerk named Zhou Lichun led a delegation of several hundred peasants to ask the magistrate for a new suspension. The group sacked the house of the tax collector. When the magistrate turned down their request:

The protesters attacked the county office and delivered a sound thrashing to the magistrate himself. Government troops were dispatched to apprehend Zhou Lichun, but the protection of a united peasant force, armed with farm tools and representing more than twenty villages, saved him from immediate arrest. As a result of this incident, Zhou emerged as a major strongman in the area, a magnet toward whom martial experts, bandits, and ordinary peasants gravitated in large numbers. (Perry 2002: 49)

Over the next year, secret societies were organizing for more general political resistance in both Shanghai and its hinterland. Zhou Lichun became a major broker among hinterland societies, linking them into an effective rebel force. During September 1853, connected rural and urban forces took Shanghai and a number of county capitals, declaring tax holidays as they did so. Only when Shanghai's conquerors themselves tried taxing the city to support their new government did an open split occur. An imperial army finished off the rebellion and executed Zhou Lichun.

In a striking parallel, Chinese Communists gained support for their seizure of power in part by equalizing taxation, but then faced significant resistance to their own tax collection once they had established their new regime (Perry 1985). Their policy of extracting rural surpluses to feed urbanites and invest in manufacturing aggravated the pressure on China's peasants. Despite their reputation for passivity, peasants often understood and exploited the rules with finesse. Kevin O'Brien points out that rightful resistance at the village level often includes the threat to take rule violations to a higher level:

> rightful resisters sometimes point to regulations limiting "farmers' burdens" to fend off unapproved fees or demands for graft that exceed amounts previously agreed to. In one of the poorest villages in Henan's Sheqi County, for example, a group of plucky villagers presented county officials with state council regulations distributed by the prefectural government when protesting thirty-seven fees that far exceeded the 5 percent limit announced in 1991. The complainants' unspoken threat was that if county officials dared to rebuff them, they would take their case up the hierarchy and insist that prefectural officials enforce central regulations they themselves had publicized. (O'Brien 1996: 36-7)

In addition to weapons of the weak, Chinese peasants sometimes deploy weapons of the semi-strong against corrupt officials.

Thomas Bernstein and Xiaobo Lü have looked closely at tax collection and its abuses – as well as resistance to both – in contemporary China. They uncover extensive collective violence in the form of broken negotiations; Table 9.2 describes the major clusters from May to August 1997. During those four months alone, close to a million people engaged in violent confrontations with Chinese authorities over issues of taxes broadly defined: not only direct levies, but also prices set for requisitioned crops, prices set for inputs to those crops, and fees collected from peasants by officials. Scattered attacks occurred through much of rural China, but higher levels of coordination emerged in the clusters of Table 9.2.

Many incidents began when groups of aggrieved peasants leapfrogged local authorities by going *en masse* to petition those officials' superiors (Bernstein & Lü 2002, chap. 5). A classic division of labor formed, with peasants mostly attacking, appropriating, or occupying property and with security forces mostly attacking people. Considering the number of people participating in these protests, the few hundred casualties were very slight. They bespeak interactions in which most of the conversation, if angry, remained nonviolent. They describe broken negotiations.

Brokerage, certification–decertification, polarization, network activation, and object shift all played their part in China's tax conflicts. Although they report few cases in which established cadres led tax protests, Bernstein and Lü describe leaders such as Zhang De'an of Renshou County, who toward the end of

Table 9.2. *Major Chinese Peasant Protests, May–August 1997*

May	*Henan* – In Yiyang and Changde prefectures, a total of about 200,000 peasants assembled in 80 locations, often demonstrating and submitting petitions, and sometimes burning vehicles or attacking county governments, with three deaths and 54 reported injuries.
May	*Hubei* – An estimated 120,000 peasants staged at least 70 demonstrations opposing peasant exploitation and official expropriation; in Tianmen county, 3,000 villagers attacked party–government buildings, with 90 injuries.
May–June	*Anhui* – Some 70,000 peasants in 40 townships engaged in 60 separate challenges to authorities, variously attacking official buildings, seizing guns and ammunition, blocking a cargo train, seizing goods, and confronting the railroads' security officers, with 40 injuries and eleven deaths, including five police.
May–June	*Jiangxi* – Peasants in 70 townships, totaling around 100,000, mounted a hundred challenges to authorities, occupying party and government buildings, attacking supply and marketing cooperatives, looting fertilizer and cement. In Yifeng County, 800 people attacked the Public Security bureau; elsewhere, crowds surrounded important officials, whom the military rescued.
July–Aug	*Hubei* – Across 75 townships, perhaps 200,000 peasants demonstrated, petitioned, and protested against improper payments for crops, high-priced inputs, and illegal taxes. Authorities called eight of the episodes "riots" or "rebellions"; in one bloody fight, 40 peasants were killed or wounded.
July–Aug	*Jiangxi* – On the order of 200,000 peasants in 78 townships protested against payment in IOUs, high-priced inputs, low prices for grain, and increased taxes; participants variously attacked (or even burned) party–government buildings, for a total of 200 peasants and 50 security officers wounded. In Yongfeng, security officers fired on the crowd, causing 70 casualties.

Source: Bernstein & Lü (2002, Table 5.1).

1992 began connecting aggrieved peasants from multiple villages in protests over tax burdens and eventually gained election to township office; he clearly operated as a broker. Moreover, Zhang De'an received certification from provincial and county officials as a legitimate speaker for justifiably aggrieved constituents.

There and elsewhere, polarization, network activation, and object shift likewise occurred as tax protesters moved from local grumbling to scattered attacks to the large-scale negotiation with higher authorities that intermittently turned violent. No doubt the nightmare of coordinated destruction in the style of old-regime China – or, for that matter, the Chinese Revolution itself – haunted some officials. But the large-scale rural violence actually faced by officials of the 1990s took the form of broken negotiations.

Of course, it will take much more digging into the records of the world's largest country to determine how much collective violence in the form of violent rituals, coordinated destruction, opportunism, brawls, and scattered attacks accompanied China's violence of broken negotiations. Yet even the scattered evidence now available confirms that, like their imperial ancestors, contemporary Chinese citizens do not take corruption, injustice, and incompetence in their rulers lightly. As with all the other forms of collective violence this book has reviewed, we find the violence of broken negotiations emerging from well-defined and more encompassing political struggles.

Switches to and from Broken Negotiations

Broken negotiations locate in the upper left-hand corner of our coordination-salience space: relatively high on coordination among damage doers, relatively low on salience of damage in all interactions among the parties. A distinct decline in coordination switches broken negotiations into scattered attacks, whereas a distinct increase in salience converts broken negotiations into coordinated destruction. Major revolutions feature multiple switches of these kinds as well as simultaneous pursuit of several different kinds of collective violence. Consider the west of France in 1793 (Tilly 1964). In March 1793, a weaver and a drover from the Angevin village of St. Pierre-de-Chemillé, not far south of the Loire, told Revolutionary officials what had happened before they had fled their home town:

Wednesday, 13 March, toward 5 P.M., a large number of men in a band, armed with guns, hooks, forks, scythes, etc., all wearing white cockades and decorated with small, square, cloth medals, on which are embroidered different shapes, such as crosses, little hearts pierced with pikes, and other signs of that kind, appeared in the central settlement of St. Pierre. All these fellows shouted "Long live the King and our Good Priests! We want our King, our priests and the old regime!" And they wanted to kill off all the Patriots, especially the present witnesses. All that troop, which was of a frightening size, threw itself at the Patriots, who were assembled to resist their attempt, killed many, made many of them prisoners, and dispersed the rest. (Departmental Archives of Maine-et-Loire, Angers, 1 L 1018)

For two years, hostile parties of Patriots (supporters of the Revolution) and Aristocrats (opponents of major revolutionary changes) had been forming and polarizing in that section of Anjou. In the attack on St. Pierre, the Aristocrats marked the boundary separating them from their enemies by donning white cockades and religious emblems in opposition to the red-white-and-blue cockades and blue uniforms favored by Patriots.

Since 1790, the two parties had confronted each other over elections to public offices, sales of church properties, requirements that parish priests take oaths of allegiance, service in the National Guard, and a dozen lesser issues. Although most of the fighting before March 1793 involved no more than threats and angry words, a number of confrontations generated visible violence: scuffles, taking of prisoners, attacks on the other party's property. In addition to Maine-et-Loire (the Revolutionary department corresponding approximately to Old Regime Anjou), similar struggles were taking place in the adjacent departments of Deux-Sèvres, Loire-Inférieure, and Vendée.

In March 1793, Anjou's Aristocrats were opposing military conscription decreed by the national government to support its expanding foreign wars. A cluster of local attacks, including the assault on the Patriots of St. Pierre-de-Chemillé, soon consolidated into a ragged but effective counterrevolutionary guerrilla force. The great insurrection of the Vendée had begun. Civil war raged in Anjou and adjacent regions to year's end. The war, and the subsequent "pacification" of the rebel area by government troops, constituted by far the most lethal domestic episode of the French Revolution. New risings in 1794, 1795, and 1799 sounded much smaller echoes of the 1793 rebellion. Counting troops and civilians on both sides over the entire series of struggles, perhaps 150,000 people died in the Vendée region as a direct result of military action (Guenniffey 2000: 234–5).

If we projected the whole film of the Vendée region's struggles from 1789 to 1793 on the large screen that previous chapters have been constructing, we would certainly see multiple instances of brawling and opportunism. We would even witness a violent ritual or two. But the main actions on the screen would shift from scattered attacks to broken negotiations, then to coordinated destruction. A move from scattered attacks to broken negotiations results from mechanisms in our *incorporation* cluster – notably, network-based escalation, setting-based activation, and brokerage. In the Vendée, those mechanisms were producing a shift from scattered attacks to broken negotiations during 1791 and 1792.

On both sides of the Vendée's widening gap, people were increasingly mobilizing within networks of patronage and solidarity already established under the Old Regime, seeking each other's aid against the enemy. The settings of churches, public meetings, and military musters increasingly became the sites of confrontation. Mercantile bourgeois on one side, priests and parish leaders on the other, engaged increasingly in brokerage that produced connections among Patriots and among Aristocrats in multiple localities.

Additional mechanisms raised the levels of coordination among parties to the Vendée's violence. Certification of activists on one side by revolutionary authorities and of their opponents by religious authorities not only reinforced the effects of network escalation and setting-based activation but also promoted object shift, as local struggles merged into more general alignments of the region's Patriots against its Aristocrats. Result: higher levels of coordination, and greater prevalence of broken negotiations as the mode of collective violence.

A shift from broken negotiations to coordinated destruction results from causal mechanisms in our *activation* cluster; they increase the salience of damage doing within all interactions by activating available boundaries, stories, and relations. Rising stakes of conflict, increasing uncertainty across boundaries, and entry of violent specialists into action all promote activation. All of them occurred in the Vendée during 1792 and 1793.

The national government's intensifying campaign against uncooperative priests, the tying of public office to National Guard membership, and the conscription of local men for distant wars all raised the stakes for villagers who had previously managed for the most part to boycott government-backed priests, hide and patronize priests who had refused the oath of allegiance, control local affairs without compromising commitments to Revolutionary leaders and programs, and generally avoid the top-down penetration of local communities that was occurring widely elsewhere in France. Uncertainty rose dramatically as both sides called in allies and maneuvered for advantage. Although Patriots had long since formed their violent specialists in small detachments of National Guards and occasional interventions of regular army troops, from the rebellion's opening days the first local acts commonly included seizing arms from the Patriots and enlisting military veterans – among them nobles – as leaders of rebel bands.

French debates over the causes and effects of the Vendée's violent struggles remain surprisingly fierce more than two centuries after the fact. They have become set pieces in larger disagreements about the meaning of revolution, the dangers of state power, and the connections between terror and reforming zeal (Furet 1995; Gérard 1999; Kaplan 1993; Malia 1998, 2001; Mayer 2000). For some, the Vendée's bloodletting arrived as an inevitable consequence of the attempt to impose a revolutionary regime on an unready people; for others, it resulted from tragic but avoidable contingencies. As usual, explanations of large-scale violence mingle with judgments of political morality.

Even in this case of terrible slaughter, however, we can actually sharpen our assessments of right and wrong by singling out for scrutiny the assertions of fact, of possibility, and of cause–effect relations that hide within those assessments. This book has concentrated on getting such cause–effect relations right. It has done so by identifying mechanisms and processes that prevail in different varieties of collective violence.

10

Conclusions

Antidotes for Euphoria

If someday you find yourself suffering from euphoria, you can cure it quickly by stacking up authoritative recent reports on the world's condition and dipping into them at random. Try a combination of the annual Human Rights Watch *World Report*, the Freedom House *Freedom in the World*, the Stockholm International Peace Research Institute *SIPRI Yearbook*, the United Nations Development Program *Human Development Report*, and – for a little less gloom – the World Bank *World Development Report*. You will encounter vicious violence galore.

Consider these pithy excerpts from the Human Rights report for the year 1999:

Sierra Leone: The January offensive brought to the capital the same atrocities witnessed in Sierra Leone's rural provinces over the last eight years, as the RUF [Revolutionary United Front] murdered at least two thousand civilians. Victims were usually chosen at random, though there was some targeting of particular groups, such as Nigerian nationals, unarmed police officers, journalists, and church workers. The horrific practice of mutilation and, in particular amputation of hands, arms, lips, legs and other parts of the body was widespread until the signing of the Lome peace accord. In January, the rebels cut off the limbs of some one hundred civilians, including twenty-six double arm amputations. An unknown number died before being able to receive medical attention. The rebel attacks around Masiaka and Port Loko produced at least another forty-four victims of mutilation, including seven double arm amputations. In a village near Masiaka, fifty-seven civilians were burned alive in late April.

Peru: On May 28, more than forty Shining Path guerrillas arrived in four trucks in the town of Uchiza in the Upper Huallaga region of San Martin. After attempting to break into the National Bank, which was closed, the attackers were surprised by the police and reportedly opened fire indiscriminately, killing Jesús Espinoza León, a teacher and trade unionist, schoolchildren Ceriño Herrada Valverde and Giuliana Fasabi, and a police bank guard. After a gun battle with police, the attackers fled when police and army reinforcements arrived. One of the truck drivers forced by the guerrillas to drive them to Uchiza was reportedly shot and wounded while trying to escape his captors.

Sri Lanka: On September 18, apparently in retaliation for the deaths of civilians killed in air force strikes on Puthukudiyiruppu three days earlier, suspected LTTE [Liberation Tigers of Tamil Eelam] members hacked to death some forty-eight Sinhalese villagers and shot six others in attacks on three villages in eastern Sri Lanka. The killings sparked large anti-LTTE demonstrations in Colombo. Increased recruitment of children was also reported from LTTE-controlled areas of the country.

Kyrgyzstan: In August, armed militants, apparently en route to Uzbekistan, clashed with Kyrgyz government troops in the southern Batken region. On August 3, the militants took four Kyrgyz citizens hostage in the village of Zardaly, Osh region. The militants released the hostages on August 13 following the reported payment by the government of an unspecified ransom. The crisis escalated two days later when the Kyrgyz army, backed by Uzbek warplanes, began to attack suspected strongholds of the militants both in Kyrgyzstan and Tajikistan. In response, on August 22, another group of militants, reportedly numbering between 500 and 1,000, entered Kyrgyzstan via the border with Tajikistan and took approximately twenty persons hostage, including four Japanese geologists and a general of the Kyrgyz army, Anarbek Shamkeev. The militants released four ethnic Kyrgyz hostages on August 31 and reportedly demanded the release of wrongfully jailed Muslim believers held in Uzbekistan, including those held in connection with a series of bomb explosions in Uzbekistan in 1999. The Russian government agreed to consider supplying military equipment to the Kyrgyz army, but ruled out sending troops to the region.

United States: In February, West African Amadou Diallo was shot at forty-one times and struck by nineteen bullets fired by New York City Police Department (NYPD) officers. Diallo, who was unarmed, was shot by officers from the NYPD's Street Crime Unit. The shooting put the unit's practices, and the NYPD generally, under increased scrutiny, and the police commissioner and the mayor on the defensive.

Among the types of collective violence this book has surveyed, Human Rights Watch rarely chronicles ritual violence, brawls, or scattered attacks. In compensation, its pages overflow with opportunism, broken negotiations, and (especially) coordinated destruction. The January 1999 attacks on Freetown, Sierra Leone, for example, clearly resulted from high levels of coordination and interactions in which damage doing was salient; they qualified as coordinated destruction. A boy abducted from Freetown the previous year at the age of 14 earned the nickname Poison by his prowess in combat:

Poison fought in Kono in the east, the source of West Africa's most prized diamonds and of Sierra Leone's decade-long war. Then in January 1999, he joined his brethren of the Revolutionary United Front in the most violent attack ever on Freetown, in which thousands of civilians were killed, raped or had their arms chopped off.

"I was ordered to kill by my commander," he recalled, leaving at that his recollection of the fateful month. (Onishi 2002: 1)

Each year, reports of collective violence in these fierce modes flood into Human Rights Watch from every part of the world.

The Freedom House publication *Freedom in the World* packs more bad news. Although by its fairly undemanding criteria the number of democratic regimes has risen in recent years, regimes it rated as democratic in 2000 included not only the United States but also Sierra Leone, Peru, Sri Lanka, and Kyrgyzstan. Of Sri Lanka, the report notes:

Since the civil war began, government security forces, state-backed Sinhalese and Muslim civilian militias, and armed Tamil groups, particularly the LTTE, have committed massacres, disappearances, extrajudicial executions, rape, and torture against civilians, mainly Tamils. Press accounts indicate the war has killed 50,000 to 60,000 people, including many civilians. Civilians are occasionally killed during government bombing raids or by artillery fire from both sides. In September, authorities blamed the LTTE for the massacre of 56 Sinhalese civilians in eastern Ampara district, in apparent revenge for the accidental death of 22 Tamil refugees by government jet bombings in northeastern Mullaitivu district. Similar tit-for-tat killings of civilians occurred relatively frequently earlier in the war. In November, the military and the LTTE blamed each other for an attack on a Roman Catholic shrine in the northwestern town of Madhu that killed some 42 civilian refugees. (Karatnycky 2000: 450–1)

Freedom House rates Sri Lanka and the other governments on this bloody roster as democratic because the governments conduct binding, contested elections for national office in which most adults have voting rights – regardless of how much the current holders of power manipulate those elections. This book has adopted a more demanding definition of democracy: the extent to which members of the population under a government's jurisdiction maintain broad and equal relations with governmental agents, exercise collective control over governmental personnel and resources, and enjoy protection from arbitrary action by governmental agents.

By that standard, Sierra Leone, Sri Lanka, and Kyrgyzstan all fall below the democratic bar, with Peru occupying an uncertain position near the threshold. Only the United States clearly falls in the upper half of the world's polities by these standards – and even there, such events as the Amadou Diallo killing signal the country's limits on protections and civilian control. No large regime, including that of the United States, has ever come close to absolute democracy.

The *SIPRI Yearbook*, for its part, publishes a comprehensive catalog of the world's larger interstate and civil wars. For the Stockholm-based group that produces the yearbook, a "major armed conflict" is:

use of armed force between two or more organized armed groups, resulting in the battle-related deaths of at least 1000 people in any single year and in which the ... [conflict] concerns control of government, territory or communal identity. (SIPRI 2001: 15)

By the SIPRI definition, hijackers' destruction of New York's World Trade Center on 11 September 2001 did not qualify as a major armed conflict despite its thousands of deaths. Among the violent episodes excerpted earlier, Sierra Leone, Peru, and Sri Lanka made the SIPRI armed conflict list for 1999, while Kyrgyzstan and the United States did not. Clearly, SIPRI sets a high threshold. Yet its experts still found 27 major armed conflicts raging in 1999, including eleven for Africa, nine for Asia, four for the Middle East, two for the Americas (Peru and Colombia), and two for Europe (Kosovo and Chechnya).

The UNDP *Human Development Report* and the World Bank's *World Development Report,* carefully perused, provide important supplementary evidence. They offer the means of verifying that the victims of those wars and of other large-scale collective violence concentrate disproportionately in countries where most people also live miserably in other regards. In addition, availability of valuable, portable resources (such as Sierra Leone's diamonds and Colombia's cocaine), of large emigrant populations that supply aid to rebels and/or provide outlets for contraband, and of external governments' support for dissidents all increase the likelihood of large-scale violent conflicts (Collier & Hoeffler 2001; Echeverry et al. 2001).

By now, readers of this book should recognize that the correlations do not result from a general propensity of poor people to lash out in violence. They arise from the tyrannies large and small that flourish in low-capacity undemocratic regimes. Tyranny also arises in high-capacity and democratic regimes, but there collective violence accompanies much smaller proportions of all public political interactions. High-capacity undemocratic regimes tend to make a three-way split of collective violence. Their violent episodes divide sharply among external wars, citizen–state interactions, and various forms of scattered attacks – including those that authorities call terrorism.

Democratic regimes, whether low-capacity or high-capacity, often engage in external wars, but otherwise their collective violence generally takes more intermittent and fragmented forms than the collective violence of undemocratic regimes. We may deplore the violence that occasionally disrupts domestic politics in democracies, but the overall record gives lovers of domestic peace strong reasons for preferring high-capacity democratic regimes.

We begin to see explanations for the puzzles we encountered at the book's outset.

Conclusions

1. Why does collective violence (unlike suicides and individual homicides) concentrate in large waves – often with one violent encounter appearing to trigger the next – and then subside to low levels for substantial periods of time?
2. How and why do people who interact without doing outright damage to each other shift rapidly into collective violence and then (sometimes just as rapidly) back into relatively peaceful relations?
3. In particular, how and why do people who have lived with their categorical differences (often cooperating and intermarrying) for years begin devastating attacks on each other's persons and property?
4. Why do different kinds of political regimes (e.g., democratic and authoritarian regimes) host such different levels and forms of collective violence?
5. How and why do peacekeeping specialists such as police and soldiers so regularly and quickly switch between violent and nonviolent action?

Conventional answers to those questions take them up one at a time, offering either ideal or behavioral replies. Common ideal answers to question 1, for example, argue that collective fears or destructive ideologies drive waves of violence, which subside as fears dissipate or ideologies lose their appeal. Common behavioral answers counter that unsupervised concentrations of young males or other violence-prone categories of people generate bursts of collective violence, which only decline as satiation reduces the appeal of violence, clusters of damage doers break up, or new social controls lock into place. Previous chapters have argued instead that alterations in social relations produce not only surges and declines in collective violence but also the whole range of switching behavior identified by questions 2 through 5.

"Argued" is the right word. Remember what this book has *not* done. It has not presented a comprehensive list of logically consistent principles and deduced empirical propositions from them. It has not laid out a set of precisely defined variables, established measures for those variables, or presented data estimating relations among the variables. It has not located a systematic array of cases within its salience–coordination space and shown that differences among the cases correspond to implications of the general arguments. It has made no effort to construct complete explanations of whole episodes. It has not documented its assertions by summing up previous research point by point; neither, for that matter, has it identified or challenged competing explanations of collective violence that other scholars have proposed. It has not tested a single hypothesis.

Instead, the book has drawn on a wide variety of theoretical and empirical resources to do three things: first, to construct a way of thinking about collective violence that helps account for its variation and change; second, to identify particular mechanisms and processes that recurrently cause variation and change in collective violence; third, to illustrate the first and second amply with concrete instances. If such a book succeeds it is by opening doors, not by closing them. With those limitations in mind, let us take up each of the organizing questions in turn.

Waves of Violence

Why does collective violence (unlike suicides and individual homicides) concentrate in large waves – often with one violent encounter appearing to trigger the next – and then subside to low levels for substantial periods of time? In very general terms, waves of violence occur, then subside, because of switching in coordination and/or salience. This true-by-definition statement clarifies what we must explain, and how to explain it.

A rapid move from scattered attacks to broken negotiations, for example, illustrates a rise in coordination. It results from processes in our *incorporation* cluster, notably network-based escalation, setting-based activation, and brokerage. Mechanisms of certification and upward object shift also regularly increase coordination, as outside authorities lend recognition to one or more participants in violent interactions and as the boundary separating antagonists moves from local to regional, national, or even international divisions. Conversely, disruption of connecting networks, blocked access to violence-prone settings, disappearance of political entrepreneurs, severance of ties among them, decertification of crucial participants, and downward object shift (e.g., when local divisions begin taking priority over national divisions) all reduce levels of coordination among participants in violent interaction. We have seen a devastating version of this downward shift as opportunism took over from coordinated destruction in Rwanda.

Changes in uncertainty about interactions across established us–them boundaries exert strong effects on switching between violent and nonviolent interaction. To expand a summary from Chapter 3, uncertainty over identity boundaries can rise through a number of different processes.

- Overarching political authorities lose their ability to enforce previously constraining agreements binding actors on both sides of the boundary (example from previous chapters: subordination of Catholics weakens in eighteenth-century Ulster as a prospering linen industry alters patterns of inequality).

- Those same authorities take actions that threaten survival of crucial connecting structures within populations on one side of the boundary while appearing to spare or even benefit those on the other side (example: between 1829 and 1835, British authorities expand Catholic political rights while banning both the Catholic Association and the Protestant Orange Order).
- The declining capacity of authorities to police existing boundaries, control use of weapons, and contain individual aggression facilitates cross-boundary opportunism, including retaliation for earlier slights and injustices (example: police withdraw from black neighborhoods during early stages of Los Angeles and Detroit confrontations of the 1960s).
- Leaders on one side of the boundary or the other face resistance or competition from well-organized segments of their previous followers (example: Algerian Islamic purists turn simultaneously against secular leaders and defecting villagers).
- External parties change, increase, or decrease their material, moral, and political support for actors on one side of the boundary or the other (example: French revolutionary authorities send troops to the Vendée in support of beleaguered Patriots).

All of these instances promoted shifts from scattered attacks toward coordinated destruction. Both coordination and salience rose significantly.

A move from broken negotiations to coordinated destruction, in contrast, results mainly from a rise in salience. Moves from uneasy peace to interstate war and back often occur very rapidly as already well-coordinated parties turn to or away from violent interaction. But rebellions, strike waves, and even ethnic struggles frequently make similar rapid switches between violence and nonviolence. Increases in salience result from mechanisms in our *activation* cluster; they increase the salience of damage doing within all interactions by activating available boundaries, stories, and relations. Rising stakes of conflict, increasing uncertainty across boundaries, and entry of violent specialists into action all promote activation. Mechanisms in the activation cluster include polarization and signaling spirals.

The three forms of coordinated destruction – campaigns of annihilation, conspiratorial terror, and lethal contests – all result from similar mechanisms, but they differ dramatically in the power balances among participants. Violence-plagued Colombia has, for example, experienced all three forms of coordinated destruction: gunning down of dissident peasants (campaigns of annihilation), kidnapping and hostage taking (conspiratorial terror), and open civil war (lethal contests). The three mutate into one other and feed each other. Rather than representing three distinct phenomena, they spring from similar causes.

Exits from coordinated destruction illustrate these general points. In rare circumstances, coordinated destruction shifts into violent ritual: increases in both coordination and salience occur. In such processes, third parties contain the violent conflict, monitors intervene in it, boundaries among participants, monitors, and spectators sharpen, as third parties and monitors jointly control the rules of combat as well as the stakes of the conflict's outcome. Thus, over the last two centuries, British and Irish authorities have now and then managed temporarily to channel Ulster's conflicts into contained (if still competitive and violent) ritual shows of strength.

At coordinated destruction's already high level of coordination, the extent of coordination among violent actors increases as (1) political entrepreneurs create connections among previously independent individuals and groups; (2) authorities control the stakes (rewards and punishment) of the outcomes; (3) categories (e.g., gender or nationality) dividing major blocs of participants also figure widely in routine social life; and (4) major participants organize and drill outside of violent encounters. The mechanisms involved include boundary activation, polarization, competitive display, monitoring, containment, and certification. Once again, two centuries of Irish conflict show us repeated waxing and waning in these regards.

Exits from coordinated destruction, however, also produce shifts into broken negotiations, scattered attacks, opportunism, and nonviolent interaction. All those shifts result from declines in coordination and/or salience. They often occur rapidly precisely because participants' relations – to political entrepreneurs, violent specialists, monitors, and third parties – themselves alter quickly. Remember how quickly England's landless laborers shifted from direct confrontations with farmers to scattered arson and machine breaking as troops began breaking up laborers' gatherings during the Swing Rebellion of 1830. As for shifts from coordinated destruction to opportunism, hostage taking in Chechnya provides a chilling case in point.

Waves of collective violence also result in part from the attachment of claim making to intermittent events that are not intrinsically violent: holidays, elections, royal successions, public rituals, proclamations of new laws, and the like. Commemorations have figured enormously in the violence attending Northern Ireland's party processions, but we have seen similar scheduling effects in the Carnival of Romans, Chinese student actions at Tiananmen, and football hooliganism.

Conclusions

Waves of collective violence depend, finally, on fluctuations in the sources of material and organizational support for participants. Flows of arms, arrivals or departures of militias, outside certification or decertification, injections of new funds, external provisions (of food, shelter, or medical care), and movements of respected leaders commonly occur intermittently, thus introducing rapid increases or decreases in violent interactions. These effects underline the organizational bases of most collective violence. For all these reasons, the greater the salience and coordination of collective violence, the more frequent its compounding into intermittent waves separated by periods of little or no violent interaction. Brawls and scattered attacks bunch less than violent rituals and coordinated destruction.

Violent and Nonviolent Coexistence

How and why do people who interact without doing outright damage to each other shift rapidly into collective violence and then (sometimes just as rapidly) back into relatively peaceful relations? We have witnessed such rapid shifts in France's Vendée rebellion, in Chinese anti-tax mobilizations, in Barcelona's Tragic Week, in London's brawls, in road rage, and in a great many other violent episodes. The same reasoning applies as in the explanation of violent waves. Increases in uncertainty, signaling spirals, polarization, brokerage, and certification–decertification paradoxically produce similar effects.

Rising uncertainty spurs wielders of violent means on either side of an us–them boundary to direct their means of destruction at those on the boundary's other side. Negative signaling spirals simultaneously magnify uncertainty, polarize participants, and fortify boundaries. Polarization itself (as with, e.g., the flight of moderates and boundary straddlers) increases the propensity of all participants in interaction to employ violent means. Brokerage connects local conflicts into larger-scale confrontations; it often brings in violent specialists as well. Certification of participants as valid interlocutors augments their leverage within the conflict, which under a wide range of circumstances increases their readiness to use violent means across existing boundaries.

On the whole, the complements of these mechanisms – declines in uncertainty, positive signaling spirals, and so on – move intense conflicts toward more nonviolent forms and also toward lower levels of coordination and/or salience. All these mechanisms can produce rapid switches between high and low levels of collective violence. We have watched both the upswing and the downswing occur repeatedly in Northern Ireland, but we have also observed them in the Swing Rebellion and Chinese tax resistance.

In particular, how and why do people who have lived with their categorical differences (often cooperating and intermarrying) for years begin devastating attacks on each other's persons and property? In addition to the switching mechanisms just described, disappearance of stabilizing third parties appears to play a crucial part in what Anton Blok (2001) follows Freud in calling the "narcissism of minor differences." Third parties such as village elders, mafiosi, police, and local patrons can disappear through defection, destruction, or outside intervention. Brokerage, boundary activation, and polarization that reorient people to available but previously inactive boundaries reinforce the effects of neutralizing third parties. In combination, brokerage, boundary activation, polarization, and neutralization of third parties occurred (literally) with a vengeance during the Rwandan genocide of spring 1994. In that case, opportunism began to displace coordinated destruction when and where brokerage by Hutu Power activists failed.

Similarly, the American ghetto conflicts of the 1960s (described in Chapter 6) shifted quickly from scattered attacks to coordinated destruction to opportunism as the absence or withdrawal of police and local leaders reshaped people's opportunities. Initial standoffs between blacks and whites soon gave way to more fragmented destruction as brokers lost what little control they exercised in the early phases. The disappearance of stabilizing third parties disrupted the usual nervous coexistence of disparate populations in Los Angeles, Washington, Detroit, and elsewhere.

The evidence we have reviewed raises serious doubts about ideal and behavioral explanations of such internecine struggles. New information and ideas do sometimes figure in the switch to violent attacks, as hostile neighbors start to believe that distraction of authorities and mutual acquaintances has made retaliation for old wrongs feasible. But most of the time, brokers who sharpen previously blurred us–them boundaries and connect wielders of violent means draw on long-established practices and understandings. Nor does the steam boiler analogy – pressure built up until everything exploded – do justice to the subtle processes of connection and coordination we have discovered in Rwanda, Ireland, France, and elsewhere.

The most plausible behavioral accounts of such rapid switching center on the lifting and reimposition of social controls, following the assumption that impulses to attack remain more or less constant. But even if we concede the importance of hostile impulses, the relational processes of lifting and reimposition turn out to be critical to the explanation of mutual destruction. The same people, differently connected, move rapidly into and out of attacks on their neighbors.

Conclusions

The prevalence of mixtures and mutations underlines a basic point of this book: distinctions among violent rituals, coordinated destruction, opportunism, brawls, scattered attacks, and broken negotiations help order the search for regularities, but they do not box off different types of social processes. Similar mechanisms and processes operate in different combinations, sequences, and initial conditions at various locations in our salience–coordination space. Varying combinations, sequences, and initial conditions, however, produce drastically different levels, frequencies, and forms of collective violence. Nowhere is that sort of variation more visible than in contrasts among different kinds of political regimes.

Regime Differences

Why do different kinds of political regimes (e.g., democratic and authoritarian regimes) host such different levels and forms of collective violence? Regimes affect the character and intensity of collective violence in several distinct ways.

- By establishing prescribed, tolerated, and forbidden forms of public claim making, thereby shaping both occasions for violent encounters and opportunities for nonviolent alternatives; we have seen strong regime effects on forms and outcomes of collective violence in the Carnival of Romans, Ireland's party processions, Japanese ritual vengeance, the Tiananmen confrontations, and the evolution of public displays from John Wilkes's election marches to twentieth-century demonstrations.
- By facilitating, tolerating, and repressing different categories of political actors and thus offering threats and opportunities to different segments of the population; we have seen Japanese rulers authorizing samurai (but not commoners) to pursue blood vengeance in 1701, British colonial officers dealing selectively with American opponents of press gangs in the 1740s, French authorities reacting to forest-invading peasants in the 1840s, and – in the 1980s – Iranian authorities stamping out street vendors and Indian authorities tolerating or even sponsoring sectarian thugs.
- By creating, controlling, co-opting, and/or deploying violent specialists; we have watched fourteenth-century Italian city-states hiring mercenaries to their peril, British authorities staging spectacular executions of felons during the eighteenth century, French troops conquering Algeria during the 1830s, and the police of Narayanpur (Uttar Pradesh) smashing uppity peasants in 1980.

- By appropriating, protecting, redistributing, or ignoring valuable resources that are subject to exploitation and opportunity hoarding; we have noted massive resistance to conscription in the Vendée during 1793 as well as large-scale resistance to taxation in rural China during 1997.

As we have seen abundantly, the extent and manner of a government's performance in these regards vary enormously as a function of governmental capacity and degree of democracy. People in low-capacity undemocratic regimes usually suffer the most extensive losses from collective violence because their regimes allow so much room for petty tyranny (on the part of officeholders, warlords, and other predators) and also provide opportunities for profit taking outside intervention. Glimpses of Somalia, Uganda, Sierra Leone, and other low-capacity undemocratic regimes have shown us how Africans suffer violence because such regimes prevail on their continent.

Despite their frequent engagement in international war and their focal positions in violence-promoting worldwide exchanges of contraband, high-capacity democratic regimes usually host much less domestic collective violence than other sorts of regime. Our review of violence in demonstrations (most of which passed without direct damage to persons or property) documented the importance of broken negotiations as a cause of collective violence in democratic regimes as well as the reasons for the usually nonviolent character of democratic struggle.

In between the extremes lie high-capacity undemocratic and low-capacity democratic regimes, which generate similar levels but very different sorts of collective violence. We have seen striking differences between the collective violence of low-capacity but relatively democratic American regimes preceding the Civil War and of high-capacity undemocratic China today. In such high-capacity regimes, a much higher proportion of all collective violence pits governmental agents against citizens rather than setting groups of citizens at each other's throats. Accordingly, low-salience scattered attacks and broken negotiations figure more prominently in low-capacity democratic regimes than in high-capacity undemocratic regimes. Where governmental agents (especially violent specialists) do participate in the collective violence of low-capacity democratic regimes, they often become objects of attacks themselves.

Switches of Violent Specialists

How and why do peacekeeping specialists such as police and soldiers so regularly and quickly switch between violent and nonviolent action? We have repeatedly encountered the irony: peacekeeping specialists are also specialists in violence. On the average, they deliver damage more efficiently and effectively than other kinds of political actors. They deliver damage under discipline that allows them to shift rapidly between violence and nonviolence. Often they do so at the behest of employers who themselves never engage directly in damaging acts. But violent specialists who escape governmental control or who enjoy great latitude so long as they perform the damaging tasks assigned to them frequently use their power to gain advantages of their own. We have seen the police of Narayanpur, India, taking just such advantage of their armed force.

Outside of government, violent specialists regularly generate protection rackets, separate zones of conquest and exploitation, local struggles with rival specialists, and retaliatory actions on their own. Even those aspirants to power who personally abstain from violent acts frequently recruit or hire their own violent specialists. Hyderabad's wrestler–enforcers, Ekaterinburg's Uralmashevskaya gang, and Rwanda's Interahamwe militia have, alas, plenty of counterparts elsewhere in the world.

Terror?

Violent specialists often operate through their own versions of terror: asymmetrical deployment of threats and violence against enemies outside the forms of contention routinely operating within the current regime. We have encountered different variants of the strategy not only in India, Russia, and Rwanda but also in Ireland, El Salvador, Algeria, Colombia, Uganda, the Caucasus, and South Africa. From among cases this book has analyzed, we could easily add Great Britain's public executions of the eighteenth century and the Terror of 1790s France. We could also go back in history to the ways that Europe's steppe nomads extorted tribute from the sedentary agricultural populations on which they fed; Mongols, for example, frequently seized hostages as guarantees that their victims would continue to pay tribute (Dewey 1988). The roll call makes clear that terror in this sense consists of a single party's conflict strategy rather than a causally coherent category of collective violence. Asymmetrical, unconventional threats and damage occur in coordinated destruction, broken negotiations, scattered attacks, and opportunism alike.

The U.S. Department of State adds another annual report to the grim yearbooks we reviewed earlier: a document called *Patterns of Global Terrorism*. The State Department defines terrorism as "politically motivated violence perpetrated against noncombatant targets by subnational groups or clandestine agents, usually intended to influence an audience" (Ruby 2002: 10). Any such definition

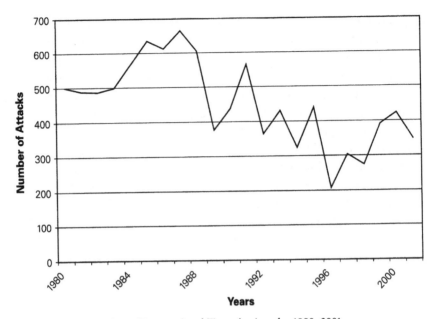

Figure 10.1 Number of International Terrorist Attacks, 1980–2001.

has the disadvantage of requiring information on motivations and intentions; we have seen how rarely solid evidence on motivations and intentions becomes available for collective violence. Still, if we interpret the criteria as singling out attacks on noncombatant targets by other than regularly constituted national military forces, especially when someone broadcasts political claims on behalf of the attackers, then we will come close to the report's implicit selection principles.

The State Department report covers only those attacks that their specialists regard as crossing international lines – because the attackers came from outside the country, because they received substantial backing from outside, or because they assaulted foreigners. Figure 10.1 shows trends in the number of such incidents from 1980 through 2001 (U.S. Department of State 2000, 2001, 2002).

As Chapter 3 reported, the frequency of designated international terrorist incidents reached a high point in 1988 and generally declined thereafter. When they voiced demands, attackers most often called for autonomy or independence for some subnational population or region, replacement of existing governments, or redress of wrongs done to some organization. On the whole, international terrorist incidents rose and fell with the activity of independence movements. Whether the secondary rise that has occurred since 1996 will continue into the twenty-first century – and whether it represents a new sort of political campaign – remains to be seen.

Conclusions

We began this chapter with a close look at 1999. For that same year, the State Department's annual count included 392 attacks, with 233 persons killed and 706 wounded, as compared with 741 killed and 5,952 wounded in 1998 (U.S. Department of State 2000: 8). The lower casualties of 1999 resulted from a shift to hostage taking and attacks on property, especially business property such as oil pipelines. Nevertheless, bombing remained by far the most frequent form of attack, with almost half the total.

The report distinguishes carefully between sites of terrorist attacks and bases for attacks on American interests. In the first regard, Asia and Africa each suffered far more attacks and casualties than the entire rest of the world put together. As for bases, the report singles out Afghanistan, Pakistan, Iran, and Syria as the principal shelters and supports of international terrorist groups. Of Afghanistan, for example, it claims: "While not directly hostile to the United States, the Taliban, which controls the majority of Afghan territory, continues to harbor Usama Bin Ladin and a host of other terrorists loosely linked to Bin Ladin, who directly threaten the United States and others in the international community." In 1999, then, the State Department anticipated a distinction that took on enormous political force after Muslim suicide squads crashed packed passenger jets into the Pentagon and the World Trade Center on 11 September 2001: on one side, terror affecting U.S. interests; on the other side, essentially local and regional conflicts.

During the 1980s and 1990s, the great bulk of the world's terrorism (as defined by State Department experts) occurred outside the range of U.S. interests. For the countries that began this chapter, the 1999 report included the following "significant terrorist incidents."

Sierra Leone

6 January: The Italian Embassy reported that Armed Forces Revolutionary Council (AFRC) rebels kidnapped two Italian missionaries. The missionaries were rescued on 13 January by government-sponsored forces.

25 January: Military sources reported that Revolutionary United Front rebels robbed and kidnapped a Japanese businessman. On 29 January the RUF released the hostage.

12 February: The Rome-based news agency, MISNA, reported that the RUF kidnapped an Italian missionary from a church. No demands were made. The rebels released the hostage unharmed on 8 April.

4 August: UN officials reported that an AFRC faction kidnapped 33 UN representatives near Occra Hills ....

15 October: In Masombo the Missionary News Agency reported that unidentified persons kidnapped three clergymen – two Italian and one Sierra Leonian. No one claimed responsibility, and no demands were made. AFRC rebels are suspected.

7 December: Near Buedu, RUF militants kidnapped one German national and one Belgian citizen, both of whom work for the humanitarian group Doctors Without Borders.... No one was injured in the attack. The rebels released both hostages unharmed on 16 December. No ransom was paid.

Kyrgyzstan

6 August: In the Batken district, according to local press, unidentified Tajikistani rebels kidnapped four Kyrgyzstani Government officials. On 13 August the rebels released the hostages unharmed for an unspecified amount of ransom.

22 August: In Bishkek, government officials reported that unidentified Uzbekistani gunmen kidnapped four Japanese geologists, their interpreter, and eight Kyrgyzstani soldiers. On 13 October four Kyrgyzstani soldiers were released unharmed. On 18 October another two Kyrgyzstani hostages were freed. On 25 October the remaining hostages were released unharmed. No ransom was paid.

For Sri Lanka, the report included no "significant terrorist incidents" but stated nevertheless that:

The separatist group Liberation Tigers of Tamil Eelam (LTTE), which the United States has designated a Foreign Terrorist Organization, maintained a high level of violence in 1999, conducting numerous attacks on government, police, civilian, and military targets. President Chandrika Kumaratunga narrowly escaped an LTTE assassination attempt in December. The group's suicide bombers assassinated moderate Tamil politician Dr. Neelan Tiruchelvam in July and killed 34 bystanders at election rallies in December. LTTE gunmen murdered a Tamil Member of Parliament from Jaffna representing the Eelam People's Democratic Party and the leader of a Tamil military unit supporting the Sri Lankan Army. (U.S. Department of State 2000: 17)

In the case of Peru, State Department experts likewise cataloged no significant terrorist incidents, but reported that:

The [Sendero Luminoso] continued to attack government targets in the Peruvian countryside. Deadly clashes between the SL and the military continued in the central and southern regions as soldiers pursued two columns of approximately 60 to 80 rebels, led by "Comrade Alipio," through the southern jungle region. A particularly deadly skirmish occurred in November, leaving five soldiers and six guerrilla fighters dead. The MRTA has not conducted a major terrorist operation since the end of the hostage crisis at the Japanese Ambassador's residence in Lima in April 1997. (U.S. Department of State 2000: 33)

Concerned with events elsewhere whose interactions crossed international boundaries, the report inventoried no terrorism within the United States. For the countries covered, however, it implicitly made two observations of great importance for this book's argument. One was negative, the other positive. Negatively, no one sort of action, person, group, or political cause dominated the episodes that State Department specialists called terror. Positively, the events in question ranged widely across the different sorts of collective violence we have reviewed – no brawls or violent rituals, but plenty of coordinated destruction, opportunism, scattered attacks, and broken negotiations. Perhaps most striking is the increasing prominence of kidnapping in the repertoire of so-called terrorists; it suggests that opportunism is on the rise.

Remember the practice of hostage taking in Chechnya, with which Chapter 6 began. At one point, American journalists singled out the practice as a prime example of terrorism. Yury Zakharovich, Moscow correspondent for *Time* magazine, put it this way:

They did not search for an excuse for terrorism, but tried to trace how this terrorism had been provoked by the war. Violence breeds new violence. This circle horrified journalists because it became endless. One can trace this dominant motive when journalists covered a famous Basayev action in Buddenosk. (Tishkov 2001: 346)

American journalists, that is, interpreted terroristic attacks as resulting from senseless spirals of action and reaction. Seen from close in, however, the terrorism in question looked much more like a combination of political bargaining and profit taking. As Valery Tishkov points out, Chechen captors regularly mutilated their hostages; sometimes subjected them to lingering, spectacular deaths; and usually made sure other people learned about their cruelty. They certainly practiced terror, but they used terror to extort revenue and concessions from their enemies. Not all users of terror, by any means, bargain coolly over the lives of their victims. Some do. That is the point: terror is a strategy, not a creed.

The use of terror spreads across a wide variety of groups, ideologies, and targets. In the United States alone, anti-abortion activists, defenders of the environment, and a wide variety of anti-government clusters have aimed assassination, bombing, and wholesale property destruction against their enemies during recent decades. Terror-inducing attacks often take place as one element of a larger conflict; World War II bombings of Dresden, London, Hiroshima, and Nagasaki all had the tinge of terror. As Ireland has shown us in the greatest detail, the same actors sometimes alternate between relatively conventional and terroristic conflict strategies. We could make the same case for Sierra Leone, Peru, Sri Lanka, Kyrgyzstan, the United States, and the Basque Country. It is a serious but common error to assume that a class of people called terrorists, motivated by ideological extremism, perform most acts of terror. As the saying goes, one person's terrorist is another person's freedom fighter.

Nevertheless, the common sense that users of terror tactics form a class apart has some foundation. Regimes have often authorized violent specialists such as paramilitary forces, secret police, and subsidized thugs to silence their opponents, but over the last few centuries those killers have usually operated in the shadows. When unauthorized groups have employed terror, furthermore, they have commonly belonged to two categories of political actors: groups actively aligned with international enemies of the regimes they are attacking (the case of most suicide attackers in recent decades) or factions of larger dissident coalitions that have broken away from moderate control (frequently the case of armed activists in Ireland and the Basque Country). In short, the same sorts of political processes that generate other forms of coordinated destruction produce the special forms that authorities and horrified observers call terrorism.

Let that conclusion sound the book's main theme: collective violence occupies a perilous but coherent place in contentious politics. It emerges from the ebb and flow of collective claim making and struggles for power. It interweaves incessantly with nonviolent politics, varies systematically with political regimes, and changes as a consequence of essentially the same causes that operate in the nonviolent zones of collective political life. Understanding those causes will help us minimize the damage that human beings inflict on each other. In our own violent time, advocates of nonviolent political struggle need all the help they can get.

References

Acemoglu, Daron, Simon Johnson, & James A. Robinson (2001). "The Colonial Origins of Comparative Development: An Empirical Investigation," *American Economic Review* 91: 1369–1401.

Allcock, John B. (2000). *Explaining Yugoslavia*. New York: Columbia University Press.

Archer, John E. (1990). *By a Flash and a Scare: Incendiarism, Animal Maiming, and Poaching in East Anglia, 1815–1870*. Oxford: Clarendon.

Armstrong, Gary (1998). *Football Hooligans. Knowing the Score*. Oxford: Berg.

Aya, Rod (1990). *Rethinking Revolutions and Collective Violence. Studies on Concept, Theory, and Method*. Amsterdam: Het Spinhuis.

Balbus, Isaac (1973). *The Dialectics of Legal Repression: Black Rebels Before the American Criminal Courts*. New York: Russell Sage Foundation.

Ballbé, Manuel (1985). *Orden público y militarismo en la España constitucional (1812–1983)*. Madrid: Alianza.

Banfield, Edward C. (1970). *The Unheavenly City. The Nature and Future of Our Urban Crisis*. Boston: Little, Brown.

Barbier, Edmond-Jean-François (1847–1856). *Journal d'un bourgeois de Paris sous le règne de Louis XV* (4 vols.). Paris: Renouard.

Barrington, Lowell (1995). "The Domestic and International Consequences of Citizenship in the Soviet Successor States," *Europe-Asia Studies* 47: 731–63.

Barry, Dan, & Kevin Flynn (2001). "Firefighters in Angry Scuffle with Police at Trade Center," *New York Times* (3 November): A1, B10.

Bayart, Jean-François, Stephen Ellis, & Béatrice Hibou (1999). *The Criminalization of the State in Africa*. Oxford: James Currey.

Bayat, Asef (1997). *Street Politics. Poor People's Movements in Iran*. New York: Columbia University Press.

Bayley, David H. (1985). *Patterns of Policing. A Comparative International Analysis*. New Brunswick, NJ: Rutgers University Press.

Bearman, Peter S. (1991). "Desertion as Localism: Army Unit Solidarity and Group Norms in the U.S. Civil War," *Social Forces* 70: 321–42.

Beattie, John (1986). *Crime and the Courts in England, 1660–1800*. Princeton, NJ: Princeton University Press.

Beissinger, Mark (1993). "Demise of an Empire-State: Identity, Legitimacy, and the Deconstruction of Soviet Politics," in Crawford Young (Ed.), *The Rising Tide of Cultural Pluralism*. Madison: University of Wisconsin Press.

(2001). *Nationalist Mobilization and the Collapse of the Soviet State*. Cambridge University Press.

Bensel, Richard (1990). *Yankee Leviathan: The Origins of Central State Authority in America, 1859–1877*. Cambridge University Press.

Bergesen, Albert (1980). "Official Violence during the Watts, Newark, and Detroit Race Riots of the 1960s," in Pat Lauderdale (Ed.), *A Political Analysis of Deviance*. Minneapolis: University of Minnesota Press.

Berkeley, Bill (2001). *The Graves Are Not Yet Full. Race, Tribe and Power in the Heart of Africa*. New York: Basic Books.

Bernardi, Claudio (2000). "Corpus Domini: Ritual Metamorphoses and Social Changes in Sixteenth- and Seventeenth-Century Genoa," in Nicholas Terpstra (Ed.), *The Politics of Ritual Kinship. Confraternities and Social Order in Early Modern Italy*. Cambridge University Press.

Bernstein, Mary (1997). "Celebration and Suppression: The Strategic Uses of Identity by the Lesbian and Gay Movement," *American Journal of Sociology* 103: 531–65.

Bernstein, Thomas P., & Xiaobo Lü (2002). *Taxation without Representation in Contemporary Rural China*. Cambridge University Press.

Besley, Timothy (1995). "Nonmarket Institutions for Credit and Risk Sharing in Low-Income Countries," *Journal of Economic Perspectives* 9: 169–88.

Blackstock, Allan (2000). "'The Invincible Mass': Loyal Crowds in Mid Ulster, 1795–96," in Peter Jupp & Eoin Magennis (Eds.), *Crowds in Ireland c. 1720–1920*. London: Macmillan.

Blok, Anton (1974). *The Mafia of a Sicilian Village, 1860–1960*. New York: Harper & Row.

(2001). *Honour and Violence*. Cambridge: Polity.

Boehm, Christopher (1987). *Blood Revenge. The Enactment and Management of Conflict in Montenegro and Other Tribal Societies*. Philadelphia: University of Pennsylvania Press. [First published in 1984 by University Press of Kansas.]

Bonneuil, Noël, & Nadia Auriat (2000). "Fifty Years of Ethnic Conflict and Cohesion, 1945–94," *Journal of Peace Research* 37: 563–81.

Bose, Sugata, & Ayesha Jalal (1998). *Modern South Asia. History, Culture, Political Economy*. London: Routledge.

Bowles, Samuel, & Herbert Gintis (1998). "The Evolution of Strong Reciprocity," Working Paper 98-08-073, Santa Fe Institute Economics Research Program.

te Brake, Wayne (1998). *Shaping History. Ordinary People in European Politics 1500–1700*. Berkeley: University of California Press.

Brass, Paul R. (1997). *Theft of an Idol. Text and Context in the Representation of Collective Violence*. Princeton, NJ: Princeton University Press.

Brewer, John (1976). *Party Ideology and Popular Politics at the Accession of George III*. Cambridge University Press.

Brewer, John, & John Styles (Eds.) (1980). *An Ungovernable People. The English and their Law in the Seventeenth and Eighteenth Centuries*. New Brunswick, NJ: Rutgers University Press.

References

Brewer, John D., et al. (1988). *The Police, Public Order and the State. Policing in Great Britain, Northern Ireland, the Irish Republic, the USA, Israel, South Africa and China.* New York: St. Martins.

Broeker, Galen (1970). *Rural Disorder and Police Reform in Ireland, 1812–36.* London: Routledge & Kegan Paul.

Bromberger, Christian (1998). *Football, la bagatelle la plus sérieuse du monde.* Paris: Bayard.

Brown, Richard Maxwell (1975). *Strain of Violence. Historical Studies of American Violence and Vigilantism.* New York: Oxford University Press.

Bruneteaux, Patrick (1993). "Le désordre de la répression en France 1871–1921. Des conscrits aux gendarmes mobiles," *Genèses* 12: 30–46.

Buford, Bill (1991). *Among the Thugs.* New York: Vintage.

Burt, Ronald S., & Marc Knez (1995). "Kinds of Third-Party Effects on Trust," *Rationality and Society* 7: 255–92.

Button, James W. (1978). *Black Violence. Political Impact of the 1960s Riots.* Princeton, NJ: Princeton University Press.

Caferro, William (1998). *Mercenary Companies and the Decline of Siena.* Baltimore: Johns Hopkins University Press.

Charlesworth, Andrew (1978). *Social Protest in a Rural Society: The Spatial Diffusion of the Captain Swing Disturbances of 1830–1831* (Historical Geography Research Series, no. 1). Liverpool: Department of Geography, University of Liverpool.

(Ed.) (1983). *An Atlas of Rural Protest in Britain, 1548–1900.* London: Croom Helm.

Charlesworth, Andrew, et al. (Eds.) (1996). *An Atlas of Industrial Protest in Britain 1750–1990.* London: Macmillan.

Chesnais, Jean-Claude (1976). *Les Morts Violentes en France depuis 1826. Comparaisons Internationales.* Paris: Presses Universitaires de France.

(1981). *Histoire de la violence en Occident de 1800 à nos jours.* Paris: Robert Laffont.

Chesterman, Simon (Ed.) (2001). *Civilians in War.* Boulder, CO: Lynne Rienner.

Chevigny, Paul (1999). "Police Brutality," in Lester Kurtz (Ed.), *Encyclopedia of Violence, Peace, and Conflict,* vol. III, pp. 1–10. San Diego: Academic Press.

Chittolini, Giorgio (Ed.) (1994). *Two Thousand Years of Warfare.* Danbury, CT: Grolier.

Clausewitz, Carl von (1968). *On War* (Ed. by Anatol Rapoport). Harmondsworth: Penguin. [First published in 1832.]

Cockburn, J. S. (1991). "Patterns of Violence in English Society: Homicide in Kent 1560–1985," *Past and Present* 130: 70–106.

Cohn, Samuel R. (1993). *When Strikes Make Sense – And Why.* New York: Plenum.

Collier, Paul, & Anke Hoeffler (2001). "Greed and Grievance in Civil War," unpublished paper, World Bank, Washington, DC.

Conley, Carolyn A. (1999a). *Melancholy Accidents. The Meaning of Violence in Post-Famine Ireland.* Lanham, MD: Lexington.

(1999b). "The Agreeable Recreation of Fighting," *Journal of Social History* 33: 58–72.

Conot, Robert (1967). *Rivers of Blood, Years of Darkness.* New York: Bantam.

Contamine, Philippe (1984). *War in the Middle Ages.* Oxford: Blackwell.

Corvisier, André (1976). *Armées et sociétés en Europe de 1494 à 1789.* Paris: Presses Universitaires de France.

Courtwright, David T. (1996). *Violent Land. Single Men and Social Disorder from the Frontier to the Inner City*. Cambridge, MA: Harvard University Press.

Covini, Maria Nadia (2000). "Political and Military Bonds in the Italian State System, Thirteenth to Sixteenth Centuries," in Philippe Contamine (Ed.), *War and Competition between States*. Oxford: Clarendon.

Creveld, Martin van (1989). *Technology and War From 2000 B.C. to the Present*. New York: Free Press.

(1991). *The Transformation of War*. New York: Free Press.

Crosby, Alfred W. (1989). *America's Forgotten Pandemic: The Influenza of 1918*. Cambridge University Press.

Davenport, Christian (2000). "Introduction," in Christian Davenport (Ed.), *Paths to State Repression. Human Rights Violations and Contentious Politics*. Lanham, MD: Rowman & Littlefield.

Davis, Natalie Zemon (1975). *Society and Culture in Early Modern France*. Berkeley: University of California Press.

Dekker, Rudolf (1982). *Holland in beroering. Oproeren in de 17de en 18de eeuw*. Baarn: Amboeken.

Delale, Alain, & Gilles Ragache (1978). *La France de 68*. Paris: Seuil.

Deneckere, Gita (1997). *Sire, het volk mort. Sociaal protest in België (1831–1918)*. Antwerp: Baarn. [Ghent: Amsab.]

Des Forges, Alison, et al. (1999). *Leave None to Tell the Story. Genocide in Rwanda*. New York: Human Rights Watch.

Dewey, Horace (1988). "Russia's Debt to the Mongols in Suretyship and Collective Responsibility," *Comparative Studies in Society and History* 30: 249–70.

Diani, Mario, & Ron Eyerman (Eds.) (1992). *Studying Collective Action*. Newbury Park, CA: Sage.

Duyvendak, Jan Willem (1994). *Le poids du politique. Nouveaux mouvements sociaux en France*. Paris: L'Harmattan.

Echeverry, Juan Carlos, Natalia Salazar, & Verónica Navas (2001). "El conflicto colombiano en el contexto internacional," in Astrid Martínez (Ed.), *Economía, Crimen y Conflicto*. Bogotá: Universidad Nacional de Colombia.

Economist (2002). "Uganda's Rebel Child-Soldiers. The Lord's Army Resists," *Economist* (20 April): p. 44.

Edwards, Bob, Michael W. Foley, & Mario Diani (Eds.) (2001). *Beyond Tocqueville. Civil Society and the Social Capital Debate in Comparative Perspective*. Hanover, PA: University Press of New England.

Egret, Jean (1962). *La pré-Révolution française*. Paris: Presses Universitaires de France.

Ellis, Stephen (1999). *The Mask of Anarchy. The Destruction of Liberia and the Religious Dimension of an African Civil War*. New York: New York University Press.

Emsley, Clive (1983). *Policing and Its Context, 1750–1870*. London: Macmillan.

Emsley, Clive, & Barbara Weinberger (Eds.) (1991). *Policing in Western Europe. Politics, Professionalism, and Public Order, 1850–1940*. New York: Greenwood.

Farge, Arlette (1979). *Vivre dans la rue à Paris au XVIIIe siècle*. Paris: Gallimard-Julliard.

Farrell, Sean (2000). *Rituals and Riots. Sectarian Violence and Political Culture in Ulster, 1784–1886*. Lexington: University Press of Kentucky.

References

Favre, Pierre (Ed.) (1990). *La Manifestation*. Paris: Presses de la Fondation Nationale des Sciences Politiques.

Favre, Pierre, Olivier Fillieule, & Nonna Mayer (1997). "La fin d'une étrange lacune de la sociologie des mobilisations. L'étude par sondage des manifestants. Fondements théoriques et solutions techniques," *Revue Française de Science Politique* 47: 3–28.

Feagin, Joe R., & Harlan Hahn (1975). *Ghetto Revolts. The Politics of Violence in American Cities*. New York: Macmillan.

Fearon, James D. (1995). "Ethnic War as a Commitment Problem," unpublished paper, Stanford University.

Feeley, Malcolm M., & Deborah L. Little (1991). "The Vanishing Female: The Decline of Women in the Criminal Process, 1687–1912," *Law & Society Review* 25: 719–57.

Fillieule, Olivier (1997a). *Stratégies de la rue. Les manifestations en France*. Paris: Presses de la Fondation Nationale des Sciences Politiques.

(Ed.) (1997b). "Maintien de l'ordre," *Cahiers de la Sécurité Intérieure* (special issue).

Fillieule, Olivier, & Fabien Jobard (1998). "The Policing of Protest in France: Toward a Model of Protest Policing," in Donatella della Porta & Herbert Reiter (Eds.), *Policing Protest. The Control of Mass Demonstrations in Western Democracies*. Minneapolis: University of Minnesota Press.

Fine, Sidney (1989). *Violence in the Model City. The Cavanagh Administration, Race Relations, and the Detroit Riot of 1967*. Ann Arbor: University of Michigan Press.

Fogelson, Robert M. (1971). *Violence as Protest. A Study of Riots and Ghettos*. Garden City, NJ: Doubleday & Co.

Fontenay, Michel (1988). "Corsaires de la foi ou rentiers du sol? Les chevaliers de Malte dans le 'corso' méditerranéen au XVIIe siècle," *Revue d'Histoire Moderne et Contemporaine* 35: 361–84.

Foweraker, Joe, & Todd Landman (1997). *Citizenship Rights and Social Movements. A Comparative and Statistical Analysis*. Oxford University Press.

Franklin, Benjamin (1972). *The Papers of Benjamin Franklin, vol. 14, January 1 through December 31, 1768* (Ed. by William B. Willcox). New Haven, CT: Yale University Press.

Franzosi, Roberto (1998). "Narrative as Data: Linguistic and Statistical Tools for the Quantitative Study of Historical Events," *International Review of Social History* 43 (suppl. 6): 81–104.

Freedom House (2002). "Freedom in the World 2002: The Democracy Gap," ⟨www.freedomhouse.org/research/survey2002.htm⟩, 29 March 2002.

Furet, François (1995). *Le passé d'une illusion. Essai sur l'idée communiste au XXe siècle*. Paris: Robert Laffont.

Gambetta, Diego (1993). *The Sicilian Mafia. The Business of Private Protection*. Cambridge, MA: Harvard University Press.

Gamson, William A., Bruce Fireman, & Steven Rytina (1982). *Encounters with Unjust Authority*. Homewood, IL: Dorsey.

Geller, Daniel S., & J. David Singer (1998). *Nations at War. A Scientific Study of International Conflict*. Cambridge University Press.

Gérard, Alain (1999). *"Par principe d'humanité..." La Terreur et la Vendée*. Paris: Fayard.

Gerner, Deborah J., et al. (1994). "Machine Coding of Event Data Using Regional and International Sources," *International Studies Quarterly* 38: 91–119.

Gilje, Paul A. (1996). *Rioting in America*. Bloomington: Indiana University Press.

Giugni, Marco (1995). *Entre stratégie et opportunité. Les nouveaux mouvements sociaux en Suisse*. Zürich: Seismo.

Giulianotti, Richard, Norman Bonney, & Mike Hepworth (Eds.) (1994). *Football, Violence, and Social Identity*. London: Routledge.

Glassie, Henry (1982). *Passing the Time in Ballymenone. Culture and History of an Ulster Community*. Philadelphia: University of Pennsylvania Press.

Gowa, Joanne (1999). *Ballots and Bullets. The Elusive Democratic Peace*. Princeton, NJ: Princeton University Press.

Granovetter, Mark (1995). "The Economic Sociology of Firms and Entrepreneurs," in Alejandro Portes (Ed.), *The Economic Sociology of Immigration. Essays on Networks, Ethnicity, and Entrepreneurship*. New York: Russell Sage Foundation.

Greer, Donald (1935). *The Incidence of the Terror During the French Revolution. A Statistical Interpretation*. Cambridge, MA: Harvard University Press.

Greif, Avner (1994). "Cultural Beliefs and the Organization of Society: A Historical and Theoretical Reflection on Collectivist and Individualist Societies," *Journal of Political Economy* 102: 912–50.

Grimal, Jean-Claude (2000). *Drogue: l'autre mondialisation*. Paris: Gallimard.

Grimsted, David (1998). *American Mobbing, 1828–1861. Toward Civil War*. New York: Oxford University Press.

Guenniffey, Patrice (2000). *La Politique de la Terreur. Essai sur la Violence Révolutionnaire, 1789–1794*. Paris: Fayard.

Gurr, Ted Robert (1993). *Minorities at Risk. A Global View of Ethnopolitical Conflicts*. Washington, DC: United States Institute of Peace Press.

    (2000). *Peoples versus States. Minorities at Risk in the New Century*. Washington, DC: United States Institute of Peace Press.

Gurr, Ted Robert, & Barbara Harff (1994). *Ethnic Conflict in World Politics*. Boulder, CO: Westview.

Guttman, Matthew C. (1993). "Rituals of Resistance: A Critique of the Theory of Everyday Forms of Resistance," *Latin American Perspectives* 20: 74–92.

Gwertzman, Bernard, & Michael T. Kaufman (Eds.) (1991). *The Collapse of Communism*, rev. ed. New York: Random House.

Hair, P. E. H. (1971). "Deaths from Violence in Britain: A Tentative Secular Survey," *Population Studies* 25: 5–24.

Hanagan, Michael (1999). "Industrial versus Preindustrial Forms of Violence" in Lester Kurtz (Ed.), *Encyclopedia of Violence, Peace, and Conflict*, vol. II, pp. 197–210. San Diego: Academic Press.

Hanagan, Michael P., Leslie Page Moch, & Wayne te Brake (Eds.) (1998). *Challenging Authority. The Historical Study of Contentious Politics*. Minneapolis: University of Minnesota Press.

Hanagan, Michael, & Charles Stephenson (Eds.) (1986). *Proletarians and Protest. The Roots of Class Formation in an Industrializing World* and *Confrontation, Class Consciousness, and the Labor Process*. New York: Greenwood.

Hannerz, Ulf (1969). *Soulside. Inquiries into Ghetto Culture and Community*. New York: Columbia University Press.

References

Hardy, Siméon-Prosper (1753–1789). *Mes loisirs. Journal d'événemens tels qu'ils parviennent à ma connaissance* (unpublished manuscript, 8 vols. catalogued as Fonds Français 6680–6687). Paris: Bibliothèque Nationale.

Harison, Casey (2000). "The Rise and Decline of a Revolutionary Space: Paris' Place de Grève and the Stonemasons of Creuse, 1750–1900," *Journal of Social History* 34: 403–36.

Hart, Peter (1998). *The I.R.A. & Its Enemies. Violence and Community in Cork 1916–1923.* Oxford: Clarendon.

Hay, Douglas, et al. (1975). *Albion's Fatal Tree. Crime and Society in Eighteenth-Century England.* New York: Pantheon.

Head, Randolph C. (1995). *Early Modern Democracy in the Grisons. Social Order and Political Language in a Swiss Mountain Canton, 1470–1620.* Cambridge University Press.

Henshall, Nicholas (1992). *The Myth of Absolutism. Change & Continuity in Early Modern European Monarchy.* London: Longman.

Hobsbawm, E. J., & George Rudé (1968). *Captain Swing.* New York: Pantheon.

Hochschild, Adam (1998). *King Leopold's Ghost. A Story of Greed, Terror, and Heroism in Colonial Africa.* Boston: Houghton Mifflin.

Hoerder, Dirk (1977). *Crowd Action in a Revolutionary Society: Massachusetts, 1765–1780.* New York: Academic Press.

Hofstadter, Richard, & Michael Wallace (Eds.) (1970). *American Violence. A Documentary History.* New York: Knopf.

Hoge, Warren (2001). "Ulster Protestants to End Demonstrations against Schoolchildren," *New York Times* (25 November): A8.

Holli, Melvin G. (Ed.) (1976). *Detroit.* New York: Franklin Watts.

Holsti, Kalevi J. (1991). *Peace and War: Armed Conflicts and International Order 1648–1989.* Cambridge University Press.

(1996). *The State, War, and the State of War.* Cambridge University Press.

Horowitz, Donald L. (2001). *The Deadly Ethnic Riot.* Berkeley: University of California Press.

Hug, Simon, & Dominique Wisler (1998). "Correcting for Selection Bias in Social Movement Research," *Mobilization* 3: 141–62.

Huggins, Martha Knisely (1998). *Policing. The United States and Latin America.* Durham, NC: Duke University Press.

Human Rights Watch (2000). *World Report 2000.* New York: Human Rights Watch.

Ikegami, Eiko (1995). *The Taming of the Samurai. Honorific Individualism and the Making of Modern Japan.* Cambridge, MA: Harvard University Press.

Imig, Doug, & Sidney Tarrow (Eds.) (2001). *Contentious Europeans. Protest and Politics in an Emerging Polity.* Lanham, MD: Rowman & Littlefield.

Ingrao, Charles W. (1987). *The Hessian Mercenary State. Ideas, Institutions, and Reform under Frederick II, 1760–1785.* Cambridge University Press.

James, Leon (1997). "Aggressive Driving and Road Rage. Dealing with Emotionally Impaired Drivers," (www.aloha.net/~dyc/testimony.html).

Jarman, Neil (1997). *Material Conflicts. Parades and Visual Displays in Northern Ireland.* Oxford: Berg.

Johnson, Gordon (1996). *Cultural Atlas of India.* New York: Facts on File.

Johnson, Larry C. (2001). "The Future of Terrorism," *American Behavioral Scientist* 44: 894–913.

Jones, Bruce (1995). "Intervention without Borders: Humanitarian Intervention in Rwanda, 1990–1994," *Millennium. Journal of International Affairs* 24: 225–49.

Joseph, Gilbert M., & Daniel Nugent (1994). *Everyday Forms of State Formation. Revolution and the Negotiation of Rule in Modern Mexico.* Durham, NC: Duke University Press.

Kakar, Sudhir (1996). *The Colors of Violence. Cultural Identities, Religion, and Conflict.* University of Chicago Press.

Kaldor, Mary (1999). *New & Old Wars. Organized Violence in a Global Era.* Cambridge: Polity.

Kaplan, Steven L. (1993). *Adieu 89.* Paris: Fayard.

Kaplan, Temma (1992). *Red City, Blue Period. Social Movements in Picasso's Barcelona.* Berkeley: University of California Press.

Karatnycky, Adrian (Ed.) (2000). *Freedom in the World. The Annual Survey of Political Rights and Civil Liberties.* Piscataway, NJ: Transaction.

Katz, Jack (1999). *How Emotions Work.* University of Chicago Press.

Kearney, Hugh (1989). *The British Isles. A History of Four Nations.* Cambridge University Press.

Keogh, Dermot (2001). "Ireland at the Turn of the Century: 1994–2001," in T. W. Moody & F. X. Martin (Eds.), *The Course of Irish History,* 4th ed. Lanham, MD: Roberts Rinehart.

Kertzer, David I. (1988). *Ritual, Politics, and Power.* New Haven, CT: Yale University Press.

Khawaja, Marwan (1993). "Repression and Popular Collective Action: Evidence from the West Bank," *Sociological Forum* 8: 47–71.

Kolata, Gina (1999). *Flu: The Story of the Great Influenza Pandemic of 1918 and the Search for the Virus That Caused It.* New York: Farrar, Straus & Giroux.

Koopmans, Ruud (1995). *Democracy from Below. New Social Movements and the Political System in West Germany.* Boulder, CO: Westview.

Kotek, Joël, & Pierre Rigoulot (2000). *Le siècle des camps. Détention, concentration, extermination. Cent ans de mal radical.* Paris: J.C. Lattès.

Kriesi, Hanspeter, Ruud Koopmans, Jan Willem Duyvendak, & Marco Giugni (1995). *New Social Movements in Western Europe. A Comparative Analysis.* Minneapolis: University of Minnesota Press.

Lagrange, Hugues (1989). "Strikes and the War," in Leopold Haimson & Charles Tilly (Eds.), *Strikes, Wars, and Revolutions in an International Perspective.* Cambridge University Press.

Landa, Janet Tai (1994). *Trust, Ethnicity, and Identity. Beyond the New Institutional Economics of Ethnic Trading Networks, Contract Law, and Gift-Exchange.* Ann Arbor: University of Michigan Press.

Lavery, Brian (2001a). "Target of Attack in Belfast: Little Girls Going to School," *New York Times* (6 September 2001): A12.

(2001b). "Little Children in the Middle as Adults Battle in Belfast," *New York Times* (14 October 2001): A6.

(2001c). "Northern Ireland: Protest at School Lifted," *New York Times* (10 November 2001): A8.

Le Cour Grandmaison, Olivier (2001). "Quand Tocqueville légitimait les boucheries," *Le Monde Diplomatique* (June): 12.

References

Ledeneva, Alena V. (1998). *Russia's Economy of Favours. Blat, Networking and Informal Exchange*. Cambridge University Press.

Le Roy Ladurie, Emmanuel (1979). *Le Carnaval de Romans. De la Chandeleur au mercredi des Cendres, 1579–1580*. Paris: Gallimard.

Levi, Margaret (1988). *Of Rule and Revenue*. Berkeley: University of California Press.

(1997). *Consent, Dissent, and Patriotism*. Cambridge University Press.

Levi, Margaret, & Laura Stoker (2000). "Political Trust and Trustworthiness," *Annual Review of Political Science* 3: 475–508.

Liang, Hsi-Huey (1992). *The Rise of Modern Police and the European State System from Metternich to the Second World War*. Cambridge University Press.

Lichbach, Mark Irving (1987). "Deterrence or Escalation? The Puzzle of Aggregate Studies of Repression and Dissent," *Journal of Conflict Resolution* 31: 266–97.

Lindenberger, Thomas (1995). *Strassenpolitik. Zur Sozialgeschichte der öffentlichen Ordnung in Berlin 1900 bis 1914*. Bonn: Dietz.

Linebaugh, Peter (1992). *The London Hanged. Crime and Civil Society in the Eighteenth Century*. Cambridge University Press.

Linebaugh, Peter, & Marcus Rediker (2000). *The Many-Headed Hydra. Sailors, Slaves, Commoners, and the Hidden History of the Revolutionary Atlantic*. Boston: Beacon Press.

Lis, Catharina, & Hugo Soly (1996). *Disordered Lives. Eighteenth-Century Families and Their Unruly Relatives*. Oxford: Polity.

Luard, Evan (1987). *War in International Society*. New Haven, CT: Yale University Press.

Lüdtke, Alf (1989). *Police and State in Prussia, 1815–1850*. Cambridge University Press.

(1992). *"Sicherheit" und "Wohlfahrt." Polizei, Gesellschaft und Herrschaft im 19. und 20. Jahrhundert*. Frankfurt: Suhrkamp.

Mac Suibhne, Breandán (2000). "Whiskey, Potatoes and Paddies: Volunteering and the Construction of the Irish Nation in Northwest Ulster, 1778–1782," in Peter Jupp & Eoin Magennis (Eds.), *Crowds in Ireland c. 1720–1920*. London: Macmillan.

Malcolm, Noel (1996). *Bosnia. A Short History*, rev. ed. New York University Press. [First published in 1994.]

(1998). *Kosovo. A Short History*. New York University Press.

Malia, Martin (1998). "The Lesser Evil?" *Times Literary Supplement* (March 27): 3–4.

(2001). "Revolution Fulfilled," *Times Literary Supplement* (June 15): 3–4.

Mallett, M. E. (1974). *Mercenaries and Their Masters. Warfare in Renaissance Italy*. Totowa, NJ: Rowman & Littlefield.

Mamdani, Mahmood (2001). *When Victims Become Killers. Colonialism, Nativism, and the Genocide in Rwanda*. Princeton, NJ: Princeton University Press.

Markovits, Andrei S., & Steven L. Hellerman (2001). *Offside. Soccer and American Exceptionalism*. Princeton, NJ: Princeton University Press.

Mason, T. David (1989). "Nonelite Response to State-Sanctioned Terror," *Western Political Quarterly* 42: 467–92.

Mason, T. David, & Dale A. Krane (1989). "The Political Economy of Death Squads: Toward a Theory of the Impact of State-Sanctioned Terror," *International Studies Quarterly* 33: 175–98.

Mayer, Arno J. (2000). *The Furies. Violence and Terror in the French and Russian Revolutions*. Princeton, NJ: Princeton University Press.

Mazower, Mark (2000). *The Balkans. A Short History*. New York: Modern Library.

McAdam, Doug, Sidney Tarrow, & Charles Tilly (2001). *Dynamics of Contention*. Cambridge University Press.

McCarthy, John D., & Clark McPhail (1998). "The Institutionalization of Protest in the United States," in David S. Meyer & Sidney Tarrow (Eds.), *The Social Movement Society. Contentious Politics for a New Century*. Lanham, MD: Rowman & Littlefield.

McCarthy, John D., Clark McPhail, & John Crist (1999). "The Diffusion and Adoption of Public Order Management Systems," in Donatella della Porta, Hanspeter Kriesi, & Dieter Rucht (Eds.), *Social Movements in a Globalizing World*. London: Macmillan.

McCarthy, John D., Clark McPhail, & Jackie Smith (1996). "Images of Protest: Estimating Selection Bias in Media Coverage of Washington Demonstrations 1982 and 1991," *American Sociological Review* 61: 478–99.

McDowell, R. B. (2001). "The Protestant Nation 1775–1800," in T. W. Moody & F. X. Martin (Eds.), *The Course of Irish History*, 4th ed. Lanham, MD: Roberts Rinehart. [First published in 1967.]

McKivigan, John R., & Stanley Harrold (Eds.) (1999). *Antislavery Violence. Sectional, Racial, and Cultural Conflict in Antebellum America*. Knoxville: University of Tennessee Press.

Ménétra, Jacques-Louis (1982). *Journal de ma vie* (Ed. by Daniel Roche). Paris: Montalba.

Merriman, John M. (1975). "The Demoiselles of the Ariège, 1829–1831," in John M. Merriman (Ed.), *1830 in France*. New York: Franklin Watts.

Miller, David W. (1983). "The Armagh Troubles, 1784–95," in Samuel Clark & James S. Donnelly, Jr. (Eds.), *Irish Peasants. Violence & Political Unrest, 1780–1914*. Madison: University of Wisconsin Press.

Mirala, Petri (2000). " 'A Large Mob, Calling Themselves Freemasons': Masonic Parades in Ulster," in Peter Jupp & Eoin Magennis (Eds.), *Crowds in Ireland, c. 1720–1920*. London: Macmillan.

Monin, Hippolyte (1889). *L'état de Paris en 1789. Etudes et documents sur l'Ancien Régime à Paris*. Paris: Jouanot, Noblet & Quantin.

Montague, Dena, & Frida Berrigan (2001). "The Business of War in the Democratic Republic of Congo: Who Benefits?" *Dollars & Sense* (July/August): 15–18, 34–5.

Moore, Barrington, Jr. (1979). *Injustice. The Social Bases of Obedience and Revolt*. White Plains, NY: M.E. Sharpe.

(2000). *Moral Purity and Persecution in History*. Princeton, NJ: Princeton University Press.

Morin, Edgar, Claude Lefort, & Jean-Marc Coudray (1968). *Mai 1968: la Brèche. Premières réflexions sur les événements*. Paris: Fayard.

Moss, B. H. (1993). "Republican Socialism and the Making of the Working Class in Britain, France, and the United States: A Critique of Thompsonian Culturalism," *Comparative Studies in Society and History* 35: 390–413.

Mueller, Carol (1997). "International Press Coverage of East German Protest Events, 1989," *American Sociological Review* 62: 820–32.

(1999). "Escape from the GDR, 1961–1989: Hybrid Exit Repertoires in a Disintegrating Leninist Regime," *American Journal of Sociology* 105: 697–735.

Mueller, John (2000). "The Banality of 'Ethnic War'," *International Security* 25: 42–70.

Muldrew, Craig (1993). "Interpreting the Market: The Ethics of Credit and Community Relations in Early Modern England," *Social History* 18: 163–83.

(1998). *The Economy of Obligation. The Culture of Credit and Social Relations in Early Modern England*. London: Macmillan.

References

Nahaylo, Bohdan, & Victor Swoboda (1990). *Soviet Disunion. A History of the Nationalities Problem in the USSR*. New York: Free Press.

National Advisory Commission on Civil Disorders (1968). *Report of the National Advisory Commission on Civil Disorders*. New York: Bantam.

National Commission on the Causes and Prevention of Violence (1969). *To Establish Justice, to Insure Domestic Tranquility*. Washington, DC: U.S. Government Printing Office.

Nirenberg, David (1996). *Communities of Violence. Persecution of Minorities in the Middle Ages*. Princeton, NJ: Princeton University Press.

Oberschall, Anthony (1994). "Protest Demonstrations and the End of Communist Regimes in 1989," *Research in Social Movements, Conflicts and Change* 17: 1–24.

O'Brien, Kevin (1996). "Rightful Resistance," *World Politics* 49: 31–55.

O'Donnell, Guillermo (1999). *Counterpoints. Selected Essays on Authoritarianism and Democratization*. University of Notre Dame Press.

Oliver, Pamela A., & Gregory M. Maney (2000). "Political Processes and Local Newspaper Coverage of Protest Events: From Selection Bias to Triadic Interactions," *American Journal of Sociology* 106: 463–505.

Oliver, Pamela E., & Daniel J. Myers (1999). "How Events Enter the Public Sphere: Conflict, Location, and Sponsorship in Local Newspaper Coverage of Public Events," *American Journal of Sociology* 105: 38–87.

Olivier, Johan (1991). "State Repression and Collective Action in South Africa, 1970–84," *South African Journal of Sociology* 22: 109–17.

Olzak, Susan (1989). "Analysis of Events in the Study of Collective Action," *Annual Review of Sociology* 15: 119–41.

Onishi, Norimitsu (2002). "Children of War in Sierra Leone Try to Start Over," *New York Times on the Web* (9 May).

Österberg, Eva, & Dag Lindström (1988). *Crime and Social Control in Medieval and Early Modern Swedish Towns*. Stockholm: Almqvist & Wiksell.

Paige, Karen, & Jeffery Paige (1981). *The Politics of Reproductive Ritual*. Berkeley: University of California Press.

Palmer, Stanley H. (1988). *Police and Protest in England and Ireland 1780–1850*. Cambridge University Press.

Patterson, Orlando (2001). "The Roots of Conflict in Jamaica," *New York Times on the Web* (23 July).

Perry, Elizabeth (1981). *Rebels and Revolutionaries in North China, 1848–1948*. Stanford University Press.

(1985). "Rural Violence in Socialist China," *China Quarterly* 103: 414–40.

(2002). *Challenging the Mandate of Heaven. Social Protest and State Power in China*. Armonk, NY: M.E. Sharpe.

Pillay, Navanethem (2001). "Sexual Violence in Times of Conflict: The Jurisprudence of the International Criminal Tribunal for Rwanda," in Simon Chesterman (Ed.), *Civilians in War*. Boulder, CO: Lynne Rienner.

Polletta, Francesca (1999). " 'Free Spaces' in Collective Action," *Theory and Society* 28: 1–38.

della Porta, Donatella (1995). *Social Movements, Political Violence, and the State. A Comparative Analysis of Italy and Germany*. Cambridge University Press.

della Porta, Donatella, & Herbert Reiter (Eds.) (1998). *Policing Protest. The Control of Mass Demonstrations in Western Democracies*. Minneapolis: University of Minnesota Press.

Powers, James F. (1988). *A Society Organized for War. The Iberian Municipal Militias in the Central Middle Ages, 1000–1284.* Berkeley: University of California Press.

Price, Roger D. (1982). "Techniques of Repression: The Control of Popular Protest in Mid-Nineteenth Century France," *Historical Journal* 25: 859–87.

Prunier, Gérard (1995). *The Rwanda Crisis. History of a Genocide.* New York: Columbia University Press.

(2001). "Genocide in Rwanda," in Daniel Chirot & Martin E. P. Seligman (Eds.), *Ethnopolitical Warfare. Causes, Consequences, and Possible Solutions.* Washington, DC: American Psychological Association.

Raeff, Marc (1983). *The Well-Ordered Police State. Social and Institutional Change through Law in the Germanies and Russia, 1600–1800.* New Haven, CT: Yale University Press.

Ramirez, Ruben Dario (2001). "On the Kidnapping Industry in Colombia," in Alex P. Schmid (Ed.), *Countering Terrorism through International Cooperation.* Milan: International Scientific and Professional Advisory Council of the United Nations Crime Prevention and Criminal Justice Programme.

Randall, Adrian, & Andrew Charlesworth (Eds.) (2000). *Moral Economy and Popular Protest. Crowds, Conflict and Authority.* New York: St. Martin's.

Redlich, Fritz (1964–1965). *The German Military Enterpriser and His Work Force* (2 vols.). Wiesbaden: Steiner.

Reiss, Albert J., Jr., & Jeffrey A. Roth (Eds.) (1993). *Understanding and Preventing Violence.* Washington, DC: National Academy Press.

Ribot Garcia, Luis (2000). "Types of Armies: Early Modern Spain," in Philippe Contamine (Ed.), *War and Competition between States.* Oxford: Clarendon.

Robert, Vincent (1990). "Aux Origines de la Manifestation en France (1789–1848)," in Pierre Favre (Ed.), *La Manifestation.* Paris: Presses de la Fondation Nationale des Sciences Politiques.

(1996). *Les chemins de la manifestation, 1848–1914.* Lyon: Presses Universitaires de Lyon.

Rotberg, Robert (Ed.) (1999). "Patterns of Social Capital: Stability and Change in Comparative Perspective," *Journal of Interdisciplinary History* 29(3–4) [Winter and Spring issues].

Rousseaux, Xavier (1995). "La répression de l'homicide en Europe occidentale (Moyen Age et Temps modernes)," *Genèses* 19: 122–47.

Rubin, Elizabeth (1998). "Our Children Are Killing Us," *The New Yorker* (March 23): 56–64.

Ruby, Charles L. (2002). "The Definition of Terrorism," *Analyses of Social Issues and Public Policy* 2: 9–14.

Rucht, Dieter, & Ruud Koopmans (Eds.) (1999). "Protest Event Analysis," *Mobilization* 4(2) [entire issue].

Rucht, Dieter, Ruud Koopmans, & Friedhelm Neidhardt (Eds.) (1998). *Acts of Dissent. New Developments in the Study of Protest.* Berlin: Sigma Rainer Bohn Verlag.

Rudé, George (1962). *Wilkes and Liberty.* Oxford: Clarendon.

(1971). *Hanoverian London, 1714–1808.* London: Secker & Warburg.

Ruff, Julius R. (2001). *Violence in Early Modern Europe, 1500–1800.* Cambridge University Press.

Rummel, R. J. (1994). *Death by Government.* New Brunswick, NJ: Transaction.

Samaha, Joel (1974). *Law and Order in Historical Perspective.* New York: Academic Press.

References

Samuel, Raphael (1981). *East End Underworld. 2. Chapters in the Life of Arthur Harding*. London: Routledge & Kegan Paul.

Schneider, Cathy Lisa (1995). *Shantytown Protest in Pinochet's Chile*. Philadelphia: Temple University Press.

Schneider, Eric C. (1999). *Vampires, Dragons, and Egyptian Kings. Youth Gangs in Postwar New York*. Princeton, NJ: Princeton University Press.

Schneider, John C. (1980). *Detroit and the Problem of Order, 1830–1880*. Lincoln: University of Nebraska Press.

Scott, James C. (1985). *Weapons of the Weak. Everyday Forms of Peasant Resistance*. New Haven, CT: Yale University Press.

(1990). *Domination and the Arts of Resistance. Hidden Transcripts*. New Haven, CT: Yale University Press.

(1998). *Seeing Like a State. How Certain Schemes to Improve the Human Condition Have Failed*. New Haven, CT: Yale University Press.

(2000). "The Moral Economy as an Argument and as a Fight," in Adrian Randall & Andrew Charlesworth (Eds.), *Moral Economy and Popular Protest. Crowds, Conflict and Authority*. London: Macmillan.

Scott, James C., & Benedict Kerkvliet (Eds.) (1986). *Everyday Forms of Peasant Resistance in South-East Asia*. London: Frank Cass.

Scott, K. Michelle (2000). "The Phenomenon of Road Rage: Complexities, Discrepancies, and Opportunities for CR Analysis," *Online Journal of Peace and Conflict Resolution* 3.3: 1–13.

Seligman, Adam (1997). *The Problem of Trust*. Princeton, NJ: Princeton University Press.

Shannon, Ulric (2002). "Private Armies and the Decline of the State," in Kenton Worcester, Sally Avery Bermanzohn, & Mark Ungar (Eds.), *Violence and Politics. Globalization's Paradox*. New York: Routledge.

Shapiro, Susan P. (1987). "The Social Control of Impersonal Trust," *American Journal of Sociology* 93: 623–58.

Sharlach, Lisa (2002). "State Rape. Sexual Violence as Genocide," in Kenton Worcester, Sally Avery Bermanzohn, & Mark Ungar (Eds.), *Violence and Politics. Globalization's Paradox*. New York: Routledge.

Sheller, Mimi (2000). *Democracy after Slavery. Black Publics and Peasant Radicalism in Haiti and Jamaica* (Warwick University Caribbean Studies). London: Macmillan.

SIPRI [Stockholm International Peace Research Institute] (2001). *SIPRI Yearbook 2001. Armaments, Disarmament and International Security*. Oxford University Press.

Small, Melvin, & J. David Singer (1982). *Resort to Arms. International and Civil Wars, 1816–1980*. Beverly Hills, CA: Sage.

Smith, Graham, Vivien Law, Andrew Wilson, Annette Bohr, & Edward Allworth (1998). *Nation-building in the Post-Soviet Borderlands. The Politics of National Identity*. Cambridge University Press.

Smith, Philip (1999). "Ritual and Symbolic Behavior," in Lester Kurtz (Ed.), *Encyclopedia of Violence, Peace, and Conflict*, vol. III, pp. 253–9. San Diego: Academic Press.

Sollenberg, Margareta, & Peter Wallensteen (2001). "Patterns of Major Armed Conflicts, 1990–2000," in *SIPRI Yearbook 2001. Armaments, Disarmament and International Security*, pp. 52–64. Oxford University Press.

Sommier, Isabelle (1993). "La CGT: du service d'ordre au service d'accueil," *Genèses* 12: 69–88.

Stanley, William (1996). *The Protection Racket State. Elite Politics, Military Extortion, and Civil War in El Salvador*. Philadelphia: Temple University Press.

Storch, Robert D. (1976). "The Policeman as Domestic Missionary: Urban Discipline and Popular Culture in Northern England, 1850–1880," *Journal of Social History* 9: 481–509.

Stowell, David O. (1999). *Streets, Railroads, and the Great Strike of 1877*. University of Chicago Press.

Sugimoto, Yoshio (1981). *Popular Disturbance in Postwar Japan*. Hong Kong: Asian Research Service.

Suny, Ronald Grigor (1993). *The Revenge of the Past. Nationalism, Revolution, and the Collapse of the Soviet Union*. Stanford University Press.

  (1995). "Ambiguous Categories: States, Empires, and Nations," *Post-Soviet Affairs* 11: 185–96.

Tarrow, Sidney (1989). *Democracy and Disorder: Social Conflict, Political Protest and Democracy in Italy, 1965–1975*. New York: Oxford University Press.

Tartakowsky, Danielle (1997). *Les Manifestations de rue en France, 1918–1968*. Paris: Publications de la Sorbonne.

  (1999). *Nous irons chanter sur vos tombes. Le Père-Lachaise, XIXe-XXe siècle*. Paris: Aubier.

Taylor, Christopher C. (1999). *Sacrifice as Terror. The Rwandan Genocide of 1994*. Oxford: Berg.

Thompson, E. P. (1991). *Customs in Common*. London: Merlin.

Thompson, Heather Ann (2000). "Understanding Rioting in Postwar Urban America," *Journal of Urban History* 26: 391–402.

Thomson, Janice E. (1994). *Mercenaries, Pirates, and Sovereigns. State-Building and Extraterritorial Violence in Early Modern Europe*. Princeton, NJ: Princeton University Press.

Tilly, Charles (1964). *The Vendée*. Cambridge, MA: Harvard University Press.

  (1975). "Revolutions and Collective Violence," in Fred I. Greenstein & Nelson W. Polsby (Eds.), *Handbook of Political Science* (vol. 3: Macropolitical Theory). Reading, MA: Addison-Wesley.

  (1977). "Collective Action in England and America, 1765–1775," in Richard Maxwell Brown & Don E. Fehrenbacher (Eds.), *Tradition, Conflict, and Modernization. Perspectives on the American Revolution*. New York: Academic Press.

  (1983). "Speaking Your Mind without Elections, Surveys, or Social Movements," *Public Opinion Quarterly* 47: 461–78.

  (1986). *The Contentious French*. Cambridge, MA: Harvard University Press.

  (1989). "Collective Violence in European Perspective," in Ted Robert Gurr (Ed.), *Violence in America* (vol. 2: Protest, Rebellion, Reform). Newbury Park, CA: Sage.

  (1990). *Coercion, Capital, and European States, AD 990–1990*. Oxford: Blackwell.

  (1992). "Conclusions," in Leopold Haimson & Giulio Sapelli (Eds.), *Strikes, Social Conflict and the First World War. An International Perspective*. Milan: Feltrinelli. [Fondazione Giangiacomo Feltrinelli, Annali 1990/1991.]

  (1993). *European Revolutions, 1492–1992*. Oxford: Blackwell.

  (1995). *Popular Contention in Great Britain, 1758–1834*. Cambridge, MA: Harvard University Press.

References

(1997). "Parliamentarization of Popular Contention in Great Britain, 1758–1834," *Theory and Society* 26: 245–73.

(1998a). "Where Do Rights Come From?" in Theda Skocpol (Ed.), *Democracy, Revolution, and History*. Ithaca, NY: Cornell University Press.

(1998b). *Durable Inequality*. Berkeley: University of California Press.

(1998c). "Social Movements and (All Sorts of) Other Political Interactions – Local, National, and International – Including Identities. Several Divagations from a Common Path, Beginning with British Struggles over Catholic Emancipation, 1780–1829, and Ending with Contemporary Nationalism," *Theory and Society* 27: 453–80.

(2000). "Spaces of Contention," *Mobilization* 5: 135–60.

(2001a). "Mechanisms in Political Processes," *Annual Review of Political Science* 4: 21–41.

(2001b). "Past and Future Inequalities," *Hagar* 2: 5–18.

(2001c). "Relational Origins of Inequality," *Anthropological Theory* 1: 355–72.

(2001d). "Do Unto Others," in Marco Giugni & Florence Passy (Eds.), *Political Altruism? The Solidarity Movement in International Perspective*. Lanham, MD: Rowman & Littlefield.

(2002). *Stories, Identities, and Political Change*. Lanham, MD: Rowman & Littlefield.

Tilly, Charles, Louise Tilly, & Richard Tilly (1975). *The Rebellious Century, 1830–1930*. Cambridge, MA: Harvard University Press.

Tilly, Charles, et al. (1995). "State-Incited Violence, 1900–1999," *Political Power and Social Theory* 9: 161–225.

Tishkov, Valery (1997). *Ethnicity, Nationalism and Conflict in and after the Soviet Union. The Mind Aflame*. London: Sage.

(2001). "The Culture of Hostage Taking in Chechnya," in Alex P. Schmid (Ed.), *Countering Terrorism through International Cooperation*. Milan: International Scientific and Professional Advisory Council of the United Nations Crime Prevention and Criminal Justice Programme.

Titarenko, Larissa, John D. McCarthy, Clark McPhail, & Boguslaw Augustyn (2001). "The Interaction of State Repression, Protest Form and Protest Sponsor Strength during the Transition from Communism in Minsk, Belarus, 1990–1995," *Mobilization* 6: 129–50.

Touraine, Alain (1968). *Le mouvement de mai ou le communisme utopique*. Paris: Seuil.

Trexler, Richard C. (1981). *Public Life in Renaissance Florence*. New York: Academic Press.

UNDP [United Nations Development Program] (2000). *Human Development Report 2000*. Oxford University Press.

Urlanis, Boris (1960). *Voiny i narodo-naselienie Evropy. Liudskie poteri vooruzhennykh sil Evropiisikh stran v voinakh XVII-XX vv*. Moscow: Izdatelstvo Sotsialno-ekonomicheskoi literatury.

U.S. Department of State (2000). Office of the Coordinator for Counterterrorism, "Patterns of Global Terrorism 1999," ⟨www.usis.usemb.se/terror/rpt1999/index.html⟩.

(2001). Office of the Coordinator for Counterterrorism, "Patterns of Global Terrorism 2000," ⟨www.usis.usemb.se/terror/rpt2000/index.html⟩.

(2002). Office of the Coordinator for Counterterrorism, "Patterns of Global Terrorism 2001," ⟨www.usis.usemb.se/terror/rpt2001/index.html⟩.

Uvin, Peter (1998). *Aiding Violence. The Development Enterprise in Rwanda*. West Hartford, CT: Kumarian Press.

(2001). "Reading the Rwandan Genocide," *International Studies Review* 3: 75–99.

(2002). "On Counting, Categorizing, and Violence in Burundi and Rwanda," in David I. Kertzer & Dominique Arel (Eds.), *Census and Identity. The Politics of Race, Ethnicity, and Language in National Censuses*. Cambridge University Press.

Varese, Federico (2001). *The Russian Mafia. Private Protection in a New Market Economy*. Oxford University Press.

Venkatesh, Sudhir Alladi (2000). *American Project. The Rise and Fall of a Modern Ghetto*. Cambridge, MA: Harvard University Press.

Volkov, Vadim (2000). "The Political Economy of Protection Rackets in the Past and the Present," *Social Research* 67: 709–44.

(2002). *Violent Entrepreneurs. The Use of Force in the Making of Russian Capitalism*. Ithaca, NY: Cornell University Press.

de Waal, Alex (1997). *Famine Crimes. Politics & the Disaster Relief Industry in Africa*. Oxford: James Currey.

Wakeman, Frederic (1966). *Strangers at the Gate: Social Disorder in South China, 1839–1861*. Berkeley: University of California Press.

(1985). *The Great Enterprise. The Manchu Reconstruction of Imperial Order in Seventeenth-Century China* (2 vols.). Berkeley: University of California Press.

Walker, William O. III (1999). "The Limits of Coercive Diplomacy: U.S. Drug Policy and Colombian State Stability, 1978–1997," in H. Richard Friman & Peter Andreas (Eds.), *The Illicit Global Economy and State Power*. Lanham, MD: Rowman & Littlefield.

Weigert, Kathleen Maas (1999). "Structural Violence," in Lester Kurtz (Ed.), *Encyclopedia of Violence, Peace, and Conflict*, vol. III, pp. 431–46. San Diego: Academic Press.

White, Robert W. (1993). "On Measuring Political Violence: Northern Ireland, 1969 to 1980," *American Sociological Review* 58: 575–85.

Wiktorowicz, Quintan (2001). "Centrifugal Tendencies in the Algerian Civil War," *Arab Studies Quarterly* 23: 65–82.

Wisch, Barbara, & Diane Cole Ahl (2000). "Introduction," in Barbara Wisch & Diane Cole Ahl (Eds.), *Confraternities and the Visual Arts in Renaissance Italy*. Cambridge University Press.

Wolf, Eric R. (1999). *Envisioning Power. Ideologies of Dominance and Crisis*. Berkeley: University of California Press.

Wong, R. Bin (1997). *China Transformed. Historical Change and the Limits of European Experience*. Ithaca, NY: Cornell University Press.

Woolcock, Michael (1998). "Social Capital and Economic Development: Toward a Theoretical Synthesis and Policy Framework," *Theory and Society* 27: 151–208.

World Bank (2001). *World Development Report 2000/2001. Attacking Poverty*. Oxford University Press.

Ylikangas, Heikki, Petri Karonen, & Martti Lehti (2001). *Five Centuries of Violence in Finland and the Baltic Area*. Columbus: Ohio State University Press.

Zhao, Dingxin (2001). *The Power of Tiananmen. State–Society Relations and the 1989 Beijing Student Movement*. University of Chicago Press.

Zwaan, Ton (2001). *Civilisering en decivilisering. Studies over staatsvorming en geweld, nationalisme en vervolging*. Amsterdam: Boom.

Index

autonomy, 67, 68, 77, 107
Avalon & Imperial, intersection of (Los
  Angeles), 143

Balkans, 92, 95–6, 97
bandits, 35–6, 60, 64, 104, 142
Barbier, Edmond-Jean-François, 159–60
Barcelona's Tragic Week, 188–9, 229
Barre, Siyad, 72–3
Basque Country, 237, 238
Bastille's fall, 61
battle(s)
  gang, 99–100
  reenactments, 86
  violent ritual in, 85
Battle of Aughrim, 123
Battle of the Boyne, 112, 123
Battle of the Diamond, 122
Bayat, Asef, 170–1, 188
behavior people, 5, 20
behavioral explanations, 225, 230
Beijing
  martial law in, 187
  shifting scattered attacks in, 187–8
  Tiananmen Square student protest,
    73–5, 74t, 187–8, 228, 231
Beissinger, Mark, 66
Belfast, 121, 125, 126–7
Belgium, 47, 50, 52, 102–3
Benett, John, 184–5
Berkeley, Bill, 38–9
Berlin Wall, 68–71
Bernstein, Thomas, 216–17, 217t
Bin Ladin, Osama, 235
Black Acts, 90
black nationalist groups, U.S., 27–8, 29
Blades, soccer fans, 82
Blok, Anton, 105, 230
blood feuds, 85, 94–7, 101
Bloods (gang), 38
Bloody Sunday, 115
Boas, Franz, 87
bombing, 40, 65, 144
booty, 139, 140
Bosnia, 29–30, 34, 95, 97, 105

Boston citizens vs. royal officials, 198–200
boundary(ies), 10
  activation of, 21, 34, 75, 76–7, 78, 84,
    103, 110, 132
  exploitation and, 79
  Protestant–Catholic, 123
  racial, 147
  sexual preference, 76
  uncertainty over, 226–7
  us–them, 32, 94, 98, 101, 139, 226
Brass, Paul, 37, 195–6
brawl(s), 15, 23, 67, 85, 154
  blending into French Revolution,
    163–5, 163t
  changing form of, 165, 166–9
  as collective violence, 154
  common features of, 155
  containment of, 157
  coordinated destruction and, 128, 166
  cross-boundary, 159
  effect of coordination on, 164
  in eighteenth-century France, 158–65,
    163t, 168–9
  London, 229
  Ménétra, Jacques-Louis in, 160–2, 166
  opportunism vs., 149–50
  problems of evidence in, 157–8
  rixe (brawl) as, 159, 164
  road rage as, 151–8
  into scattered attacks, 166
  selected Parisian, 163t
  signaling spirals in, 157
  social settings in, 168
  stonecutters, 163t, 164
  triple mode, 159
  twentieth-century English, 166–9
  in Ulster, 117
  violent ritual vs., 156–7
  violent specialists in, 166
British Fenian rising, 124
British government vs. Irish nationalists,
  113, 115–16
broken negotiations, 14, 16, 23, 67, 133
  by-product encounters in, 86
  Chinese rural violence as, 217–18

Index

Irish Catholics: *see* Catholics
Irish Republican Army, 70, 115, 116, 119
Ishii brothers, 93–4
Islamic, Salafi purists, 105–6
Italy
    aid for Somalia from, 72
    flagellant confraternities in, 88–9
    mercenaries in Florence, 134–5, 231

Jamaica, 47, 50, 52, 75
James, Leon, 151–2
Japan, 44, 47, 50, 52
Japanese-American internment, 44
Johnson, Lyndon, 143
journalists
    American, 237
    as hostages, 130
journeymen, French, 160–2, 166
judgments
    of political morality, 220
    required for categorizing opportunism,
        131

Kakar, Sudhir, 36–7
Katz, Jack, 154–5
Kercheval Avenue (Detroit), 146
Kerner Commission, 147, 148
Khabarov, Alexander, 37
kidnapping, 35–6
    Colombian, 106
    as opportunism, 131
    by terrorists, 237
Kigali, Rwanda, 2–3, 31, 137, 141, 149
killing
    internecine, 57
    large-scale, 59, 78–9
    shift from interstate to intrastate, 63
    small-scale, 59
kin groups, 94, 95
King, Martin Luther, 144
Knowles, Charles, 199
Kony, Joseph, 108, 133
Kosovo, 97
Kurds, 64
Kuwait, 58

Kwakiutl, potlatches of, 87–8
Kyrgyzstan, 222, 223, 236

labor, postsocialist division of, 135
laborers, agricultural vs. farmers,
    178–87
"land business," 36–7
landlords
    Anglican, 112
    Catholic, 112
    Columbia, 106
    exploitation benefiting, 112
    Malaysian villagers retaliation against,
        1–2, 3, 6, 17, 176–7
landlord–tenant political identity, 78
Lebanon, 55, 57, 58, 68
legal claims, filing of, 47
legitimate force vs. illegitimate violence,
    28, 132
lesbian activists: *see* gay and lesbian
    activists, U.S.
lethal contests, 102–4, 111, 228
Liberation Tigers of Tamil Eelam
    (LTTE), 222, 223, 236
Liberia, 55, 58, 68, 111, 131–2, 133
linen industry, Ireland, 112
London
    brawls, 229
    eighteenth-century executions in, 87,
        89–90, 231, 233
    thug (Arthur Harding), 166–8
    Titanics gang, 167
looting, 131
    American ghetto rebellions and, 143–9,
        230
    Rwandan, 141
low-capacity regimes: *see* regimes,
    low-capacity; regimes, low-capacity
    democratic; regimes, low-capacity
    undemocratic
low coordination: *see* coordinated
    destruction; coordination;
    coordination–salience space
low salience: *see* coordination–salience
    space; salience; salience, low

265

9 780521 531450